REA: THE TEST PREP AP® TEACHERS RECOMMEND

2nd Edition

AP® ENGLISH LANGUAGE AND COMPOSITION CRASH COURSE®

By Dawn Hogue, M.A.

Research & Education Association

Visit our website at: www.rea.com

Research & Education Association
61 Ethel Road West
Piscataway, New Jersey 08854
Email: info@rea.com

AP® ENGLISH LANGUAGE AND COMPOSITION CRASH COURSE®, 2nd Edition

Printed in the United States of America

Library of Congress Control Number 2018939877

ISBN-13: 978-0-7386-1239-3
ISBN-10: 0-7386-1239-1

Cover photo ©iStockphoto.com/AntonioGuillem

H18

CRASH COURSE
TABLE of CONTENTS

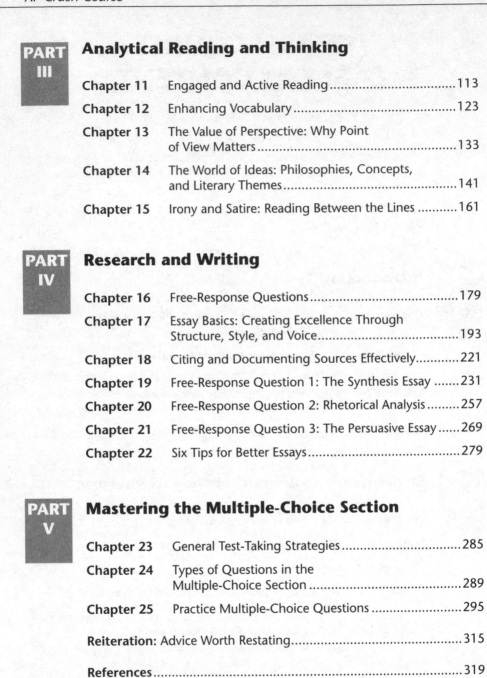

ABOUT OUR BOOK

REA's *AP English Language and Composition Crash Course®* is designed for the last-minute studier or any student who wants a quick refresher on the AP course. The *Crash Course* is based on the latest changes to the AP English Language and Composition course and exam and focuses only on the topics tested, so you can make the most of your study time.

Written by a veteran AP English Language and Composition test expert, our *Crash Course* gives you a concise review of the major concepts and important topics tested on the AP exam.

- **Part I** offers you our **Keys for Success**, so you can tackle the exam with confidence. It also explains the different genres of literature you'll encounter on the exam, and offers a list of representative authors and texts to strengthen your awareness of potential arguments included on the exam..

- **Part II** covers **Elements of Argument, Style, and Rhetoric** and includes information on elements of language, logical fallacies, and syntax and grammar basics, among other topics.

- **Part III** examines **Analytical Reading and Thinking** and gives advice on practicing engaged and active reading, enhancing your vocabulary, as well as improving your understanding of irony and satire.

- **Part IV** presents **Research and Writing** topics. It covers essay-writing basics, citing sources, and specific approaches for answering the exam's free-response questions.

- **Part V** is devoted to mastering the **Multiple-Choice Section** of the exam. Test-taking strategies and practice test questions help ensure you're ready for test day.

ABOUT OUR ONLINE PRACTICE EXAM

How ready are you for the AP English Language and Composition exam? Find out by taking **REA's online practice exam** available at *www.rea.com/studycenter*. This test features automatic scoring, detailed explanations of all answers, and diagnostic score reporting that will help you identify your strengths and weaknesses so you'll be ready on exam day.

Whether you use this book throughout the school year or as a refresher in the final weeks before the exam, REA's *Crash Course* will show you how to study efficiently and strategically, so you can boost your score.

Good luck on your AP English Language and Composition exam!

ABOUT OUR AUTHOR

Dawn Hogue taught all levels of high school English and AP English for the Sheboygan Falls School District, Sheboygan Falls, Wisconsin. She has earned numerous awards and recognition for her role in the classroom.

Ms. Hogue received her B.A. in English, graduating summa cum laude, from Lakeland University, Sheboygan, Wisconsin. She also earned her M.A. in Education from Lakeland University and her M.S. in Educational Leadership from Cardinal Stritch University, Milwaukee

She is interested in promoting technology and web resources in the classroom and maintains a website (*www.mshogue.com*) for that purpose. Ms. Hogue is an adjunct faculty member at Johns Hopkins University's Center for Talented Youth, where she works in digital spaces to help gifted students improve their writing skills.

Ms. Hogue is also the author of REA's *AP English Literature and Composition Crash Course.*

ACKNOWLEDGMENTS

In addition to our author, we would like to thank Larry B. Kling, Vice President, Editorial, for his overall guidance; Pam Weston, Publisher, for setting the quality standards for production integrity and managing the publication to completion; John Cording, Vice President, Technology, for the design and development of the REA Study Center; Diane Goldschmidt, Managing Editor, for editorial project management.

We also extend our special thanks to Elizabeth Catalfamo for copyediting, and Kathy Caratozzolo of Caragraphics for typesetting this edition.

PART I:

INTRODUCTION

Keys for Success
on the AP English Language and Composition Exam

*There are no secrets to success. It is the result of preparation,
hard work, and learning from failure.*—Colin Powell

OVERVIEW

Congratulations! You have chosen to enhance your AP English
Language study with the help of this *Crash Course*. You are a person who
wants to know more and go further. That speaks well of your intent to do
what it takes to succeed. In the chapters that follow, you will get content-
specific help, tips for success, and general insight about what you need
to know to be successful on the AP English Language and Composition
exam. This chapter gives you a glimpse into the structure and scoring of
the exam as well as general ways you can prepare yourself for the big day
in May.

STRUCTURE OF THE EXAM

Part I: Multiple Choice—There are typically 4 or 5 passages to read and
52 to 55 multiple-choice questions to answer in 60 minutes. This
section represents 45 percent of your total score.

Part II: Free Response—You are given a 15-minute reading period,
then 120 minutes to write three essays: a synthesis essay, a rhetorical
analysis essay, and a persuasive (argument) essay. This section
represents 55 percent of your total score.

Test proctors will give a ten-minute break between Part I and Part II.
(Your AP English Language and Composition instructor is not allowed to
proctor your exam.)

SCORING THE EXAM

The multiple-choice section of the exam is scored by machine. Scores on the multiple-choice section are based only on the number of questions answered correctly. Points are not deducted for incorrect answers and no points are awarded for unanswered questions.

The three essays are scored by College Board readers in early June. Readers include college professors and experienced AP English teachers who meet for this purpose. These readers score essays using scoring guides created by the College Board's test development committee for this exam. Your essay is not identified by name or geographical location.

The scores from Part I and Part II are combined to create a composite score. Scores are reported to students and designated colleges in July.

AP SCORE SCALE

5	Extremely well qualified
4	Well qualified
3	Qualified
2	Possibly qualified
1	No recommendation

Qualification means you may receive college credit or advanced placement at colleges and universities in the United States and Canada.

In their information to students, the College Board writes that, "You may be very surprised to see that your composite score can be approximately two-thirds of the total possible score and you could still earn a grade of 5!" Earning that score on other exams might translate to an "F" at worst and a "D" at best. In other words, you do not have to get all the multiple-choice questions correct or write perfect essays to get a high score on the exam.

In the 2017 figures reported by the College Board, 55 percent of all students who took the exam scored a 3 or higher. And while only about 9 percent of students scored a 5, which says a bit about the difficulty of the exam, you should focus on the high number who passed. A score of 3, 4, or 5 will commonly earn you college credits or placement, but always check with your intended colleges for their AP credit policy.

WHAT TO KNOW ABOUT EXAM DAY

What you can (should have) and cannot have in the exam room:

Yes	No
Several No. 2 pencils, sharpened, with good erasers	Cell phones, MP3 players, or any other electronic devices, including calculators
One or two reliable dark blue or black pens; avoid pens that clump or bleed	Cameras or other recording devices
A watch, so you can monitor your time. Make sure it does not beep or have an alarm or Internet access	Books, including dictionaries
Your Social Security number	Scratch paper
	Notes you've made in advance
	Highlighters
	Food or drink
	Clothing with subject-related information

PREPARING YOURSELF

1. Eat well in the weeks prior to the exam. Since the AP English Language exam is generally scheduled in the morning, get used to eating breakfast, so that you can eat a good breakfast on exam day. A good breakfast for your brain consists of fruit, lean protein, and complex carbohydrates. Also, drink water instead of sugared drinks. Energy drinks are notoriously loaded with sugar and should be avoided.

2. Get enough sleep and not just the night before the exam. Establish good sleep patterns in the weeks prior to the exam. High school students typically do not get enough sleep. Aim for 8–9 hours a night.

3. Wake up early enough to be fully awake and ready to go on exam day. Set your alarm so you don't oversleep. You don't want to be groggy!

4. Caffeine may help you be more alert, but overdoing it can make you jittery and make it difficult for you to focus. If you are not accustomed to caffeine, don't have any on exam day.

5. Wear comfortable clothes and shoes on the day of the exam. Prepare for fluctuations in room temperature by wearing layers that you can adjust.

See more in Chapter 2 about what you can do to prepare for exam day.

Don't take my word for it. Research the effect of health and wellness on academic performance. You'll enhance your informed and active reading skills by doing this research.

The Student's Tools:
What You Can
Do to Ensure Success

Diligence is the mother of good luck.—Benjamin Franklin

OVERVIEW

Any study text is useless if you don't pair it with your best intentions. This brief chapter simply outlines what you can do to enhance your own success.

A MATTER OF TIME

You may have heard the saying, "What's worth doing, is worth doing well." This is so true for your preparation for the AP English Language and Composition exam. While the title of this book is *AP English Language and Composition Crash Course*, it will be very difficult for you to literally cram in a short period of time. The information and tips you get in this book will help you either way, but it is best if you start early enough to really learn what you need to know. Except for some literary terms, there is little in this text that you can actually memorize. Instead, you need to develop your reading, writing, and thinking skills.

It is best to give yourself at least six to nine months to prepare for the exam. If that is not possible, then a few weeks of serious review with this book will definitely help you earn a higher score on the exam.

SUGGESTED STRATEGIES FOR USING THIS BOOK

1. Read the entire book, making notes about which chapters are important for you to study. New research shows that handwritten notes (versus digital or e-notes) are better to help us remember

information. Focus on what you need to know instead of what you already know.

2. Make a goal sheet, listing specific tasks for the upcoming months. Examples of these tasks might be:

   • Read and study several texts, maybe two books and four articles. (See Chapter 4 for a list of authors and texts.)

   • Practice annotating all the texts you read.

3. Good goals have time limits, so be sure to state when you plan to meet your goals.

4. Re-read this book as often as necessary to reinforce ideas. Most people will not remember everything they read the first time.

5. Make a short list of the five most important skills you need to improve before test time, such as reading complex texts or understanding satire. Find ways to practice those skills.

6. Form a study team with friends who are also taking the exam. Learn from each other. Here are some reasons to form a study team:

   • Quizzing each other on terms can help you remember them.

   • You can share your essays with your group. Peer review can help you see strengths and weaknesses in your writing, and by reading others' work, you can learn from them as well.

   • If you all read the same books, you can discuss them, which helps to understand a text more completely.

7. If you get frustrated, try these strategies:

   • Analyze the reason for your frustration. Why are you frustrated? What can you do to lessen how you feel?

   • Take a short break to refocus: go for a walk without headphones. Let nature (or the city) help you get out of yourself for awhile.

   • Talk to your study group and vent, but then find ways together to get back on track.

   • Ask your teacher for help.

MORE TIPS

- Penmanship counts! Not everyone has good penmanship, but in preparation for the exam, you should do as much as you can to improve your penmanship. If your essays are not written legibly, you are jeopardizing your score. You cannot expect tired, overworked AP exam readers to struggle with your essay needlessly because they cannot read your handwriting. When you write your practice essays, always use blue or black ink and always write with an imagined reader in mind.

- This exam is about scholarship. Think of yourself as you embark on this "quest" as an upper-level scholar—a college student, really. If you wear the garb of a scholar, even metaphorically, it will influence how you think about things.

- Your attitude is more important than you think—it influences everything, even your physical well-being. A positive attitude will give you energy and confidence. A negative attitude will:

    — Limit your ability to read carefully (you'll want to rush, skim, or get it over with);

    — Lead to frustration and fatigue;

    — Keep you from having an open mind;

    — Possibly infect others, giving them doubt about their own abilities.

- Study hard and take the exam seriously. Remember, however, that this is just one test of what you know at this point in your life. It is not the most important thing you will ever do. Try to keep it all in perspective. Try to have fun with all of this.

Classifying Nonfiction:
Genres, Patterns, and Purposes

Writing is writing, and stories are stories. Perhaps the only true genres are fiction and non-fiction. And even there, who can be sure?—Tanith Lee

OVERVIEW

The word **genre** means "type." There are many and diverse types of literature in the nonfiction realm, which seems to change daily, especially with Web platforms like Facebook and Twitter. Are profile updates or tweets considered genres? Some of you have probably read multi-genre novels, like Avi's *Nothing But the Truth* and have seen how authors weave nontraditional forms with more traditional narratives to create interesting and new types of fictional texts.

Nonfiction authors have also blurred the line between fiction and nonfiction in the latter part of the twentieth century, blending the elements of fiction (imagery, figurative language, suspense, and even dialogue) with nonfiction prose. In general, this blend is called **Creative Nonfiction**.

The essay itself is said to have originated with French writer Michel de Montaigne, whose short, topic-focused essays set the standard for what followed. For Montaigne, the act of writing the essay was the act of discovering knowledge. He was writing to know. This may also be your essay experience on the AP English Language and Composition exam, as you will be pondering and writing about topics that you may not normally think about in your daily life. You will be writing to know.

To that end, the exam presents you with many engaging texts to read, to think about, and to write about. It is impossible to predict the actual genres of the texts you'll encounter on your exam, as the field is so rich and diverse. Surely, whatever the selections are, you can be certain that they will be "stylistically engaging" and "intricately constructed," according to the College Board's AP English Language Course Description.

What does this mean? Mostly it means that while the texts should prove interesting (topically), they will present a challenge for you. They will be complex enough to put your thinking to the test, which is the point, after all, isn't it?

One purpose of this chapter is to suggest the types of literature that you may encounter on the exam and to briefly describe them. There generally are one or two questions on the exam that ask you to identify a specific genre. This chapter will help. In the "old days," nonfiction meant biography, autobiography, factual reference, and essay, as well as a few others. These days, the list is much longer. Which genre are you most interested in reading? If you think a memoir sounds interesting, you might pick up that copy of *The Year of Magical Thinking* by Joan Didion from your mother's bookshelf. It wouldn't be a bad start to your study. If your sense of history is lacking depth, you could read a biography, which would help you expand your knowledge not just of a person, but more importantly, his or her impact on events. Choose biographies of historically impactful people over those of celebrities.

Depending on how much time you have, try to read a few books to deepen your overall knowledge, which will help you in more than one way on this exam.

This chapter also details the specific patterns of exposition that you are likely to encounter in your reading. You should also be able to use these patterns in your own writing. See Chapter 17 for more information on general essay writing.

GENRE LIST

The following list is not complete, but does include the genres you are most likely to encounter on the exam based on a study of released exams. No matter what the genre, the writer's purposes can be layered and often are. A diary can provide information, chronicle a life, and also describe and persuade. The letters John and Abigail Adams wrote to each other tell us more than details of their lives; these letters are also important historical documents.

Remember also that fictional elements are now used widely in nonfiction, an overlap that makes it difficult to determine exact distinctions between fiction and nonfiction.

Genre	Attributes & Notes
Allegory	Allegory tells a literal story by using another story, a figurative one, to create ambiguity. Jonathan Swift's *Gulliver's Travels* is social criticism and satire veiled as a fantastical tale of strange lands and peoples.
Autobiography	An author's story of his or her own life; written in first person. Varies from memoir in that it generally reads less like a novel (as memoirs often do) and more like a chronological account, though there are no rules for either.
Biography	A third-person account of another's life.
Blog Post (or Weblog Post)	An entry on a personal or professional website called a blog; can be on any topic, from any point of view, and written for various audiences and various purposes. Truly a democratic genre; anyone can write a blog.
Creative Nonfiction	A relatively new genre, creative nonfiction tells true stories using the tools fiction writers use, such as plot, narratives, imagery, dialogue, and more. Topics are diverse, from personal narratives to travelogues, and more.
Critique (Criticism)	Similar to a review, a critique points out the strengths and weaknesses of a work (art, literature, speech, performance, etc.).
Debate	A traditional debate is a spoken event in which participants (two opposing teams) argue (with supporting details) a controversial issue. Political debates feature candidates (sometimes only two, sometimes many) who give their own point of view on current topics.
Diary (journal, log)	An account that is kept daily, or almost daily, by an individual to record events of his/her life and to express his/her views.

Continued →

Genre	Attributes & Notes
Excerpt	A short portion of a larger text meant to stand on its own. You may be asked to infer the broader context of an excerpt, such as from what genre it was excerpted or the identity of the intended audience.
Editorial	Written by the editor of a newspaper, traditionally, it expresses the view of the editor or the editorial board on an issue prominent in the news. An editorial is typically short (300–350 words) and generally persuasive.
Eyewitness Account	A first-person report (primary source) of an individual who witnesses an important or significant event. As each person's point of view is affected by a wide variety of limiting factors, more than one account is desired for a more objective view of reality.
Fable	A narrative meant to teach a lesson in which the characters are sometimes animal representatives of human types or specific human beings, especially if used for satirical purposes.
History/ Historical Commentary	A history is a factual account of an event or period in time. A historical commentary is one person's view of that event, so opinion is based on research, fact, or observation.
Homily	A sermon or a lecture, generally narrative in style, with a moralizing (didactic) purpose.
Image	Graph, chart or other infographic. Could also be a photograph or other type of visual image.
Letter (epistle)	Letters can take various forms, from business letters to personal correspondence. The genre now seems nearly obsolete due to email, but historically letters were preserved. Letters from writers, politicians, artists, and others are viewed as historical documents or even as literary works. Letters are also written for a wide variety of purposes: to inform, persuade, entertain, satirize, criticize, and more. The term *epistolary style* means "in letter form."

Genre	Attributes & Notes
Literary Criticism	Beyond a review, a literary criticism measures a work of literature against current standards; an analysis of a work that investigates a certain aspect of the work, such as symbolism or irony. Literary criticism may also discuss the work as seen through a specific literary theory, such as feminist, Freudian, or Marxist.
Memoir	A personal narrative that reflects upon one's own life experiences. May be less chronological and encompassing than a typical autobiography.
Monologue	One voice, generally first-person, narrates a train of thought or consciousness on one topic. Typically spoken, as on the stage, for an audience.
Personal Reminiscence	First-person account of a particular event in time.
Political Cartoon	Generally a one-celled comic, the political cartoon is primarily satire, which hopes to point out inadequacies or corruption in the political sphere.
Review	Gives the writer's informed opinion about the quality of literary works, movies or other visual media, art, music, even restaurants. Reviewers are called critics.
Satire	The satirist seeks to improve society by showing its faults through irony and humor, either with a friendly nudge or sharp-edged jabs. See Chapter 15 for more on satire.
Sermon	A speech given by the clergy to the congregation, typically didactic in nature.
Social Criticism	Various subgenres (satire, essay, speech, etc.) meant to criticize current social trends, philosophies, standards, mores, etc.
Speech	Oral essay, commentary; there is a wide variety of types of speeches. The important distinction is that a speech is spoken to an intended audience, which impacts word choice, etc.

Continued ➔

Genre	Attributes & Notes
Travelogue/ Place Essay	The setting provides the basis for the writing; the author recognizes something significant in the setting.
Treatise	A formal and systematic exposition in writing of the principles of a subject, generally longer and more detailed than an essay.

Test Tip

If you are given an excerpt on the exam, you may be asked to infer the broader context, such as from what genre it was likely excerpted or the probable identity of the intended audience.

PURPOSES OF ESSAYS (OF WRITING IN GENERAL)

While writers may have one main purpose in mind, they may achieve more than one simultaneously. You will be asked to determine the writer's purpose on the exam and should choose the author's main or dominant reason for writing.

Inform	To give information, clearly and objectively.
Persuade	To convince another to adopt a point of view or engage in an action.
Entertain	To provide humor or a pleasant escape.
Satirize	To point out flaws in people or institutions with the intent of making positive change.
Inspire	Through one's own experiences or observations, provide models that guide or give hope to others.
Reflect	To think back upon, to put into perspective. Reflection is typically personal, but considers the self in relation to others, to history, or to events in time.
Document	To mark in time, to record the significance of some event or action.

TYPES (PATTERNS) OF ESSAYS

Pattern	Purpose
Analogy	To explain something abstract or complex by showing its similarity to something simpler and more concrete. For the analogy to be effective, the writer should assume that the reader is familiar with the subject. The main purpose of the analogy is to explain.
Cause and Effect	The writer wishes to explain *why*. Types of causes are the *immediate* causes, which are encountered first, and the *ultimate* causes, which are the basic, underlying factors that explain the more apparent causes. Example: Mom was late for work today because she overslept (immediate cause). She didn't sleep well because she was worrying about her annual employment review and hoped her boss would not bring up the obvious dip in quarterly sales, which she was prepared to explain was due more to the economic recession than her ad campaign (ultimate cause). In writing a logical cause and effect essay, the writer must consider all possible relevant factors. There must be evidence for all assertions and attention to objectivity.
Classification	The author divides the subject into categories or other systems to analyze the material, such as types, sizes, number, appearance, prevalence, etc. The system needs to be logical and consistent throughout the essay.
Comparison and Contrast	When we show, in writing, the similarities and differences between two subjects, we are asking readers to look more closely at each. Sometimes the writer looks only to suggest how two things are alike (for example, how Iraqis are similar to U.S. citizens, which brings understanding). Or, she may want to show the superiority of one thing over another (such as contrasting the nutritional value of eggs from free-range chickens with those cooped up in large commercial poultry farms). See Chapter 17 for more on comparison and contrast.

Continued ➞

Pattern	Purpose
Definition	When terms need clarification because they are ambiguous, abstract, unusual, or otherwise not generally understood, the writer will seek to define them for the reader, especially if the overall explanation relies on an understanding of these terms. There are several ways to define. One is through exclusion or differentiation, which shows what is not meant by the term, also called clarification by negation. Writers can also give examples to illustrate the definition. This type of essay, or extended definition, will most likely do more than simply define. The writer seeks also to bring about a greater sense of understanding on an important topic or issue. For example, an essay defining the word "nerd" might be funny and informative, but could also challenge basic stereotypes.
Description	Description is either objective (factual, not an impression or opinion) or subjective (filtered through the writer's perspective and his/her opinion). Subjective description begins in fact. Careful description helps readers see things more clearly, understand abstract concepts more simply, and appreciate ideas and events in a more personal way. Imagery and sensory language nearly always engage the reader emotionally. In such an essay, the writer hopes to present a single, dominant impression.
Exemplification (Illustrating by use of examples)	Uses examples to put abstract or complex ideas into a simpler, more concrete form. To support an argument, a writer must choose a clearly typical example or present several examples that represent the situation fairly. Examples must be relevant or pertinent to the argument.
Hypothesis/Support	The writer presents a hypothesis or theory and provides details and examples to support it or refute it.

Pattern	Purpose
Narration	A narrative essay tells a story and uses the tools of fiction: selection of important, telling details; logical order of events (such as those in a plot), which may or may not add an element of suspense; transitions to mark time and events; a narrative point of view, which affects how readers view events; and even dialogue. These essays, while non-fiction, may read like short stories, but the characters and events are derived from real life. The overall purpose is to illuminate or explain.
Process Analysis	There are two kinds of processes: a set of directions, that is, how to do something; and an information process, which explains how something is done or how it works or operates. A process analysis essay can be written in chronological order, that is, the order of the steps in the process (first, next, after that, finally). Some processes are more complicated and require a different approach. A historian who writes about how civil rights activists registered voters would not necessarily follow a chronology of events.

Representative
Authors and Texts

*Rarely do we find men who willingly engage in hard, solid thinking.
There is an almost universal quest for easy answers and
half-baked solutions. Nothing pains some people more
than having to think.*—Martin Luther King, Jr.

OVERVIEW

In the Course Description, the College Board acknowledges that there
is "no recommended or required reading list for an AP English Language
and Composition course." However, they do give a list of authors that is
"designed to illustrate the possibilities of nonfiction prose."

The purpose of this chapter is to give you a sense of the diversity
of literature you will encounter on the AP English Language exam. In
preparing for the exam, look to read a variety of texts, even if you only
read partial texts. Many of the older works are in the public domain and
can be found online. If you have an e-reader, you can download them
easily. And don't overlook the fact that a public library is still an amazing
place. I am sure that even the smallest local library is going to have many
works by these writers on its shelves.

ABOUT THE LITERATURE

Most of the selections you will read will be nonfiction, but as that
overall genre has changed dramatically over the years, a diverse spectrum
indeed awaits you. This is not to say that you will never see a poem or a
fictional selection on the exam. You might. But it will not be typical.

So, what do you read to prepare yourself for the exam? You could not
possibly study all the authors and their works. What you should do instead

is select a few names from each major category in the list included in this chapter. Read some old, some new. Read a variety of topics. For example, if you are interested in ecology and the environment, find authors who share that interest. But if you only read these authors and their works, you will be limiting your scope.

If you are enrolled in an AP English Language and Composition course at your school, you most likely have been provided with an anthology-style textbook. If you're like my students, you read only what the teacher assigns. The book contains selections chosen purposefully for AP English Language students. Not only should you consider this book to be a free resource of great material, depending on your time, you should read and study as many of the selections as possible. Strive to read diversely: various viewpoints, various styles, various genres.

Nonfiction is, or can be, just as entertaining to read as fiction or drama. You won't find characters that are embroiled in complex plots, but real life is full of conflict and drama, and the real people who walk across the stage of life are just as interesting, if not more so.

Choose six to eight works to read and study. Think about the authors' ideas, but more importantly, the rhetorical strategies and techniques they use to get their point across to their reader. Study their style, their use of language, syntax, and diction. Study their effectiveness. These writers are listed for a reason—they're respected for what they say and how they say it. What's more, the twentieth-century authors (and beyond) are included because they represent diverse voices and experiences, which means that you are much more likely to relate to what they have to say.

Test Tip

A SOAPSTone chart is included at the end of this chapter. Fill one out for each of the major works you study in preparation for the exam. This will help you remember each one more specifically.

REPRESENTATIVE AUTHORS

While many of the writers listed are known for more than what is shown in representative works, I have chosen to list those works that seem most suited to the exam or what is generally thought to be that writer's most accomplished or famous work. For example, Oscar Wilde is best known for his plays, but he is also known for his literary criticism and his involvement with the aesthetic movement, which embraced the idea of art for art's sake.

There may be many writers on this list who are familiar to you for one reason or another. If you've seen some of these people interviewed on television or if you've read about them in your history class, you may be more motivated to read more of what they have to say.

PRE-TWENTIETH CENTURY

Writer	Representative Work(s)
Joseph Addison (1672–1719) English essayist, poet, playwright and politician	Founded *The Spectator* magazine with Richard Steele
Francis Bacon (1561–1626) English philosopher, statesman, scientist, lawyer, jurist and author	*The Advancement of Learning; Novum Organum*
James Boswell (1740–1795) Scottish lawyer, diarist, author	*The Life of Samuel Johnson,* a biography, and his journals
Thomas Carlyle (1795–1881) Scottish satirist, essayist, and historian	*Sartor Resartus; Signs of the Times*
Samuel Taylor Coleridge (1722–1834) English poet, literary critic, and philosopher	*Biographia Literaria*
Charles Darwin (1809–1882) English naturalist	*On the Origin of Species*
Frederick Douglass (circa 1818–1895) American abolitionist, editor, orator, author, and statesman	*A Narrative of the Life of Frederick Douglass, an American Slave; My Bondage and My Freedom; Life and Times of Frederick Douglass*
Ralph Waldo Emerson (1803–1882) American philosopher, essayist, and poet	Various essays can be found at *http://www.rwe.org/*
Benjamin Franklin (1706–1790) one of the Founding Fathers of the United States; also a leading author and printer, satirist, political theorist, politician, and diplomat	*The Autobiography of Benjamin Franklin*
Margaret Fuller (1810–1850) American journalist, critic, and women's rights advocate	*Woman in the Nineteenth Century*

Continued ➞

Writer	Representative Work(s)
Edward Gibbon (1737–1794) English historian and member of Parliament	*The History of the Decline and Fall of the Roman Empire*
Thomas Hobbes (1588–1679) English political philosopher	Leviathan
Harriet Jacobs (Linda Brent) (1813–1897) American writer, abolitionist speaker, and reformer	*Incidents in the Life of a Slave Girl*
Thomas Jefferson (1743–1826) third President of the United States, philosopher, and writer (among numerous other things)	primary author of the *Declaration of Independence; Declaration of the Causes and Necessity of Taking Up Arms*
Samuel Johnson (1709–1784) British author, poet, essayist, literary critic, biographer, and editor	*Dictionary of the English Language; Lives of the Most Eminent English Poets*
Charles Lamb (1775–1834) English essayist	*Specimens of English Dramatic Poets who Lived About the Time of Shakespeare; Essays of Elia*
John Locke (1632–1704) English philosopher	*An Essay Concerning Human Understanding*
Niccolò Machiavelli (1469–1527) Italian philosopher and writer; considered one of the main founders of modern political science	*The Prince*
John Stuart Mill (1806–1873) British philosopher	His collected works are easily accessed online: *http://www. gutenberg.org/browse/authors/ m#a1705*
John Milton (1608–1674) English poet, author	*Areopagitica; Paradise Lost*
Michel de Montaigne (1533–1592) French writer, essayist	His collected essays (Montaigne is considered to be the father of the modern essay.)
Thomas More (1478–1535) English lawyer, social philosopher, author, and statesman	*Utopia*

Writer	Representative Work(s)
Thomas Paine (1737–1809) American author, pamphleteer, radical, intellectual, revolutionary; one of the founding fathers of the United States	*Common Sense; The American Crisis; The Rights of Man*
Francis Parkman (1823–1893) American historian	*The Oregon Trail: Sketches of Prairie and Rocky-Mountain Life; France and England in North America*
Walter Pater (1839–1894) English essayist, critic, and fiction writer	*The Renaissance*, especially *The Conclusion*
George Bernard Shaw (1856–1950) Irish playwright, critic, journalist; Nobel Prize in Literature	*The Intelligent Woman's Guide to Socialism and Capitalism; Treatise on Parents and Children; Pygmalian*
Richard Steele (1672–1729) Irish writer and politician; remembered as co-founder, with his friend Joseph Addison, of the magazine *The Spectator*	*The Tatler; The Spectator*
Jonathan Swift (1667–1745) Anglo-Irish satirist, essayist	*Gulliver's Travels; A Modest Proposal; A Tale of a Tub; Drapier's Letters*
Henry David Thoreau (1817–1862) American author, naturalist, critic	*Walden; Civil Disobedience*
Alexis de Tocqueville (1805–1859) French political thinker and historian	*Democracy in America; The Old Regime and the Revolution*
Oscar Wilde (1854–1900) Irish writer, poet, and playwright	*Intentions; De Profundis*
Mary Wollstonecraft (1759–1797) British writer, philosopher, and feminist	*A Vindication of the Rights of Woman*

20TH CENTURY TO THE PRESENT

Writer	Representative Work(s)
Edward Abbey (1927–1989) American author and essayist noted for his advocacy of environmental issues and criticism of public land policies	*The Monkey Wrench Gang; Desert Solitaire*
Diane Ackerman (1948–) American author, poet, and naturalist	*A Natural History of the Senses*
Paula Gunn Allen (1939–2008) Native American poet, literary critic, lesbian activist, and novelist	*The Sacred Hoop: Recovering the Feminine in American Indian Traditions*
Natalie Angier (1958–) American nonfiction writer and a science journalist for the *New York Times*; also a contributor to *Time* magazine	*Natural Obsessions*
Margaret Atwood (1939–) Canadian author, poet, critic, essayist, feminist, and social campaigner	*Writing with Intent: Essays, Reviews, Personal Prose—1983–2005; Second Words: Selected Critical Prose*
James Baldwin (1924–1987) American novelist, writer, playwright, poet, essayist and civil rights activist	*Notes of a Native Son; The Fire Next Time; No Name in the Street; The Devil Finds Work; The Evidence of Things Not Seen; The Price of the Ticket*
Dave Barry (1947–) Pulitzer Prize-winning American author and columnist; humorist	*The World According to Dave Barry; Dave Barry is NOT Making This Up*
Melba Patillo Beals (1941–) American journalist and member of the Little Rock Nine, a group of African-American students who were the first to integrate Central High in Little Rock, Arkansas	*Warriors Don't Cry; White is a State of Mind*
Simone de Beauvoir (1908–1986) French existentialist philosopher and writer	*The Ethics of Ambiguity; The Second Sex*
Lerone Bennett Jr. (1928–) American scholar, author and social historian	*When the Wind Blows; History of Us*
Wendell Berry (1934–) American writer, fiction, nonfiction, and poetry	Essay collections: *Citizenship Papers; The Way of Ignorance*
Susan Bordo (1947–) modern feminist philosopher and writer	*Unbearable Weight: Feminism, Western Culture, and the Body*

Writer	Representative Work(s)
Jacob Bronowski (1908–1974) British mathematician and biologist	*The Ascent of Man; A Sense of the Future; Magic Science & Civilization; The Origins of Knowledge and Imagination*
William F. Buckley (1925–2008) American author, commentator, editor	See *https://cumulus.hillsdale.edu/ Buckley*
Judith Butler (1956–) American feminist, philosopher, and writer	*Gender Trouble: Feminism and the Subversion of Identity*
Rachel Carson (1907–1964) American marine biologist and nature writer	*Silent Spring*
G. K. Chesterton (1874–1936) British journalist, novelist, essayist	*Eugenics and Other Evils*
Winston Churchill (1874–1965) British Prime Minister, historian, and writer	*The Second World War; A History of the English-Speaking Peoples*
Judith Ortiz Cofer (1952–2016) Puerto Rican author	*Sleeping with One Eye Open: Women Writers and the Art of Survival; The Myth of the Latin Woman*
Richard Dawkins (1941–) British ethologist, evolutionary biologist, and popular science author	*The Selfish Gene*
Joan Didion (1934–) American novelist, essayist, memoir writer	*Slouching Towards Bethlehem; The Year of Magical Thinking*
Annie Dillard (1945–) Pulitzer Prize-winning American author and artist, best known for her narrative nonfiction	*Pilgrim at Tinker Creek*
Maureen Dowd (1952–) columnist for the *New York Times* and best-selling author	*Are Men Necessary?: When Sexes Collide;* also see current and archived columns in the *New York Times*
Elizabeth Drew (1935–) American political journalist and author	Washington Journal: *The Events of 1973–74; Portrait of an Election: The 1980 Presidential Campaign; On the Edge: The Clinton Presidency; Citizen McCain; George W. Bush's Washington*

Continued →

Writer	Representative Work(s)
W. E. B. Du Bois (1868–1963) American civil rights activist, historian, and author	*The Souls of Black Folk* and much more
Richard Ellmann (1918–1987) American literary critic and biographer	*Four Dubliners: Wilde, Yeats, Joyce, and Beckett*
Nora Ephron (1941–2012) American film director, producer, screenwriter, novelist, and journalist	Various screenplays: *Silkwood; When Harry Met Sally; Julie and Julia*
Timothy Ferris (1944–) American science writer	*The Science of Liberty; Coming of Age in the Milky Way*
M. F. K. Fisher (1908–1992) American writer	*Map of Another Town: A Memoir of Provence; To Begin Again: Stories and Memoirs*
Frances Fitzgerald (1940–) American journalist and author, known for her journalistic account of the Vietnam War	*America Revised; Cities on a Hill; Way Out There in the Blue: Reagan, Star Wars and the End of the Cold War; Rewriting American history, a short article in The Norton Reader; and Vietnam: Spirits of the Earth*
Tim Flannery (1956–) Australian palaeontologist and environmental activist	*The Weather Makers: The History & Future Impact of Climate Change*
Shelby Foote (1916–2005) American novelist and historian of the American Civil War	*The Civil War: A Narrative*
John Hope Franklin (1915–2009) United States historian	*Racial Equality in America; My Life and an Era: The Autobiography of Buck Colbert Franklin; Runaway Slaves: Rebels on the Plantation; Mirror to America: The Autobiography of John Hope Franklin*
Antonia Fraser (1932–) Anglo-Irish author	*The Weaker Vessel: Woman's Lot in Seventeenth-Century England; The Warrior Queens: Boadicea's Chariot; The Gunpowder Plot*
Thomas L. Friedman (1953–) American journalist, columnist, and Pulitzer Prize-winning author	*The Lexus and the Olive Tree; The World Is Flat; Longitudes and Attitudes*
Paul Fussell (1924–2012) American cultural and literary historian, professor of literature	*The Great War and Modern Memory; Thank God for the Atom Bomb and Other Essays*

Writer	Representative Work(s)
John Kenneth Galbraith (1908–2006) Canadian-American economist, writer	*A Life in Our Times*
Henry Louis Gates Jr. (1950–) American literary critic, educator, scholar, writer, editor	*Colored People; Tradition and the Black Atlantic: Critical Theory in the African Diaspora; Personal History: Family Matters*
Ellen Goodman (1941–) American journalist and Pulitzer Prize-winning syndicated columnist	*Making Sense; Value Judgments; Paper Trail*
Nadine Gordimer (1923–2014) South African writer, political activist and Nobel laureate	*The Conservationist; The Pickup; The Essential Gesture: Writing, Politics and Places*
Stephanie Elizondo Griest (1974–) Chicana author and activist from South Texas	*Around the Bloc: My Life in Moscow, Beijing, and Havana; 100 Places Every Woman Should Go*
David Halberstam (1934–2007) American Pulitzer Prize-winning journalist and author; known for his early work on the Vietnam War	*Summer of '49; The Next Century; The Fifties; October 1964*
Elizabeth Hardwick (1916–2007) American literary critic, novelist, and short-story writer	*A View of My Own* (1962); *Seduction and Betrayal* (1974); *Bartleby in Manhattan* (1983); and *Sight-Readings* (1998).
Elva Trevino Hart Mexican-American writer	*Barefoot Heart: Stories of a Migrant Child* (memoir)
John Hersey (1914–1993) Pulitzer Prize-winning American writer and journalist	*Hiroshima*
Edward Hoagland (1932–) American author best known for nature and travel writing	*Compass Points; Hoagland on Nature; Early in the Season*, plus numerous essays
Richard Holmes (1945–) British biographer	*Shelley: The Pursuit; Coleridge: Early Visions*
Bell Hooks (1952–) American author, feminist, and social activist	*Ain't I a Woman?: Black Women and Feminism; Yearning: Race, Gender, and Cultural Politics*

Continued →

Writer	Representative Work(s)
Zora Neale Hurston (1891–1960) American folklorist, anthropologist, and author	*Mules and Men; Their Eyes Were Watching God*
Evelyn Fox Keller (1936–) American author and physicist	*The Century of the Gene, Making Sense of Life: Explaining Biological Development with Models, Metaphors, and Machines*
Helen Keller (1880–1968) American author and lecturer	*The Story of My Life*
Martin Luther King Jr. (1929–1968) American clergyman and political leader	various speeches, letters, essays
Barbara Kingsolver (1955–) American novelist, author	*Animal, Vegetable, Miracle; Small Wonder: Essays, High Tide in Tucson*
Maxine Hong Kingston (1940–) Asian American author	*The Woman Warrior*
Paul Krugman (1953–) American columnist, author, and Nobel Prize-winning economist	Op-ed columns for the *New York Times*; various books and articles
Alex Kuczynski (1967–) American author and reporter for the *New York Times*, columnist for the *New York Times Magazine*	*Beauty Junkies*
Lewis H. Laphamn (1935–) American author, journalist	*Waiting for the Barbarians; Theater of War; Gag Rule; and Pretensions to Empire*
T. E. Lawrence (1888–1935) British army officer, known also as Lawrence of Arabia	*Seven Pillars of Wisdom; Revolt in the Desert*
Gerda Lerner (1920–2013) American historian and author	*Why History Matters; The Creation of Feminist Consciousness; Fireweed: A Political Autobiography*
Phillip Lopate (1943–) American author and media critic	*Waterfront: A Walk Around Manhattan; Against Joie de Vivre*
Barry Lopez (1945–) American environmental author and social critic	*Home Ground: Language for an American Landscape*
Norman Mailer (1923–2007) American writer, co-founder of "new journalism"	*The Executioner's Song; The Big Empty: Dialogues on Politics, Sex, God, Boxing, Morality, Myth, Poker and Bad Conscience in America*

Writer	Representative Work(s)
Nancy Mairs (1943–2016) American author, writes about her experiences with multiple sclerosis	*Waist High in the World*
Peter Matthiessen (1927–2014) American writer and environmental activist	*In the Spirit of Crazy Horse; Travelin' Man; Shadow Country*
Mary McCarthy (1912–1989) American author and political activist	*Memories of a Catholic School Girl; Vietnam; Ideas and the Novel*
Frank McCourt (1930–2009) Irish-American writer	*Angela's Ashes*
Bill McKibben (1960–) American environmentalist and writer	*The Bill McKibben Reader: Pieces from an Active Life; Eaarth: Making a Life on a Tough New Planet*
John McPhee (1931–) American writer and pioneer of creative nonfiction	*Annuls of the Former World; Encounters with the Archdruid; Silk Parachute*
Margaret Mead (1901–1978) American anthropologist	*Sex and Temperament in Three Primitive Societies; Male and Female*
Jan Morris (1926–) Welsh historian and travel writer	*Locations; O Canada!; Contact! A Book of Glimpses*
John Muir (1838–1914) Scottish-born American naturalist, author, and early advocate of preservation of wilderness in the United States, co-founder of the Sierra Club	*The Story of My Boyhood and Youth*
Donald M. Murray (1923–2006) American journalist and teacher	*My Twice-Lived Life: A Memoir, The Lively Shadow: Living with the Death of a Child*
V. S. Naipaul (1932–) Trinidadian novelist and essayist, awarded the Nobel Prize in literature in 2001 for his life's work	*The Writer and the World: Essays,* or anything by this writer
Joyce Carol Oates (1938–) American novelist and essayist	*Where I've Been, And Where I'm Going: Essays, Reviews, and Prose*
Barack Obama (1961–) 44th President of the United States, president of *Harvard Law Review*	Keynote address at the Democratic National Convention in 2004
George Orwell (1903–1950) English author and journalist	*Politics and the English Language; 1984*

Continued ➜

Writer	Representative Work(s)
Cynthia Ozick (1928–) Jewish American writer	*Fame & Folly: Essays, Quarrel & Quandary, The Din in the Head: Essays*
Francine Prose (1947–) American writer	*Blue Angel; The Lives of the Muses: Nine Women & the Artists They Inspired*
David Quammen (1948–) award-winning science, nature, and travel writer	*Monster of God: The Man-Eating Predator in the Jungles of History and the Mind*
Arnold Rampersad (1941–) biographer and literary critic, born in Trinidad	*Days of Grace: A Memoir; Jackie Robinson: A Biography*
Ishmael Reed (1938–) American poet, essayist, and novelist	*Barack Obama and the Jim Crow Media: The Return of the "Nigger Breakers," Mixing It Up: Taking on the Media Bullies and Other Reflections*
David Remnick (1958–) American journalist and Pulitzer Prize-winning writer	*Lenin's Tomb: The Last Days of the Soviet Empire.*
Mordecai Richler (1931–2001) Canadian author, screenwriter, and essayist	*Oh Canada! Oh Quebec! Requiem for a Divided Country; Dispatches from the Sporting Life*
Sharman Apt Russell (1954–) American nature and science writer	*An Obsession with Butterflies: Our Long Love Affair with a Singular Insect, Anatomy of a Rose: Exploring the Secret Life of Flowers*
Carl Sagan (1934–1996) American astronomer, astrophysicist, and author	*Pale Blue Dot: A Vision of the Human Future in Space, Cosmos*
Edward Said (1935–2003) Palestinian-American literary theorist	*Out of Place*
George Santayana (1863–1952) Spanish-American philosopher and author	*The Sense of Beauty; The Life of Reason*
Arthur M. Schlesinger (1917–2007) Pulitzer Prize-winning American historian and social critic	*A Thousand Days: John F. Kennedy in the White House; The Disuniting of America: Reflections on a Multicultural Society, A Life in the 20th Century, Innocent Beginnings, 1917–1950*

Writer	Representative Work(s)
David Sedaris (1956–) American humorist and writer	*Naked; Holidays on Ice; Me Talk Pretty One Day; Dress Your Family in Corduroy and Denim*
Richard Selzer (1928–2016) American surgeon and author	*The Exact Location of the Soul: New and Selected Essays; Raising the Dead: A Doctor's Encounter with His Own Mortality*
Leslie Marmon Silko (1948–) Native American author	*Yellow Woman and a Beauty of the Spirit: Essays on Native American Life Today*
Barbara Smith (1946–) American lecturer, author, and lesbian feminist	*Writings on Race, Gender and Freedom: The Truth That Never Hurts*
Red Smith (1905–1982) American sportswriter	*Views of Sport; Out of the Red*
Shelby Steele (1946–) American author and documentary filmmaker, specializing in the study of race relations	*The Content of Our Character*
Lincoln Steffens (1866–1936) American journalist, lecturer, and political philosopher; a famous muckraker	*The Shame of the Cities*
Ronald Takaki (1939–2009) American author	*Debating Diversity: Clashing Perspectives on Race and Ethnicity in America*
Lewis Thomas (1913–1993) American physician, researcher, and writer	*The Lives of a Cell: Notes of a Biology Watcher*
Barbara Tuchman (1912–1989) American historian and Pulitzer Prize-winning author	*The Guns of August*
Cynthia Tucker (1955–) American journalist and Pulitzer Prize-winning columnist	Her blog can be found at *http://blogs.ajc.com/cynthia-tucker/*
Laurel Thatcher Ulrich (1938–) Harvard University professor and women's historian	*Good Wives: Image and Reality in the Lives of Women in Northern New England, 1650–1750; A Midwife's Tale: The Life of Martha Ballard based on her diary, 1785–1812*

Continued →

Writer	Representative Work(s)
John Updike (1932–2009) American novelist and critic	*The Clarity of Things: What's American About American Art?; Due Considerations: Essays and Criticism, Still Looking: Essays on American Art*
Gore Vidal (1925–2012) American author and political activist	*Gore Vidal: Snapshots in History's Glare; Imperial America: Reflections on the United States of Amnesia*
Alice Walker (1944–) American author	*In Search of Our Mothers' Gardens: Womanist Prose; We Are the Ones We Have Been Waiting For*
Jonathan Weiner (1953–) American journalist, science writer	*Long For This World; The Next One Hundred Years: Shaping the Fate of Our Living Earth; The Beak of the Finch: A Story of Evolution in Our Time* (Pulitzer Prize)
Cornel West (1953–) African American philosopher, author, and civil rights activist	*The African-American Century: How Black Americans Have Shaped Our Century; Restoring Hope: Conversations on the Future of Black America; The War Against Parents: What We Can Do For America's Beleaguered Moms and Dads*
E. B. White (1899–1985) American writer	Essays of E.B. White
George Will (1941–) U.S. newspaper columnist, journalist, author, and baseball fan	Will has published numerous books, but search online for his editorials and columns in *Newsweek*, *The Washington Post*, and ABC News. He is syndicated across the nation.
Terry Tempest Williams (1955–) American author, naturalist, and environmental activist	*Mosaic: Finding Beauty in a Broken World*

Writer	Representative Work(s)
Garry Wills (1934–) American historian and Pulitzer Prize-winning author	*Lincoln at Gettysburg: The Words That Remade America; Inventing America: Jefferson's Declaration of Independence*
E. O. Wilson (1929–) American biologist, researcher, and Pulitzer Prize-winning author, specializing in the study of ants	*On Human Nature, The Ants, The Future of Life*
Edmund Wilson (1895–1972) American writer, literary and social critic	*The American Earthquake: A Documentary of the Twenties and Thirties, The Bit Between My Teeth: A Literary Chronicle of 1950–1965*
Tom Wolfe (1930–2018) American author and journalist, one of the founders of the New Journalism movement	*The Electric Kool-Aid Acid Test, The Right Stuff,* and 35th Jefferson Lecture in the Humanities titled "The Human Beast"
Virginia Woolf (1882–1941) English author	*A Room of One's Own, Women And Writing, Collected Essays*
Richard Wright (1908–1960) American author	*American Hunger, Black Boy*
Malcolm X (1925–1965) African-American Muslim minister, public speaker, and human-rights activist	*The Speeches of Malcolm X at Harvard; The Autobiography of Malcolm X*
Anzia Yezierska (circa 1880–1970) Polish-American novelist	*Red Ribbon on a White Horse; Bread Givers*

ANALYZING MAJOR WORKS

Use the following SOAPSTone chart for each book you read.

SOAPSTone ANALYSIS CHART

Title: _____

Author: _____

Year Published: _____   Genre: _____

	Go beyond the basics . . .
S = Speaker	Identify the voice and the point of view from which she or he is speaking. Identify the speaker's values, biases, and beliefs. Determine if the speaker can be trusted.
O = Occasion	What is the time and place? Is there a particular historical context that influences the message or the speaker? What specific set of circumstances prompted the writer to write?
A = Audience	Who will hear or read this message? What is this audience's biases or values? Is this audience open to the message?
P = Purpose	What does the writer want the reader to know, to understand, to do?
S = Subject	What is the main idea? What is this work about?
T = Tone	What is the dominant tone and what is its effect? Look primarily at the author's attitude. What words, images, or figures of speech reveal the author's attitude? Are there any shifts in tone within the document, and if so, what is the result?
Most Memorable?	

SOAPSTone ANALYSIS CHART

Title: _____

Author: _____

Year Published: _____ Genre: _____

	Go beyond the basics . . .
S = Speaker	
O = Occasion	
A = Audience	
P = Purpose	
S = Subject	
T = Tone	
Most Memorable?	

ESSENTIAL READING

Although the College Board does not provide a list of required texts, there are classic arguments AP English teachers use year after year in their courses that prove effective in preparing students for the exam. If you have time to read nothing else prior to May, the list* below will serve you well. Everything listed below is a short text, either an essay or a speech. They're listed in alphabetical order (by author name).

Keep in mind that it is not enough to just read these texts. It is crucial that you read analytically, always with your eye on the speaker's thesis and how and why he or she creates the desired effect.

You should find many of these texts in your anthology textbook for your AP class. If such a book is not available to you, visit your local public library.

1. "On Women's Right to Vote," Susan B. Anthony

2. "What to the Slave is the Fourth of July," Frederick Douglass

3. "Self Reliance," Ralph Waldo Emerson

4. "Letter from Birmingham Jail," Martin Luther King Jr.

5. from *The Prince*, "The qualities of the Prince," Niccolo Machiavelli

6. "Shooting an Elephant," George Orwell

7. "Allegory of the Cave," Plato

8. "1999 Commencement Speech," Anna Quindlen

9. "Affirmative Action: The Price of Preference," Shelby Steele

10. "A Modest Proposal," Jonathan Swift

11. "I Want a Wife," Judy Brady Syfers

12. "Ain't I a Woman?" Sojourner Truth

13. "Corn Pone Opinions," Mark Twain

14. "This Awful Slaughter," Ida B. Wells

15. "Death of a Pig," E.B. White

---

* Collated from an informal survey of college and AP English Language and Composition teachers.

Also included in this *Crash Course* are several other great examples: "From Woman in the Nineteenth Century," Margaret Fuller; "Advice to Youth," Mark Twain; and "Should We Ban Cigarettes?," Peter Singer. Each of these samples is annotated or analyzed in later chapters.

Test Tip

Read the texts included in this book and learn from the accompanying annotations or analysis. Then use what you learn to deepen your analytical reading skills.

PART II:
ELEMENTS OF ARGUMENT, STYLE, AND RHETORIC

Basic Elements of Language

Learning never exhausts the mind.—Leonardo da Vinci

OVERVIEW

Every enterprise has its own vocabulary. As you emerge into the world of work, you'll realize how specialized language can become. The purpose of this chapter is to help you recognize and understand the basic terms used in persuasive writing, in all its various modes and styles.

100 KEY TERMS

Familiarize yourself with the following list of terms. The starred (★) terms are those that have appeared more prominently on the released AP English Language exams. Throughout this text, these terms (and others) are emphasized or reiterated. As you study this book, be sure you at least have a general understanding of all terms.

Choose two terms to teach to someone else each day for several months. We tend to remember an idea better when we teach it. Involve your parents. They will be impressed with how smart you are and might be happy to help you study.

1. **abstraction**: a concept or idea without a specific example; idealized generalizations.

2. **abstract noun**: ideas or things that can mean many things to many people, such as peace, honor, etc.

3. **allegory**: a narrative or description with a secondary or symbolic meaning underlying the literal meaning. Satirists sometimes use allegory because it allows them a way to indirectly attack their satirical target. Swift's *Gulliver's Travels* is an example.

4. **alliteration**: repetition, at close intervals, of beginning sounds.

★ 5. **allusion** (allude to): a reference to something in culture, history, or literature that expands the depth of the text if the reader makes the connection.

6. **allusion, classical**: a reference to classical (especially Greek or Roman) myth, literature, or culture.

★ 7. **analogy**: compares two things that are similar in several respects in order to prove a point or clarify an idea.

★ 8. **anecdote**: a short narrative of an amusing, unusual, revealing, or interesting event. Usually, the anecdote is combined with other material such as expository essays or arguments to clarify abstract points or to create a memorable image. **Anecdotal**: evidence that relies on observations, presented in narrative.

9. **anticlimax, anticlimactic**: an event or experience that causes disappointment because it is less exciting than was expected or because it happens immediately after a much more interesting or exciting event.

10. **antecedent**: that which comes before; the antecedent of a pronoun is the noun to which the pronoun refers. (You may be expected to find this relationship on the exam.)

★ 11. **antithesis**: the opposite of an idea used to emphasize a point; the juxtaposition of contrasting words or ideas. Hope is the antithesis of despair.

12. **antithesis, balanced**: a figure of speech in which sharply contrasting ideas are juxtaposed in a balanced or parallel phrase or grammatical structure, as in *To err is human; to forgive, divine.*

★ 13. **apostrophe**: a speaker directly addresses something or someone not living, that cannot answer back.

★ 14. **appeal to authority**: one of several appeals strategies; in appealing to authority, the writer refers to expert opinion. (See Chapter 6 for more rhetorical strategies.)

15. **assertion**: the claim or point the author is making.

16. **bias**: a preference or an inclination, especially one that inhibits impartial judgment.

17. **burlesque**: a comic tool of satire, the writer uses ridiculous exaggeration and distortion.

18. **cadence**: the rhythm of phrases or sentences created through repetitive elements. (See *syntax*.)

19. **candor**: open and honest communication; truthfulness.

20. **catalog** (list): a list of details that reinforces a concept. Inductive arguments build to a conclusion based on the collective impression of lists (facts, observations).

21. **cause and effect**: essay pattern in which the writer shows the immediate and underlying causes that led to an event or situation.

22. **circular reasoning**: type of faulty reasoning in which the writer attempts to support a statement by simply repeating the statement in different or stronger terms.

★ 23. **circumlocution**: to write around a subject; to write evasively; to say nothing.

24. **colloquial**: common or regional language or behavior; referring to local custom or sayings.

25. **concession**: acknowledgment of the validity of an opposing view.

26. **concrete versus abstract**: concrete is observable, measurable, easily perceived versus abstract, which is vague and not easily defined. An example of a concrete noun is *chair*. While there are many types of chairs, chairs have one basic purpose. An example of an abstract noun is *patriot*. There are many ways to define a patriot.

27. **counterargument**: opposing argument that weakens the author's point.

28. **counterexample**: an exception to a proposed general rule.

29. **damn with faint praise**: accolades with words which effectively condemn by seeming to offer praise which is too moderate or marginal to be considered praise at all.

30. **diatribe**: in contemporary terms, a rant. An explosion of harsh language that typically vilifies or condemns an idea.

31. **diction, concrete**: the writer chooses language that is concrete, quantifiable, based on facts, easily accepted by the reader, and generally understood. It is the opposite of abstract diction.

★ 32. **digress, digression**: to move off the point, to veer off onto tangents.

33. **dilemma**: basically an either/or situation, typically a moral decision.

34. **dilemma, false**: simplifying a complex problem into an either/or dichotomy.

35. **discretion**: refined taste; tact or the ability to avoid embarrassment or distress.

36. **double entendre**: a phrase or saying that has two meanings, one generally being sexual or provocative in nature.

37. **ellipsis**: a mark or series of marks (. . .) used in writing to indicate an omission, especially of letters or words.

38. **empirical, empiricism**: knowledge based on experience or observation; the view that experience, especially of the senses, is the only source of knowledge.

39. **episodic**: appearing in episodes, a long string of short, individual scenes, stories, or sections, rather than focusing on the sustained development of a single plot.

40. **epigram**: a short quotation or verse that precedes text that sets a tone, provides a setting, or gives some other context for the text.

41. **epithet**: 1. a short, poetic nickname—often in the form of an adjective or adjectival phrase—attached to the normal name. Example: Grey-eyed Athena (Homer); 2. a term used as a descriptive substitute for the name or title of a person, such as "The Great Emancipator" for Abraham Lincoln; 3. an abusive or contemptuous word or phrase, commonly a slur. *ex. nigger*

42. **ethos**: a speaker's or writer's credibility; his or her character, honesty, commitment to the writing.

★ **43. euphemism**: a kinder, gentler, less crude, or harsh word or phrase to replace one that seems imprudent to use in a particular situation; also a word or phrase that dilutes the meaning of or evades responsibility for a more precise word or phrase (such as "assessment" for "test," "casualties" for "deaths").

44. exemplar: an example, especially one that is a model to emulate or particularly apt for the situation.

45. explicit: expressly stated; made obvious or evident; clear.

46. fact versus fiction: facts can be verified; fiction is supposed or imagined, and while it may possess truthful elements, fiction is not actual and cannot be verified.

47. fallacy, fallacious claim: an error of reasoning based on faulty use of evidence or incorrect inference.

48. figurative language: language that is not meant to be taken literally; in general: metaphor; specifically: metaphor, simile, personification, metonymy, and more.

49. footnote: an explanatory or documenting reference at the bottom of a page of text.

50. hyperbole: an exaggeration or overstatement—saying more than is warranted by the situation in order to expose reality by comparison; also, one of the main techniques in satire. (See Chapter 15 for more on satire.)

51. hypothetical examples: examples based on supposition or uncertainty.

52. idealism: the act or practice of envisioning things in an ideal form; seeing things as they could be or as you wish they were.

53. idiom, idiomatic: a figure of speech; a manner of speaking that is natural to native speakers of a language. (Example: Madder than a wet hen.)

★ **54. imagery**: language (descriptions) that evoke the senses.

55. imagery, concrete: imagery that relies on concrete language. Example: Describe the moon as full and orange instead of ominous, which can be interpreted in a variety of ways. Most people have an understanding of what a full moon is and of the color orange.

56. **implicit**: something that is implied.

57. **induction**: reasoning by which a general statement is reached on the basis of particular examples.

58. **inference**: an interpretation of the facts based on available details, drawing conclusions.

59. **ironic commentary**: the commentator or opinion writer does not mean what she writes. The writer's point is meant to be taken ironically.

60. **juxtapose (juxtaposition)**: to place side by side in order to show similarities or differences. The placement often reveals irony.

61. **list**: See catalog

62. **maxim**: a saying or expression that proposes to teach or tell a truth.

★ 63. **metaphor**: a comparison of two unlike things in order to show one more clearly or in a new way.

64. **metaphor, extended**: the metaphor extends throughout the work or passage, even forming the basis for the entire work. The key to identifying an extended metaphor is length.

65. **mock (mockery)**: to make fun of, to treat with ridicule or derision. A tool of satire. Also, a lesser, ignoble form of hero, epic, etc. A mock hero is all that a real hero is not.

66. **musing**: quiet reflection upon a topic; pondering.

67. **naïveté**: innocence in perception, lack of worldly knowledge.

68. **negation(s)**: a negative statement; a statement that is a refusal or denial of some other statement, or a proposition that is true if, and only if, another proposition is false.

69. **neutrality**: not taking a position, staying out of an argument.

70. **onomatopoeia**: words whose sounds mimic their meaning.

71. **overgeneralization** (also known as **hasty generalization**): drawing conclusions from insufficient evidence. Example: All teenagers are sullen and argumentative.

★ **72. oxymoron**: a figure of speech in which two contradictory elements are combined for effect, such as "deafening silence" or "random order."

★ **73. paradox**: the juxtaposition of incongruous or conflicting ideas that reveals a truth or insight.

★ **74. parallel structure/syntax**: the use of parallel elements in sentences or in the structure of an essay or prose passage. Examples: A sentence with successive prepositional phrases uses parallelism. An essay that has four parts, each beginning with a question followed by an answer.

75. parody: a humorous imitation of an original text meant to ridicule; used as a technique in satire.

76. pathos: the quality in literature that appeals to the audience's emotion.

77. personification: to give human attributes or qualities to something nonliving or nonhuman.

78. propaganda: information that is spread for the purpose of promoting some cause; information, especially of a biased or misleading nature, used to promote a political cause or point of view.

79. qualifying a claim/statement: "to qualify" means to show how a claim can be true in some ways, but not true in other ways.

80. rebut, rebutting, rebuttal: to give an opposing point of view or to dismantle an opponent's argument, showing its flaws.

81. refutation: an attack on an opposing view to weaken, invalidate, or make it less credible.

82. repetition: any of a variety of devices that emphasize through repetition. One example of a repetition device is anaphora, which is the repetition of the same word or words at the beginning of successive phrases, clauses, or sentences. (See Chapter 9 on syntax for more of these patterns.)

83. rhetorical question: a figure of speech in the form of a question posed for its persuasive effect without the expectation of a reply.

84. **rhetorical strategy**: various strategies and appeals that writers use to persuade. (See Chapter 6 for more details.)

85. **satire (satirize)**: a type of literature (or a rhetorical strategy) that exposes idiocy, corruption, or other human folly through humor, exaggeration, and irony. (See Chapter 15 for a more complete explanation of satire.)

86. **simile**: a metaphor using *like* or *as* in the comparison.

87. **simile, extended**: the simile progresses throughout the passage or work and may provide the basis for the work in itself.

88. **staccato phrases**: phrases composed of a series of short, sharp sounds or words.

89. **suspense**: an aspect of plot or narrative in which the author withholds information creating an urgent need to know in the reader.

90. **syllogism**: a formula of deductive argument that consists of three propositions: a major premise, a minor premise, and a conclusion.

91. **symbol**: a thing, idea, or person that stands for something else.

92. **syntax**: the order of words in a sentence; also the types and structures of sentences. (See more about syntax in Chapter 9.)

93. **thesis**: the main idea of the essay; what the writer hopes to prove is true.

94. **tone**: the speaker's (author's, narrator's) attitude toward a person, place, idea, or thing; the emotional quality of a phrase or passage.

95. **tongue-in-cheek**: humorous or ironic statement not meant to be taken literally.

96. **truism**: a statement that is obviously true and says nothing new or interesting.

97. **typography**: techniques in print (type) used for emphasis: italicizing, bold font, variation in font, etc.

★ 98. **understatement**: saying less than is warranted by the situation in order to emphasize reality.

99. **verb phrase**: the verb and its object and modifiers.

100. vernacular: the ordinary, everyday speech of a region.

101. wit: clever use of language to amuse the reader, but more to make a point.

Try to see these terms as they exist in everything you see and read. If you think of this list as merely terms you have to memorize, you will not really integrate them into your thought processes. Instead, apply what you know to how you think about everything you "read," even when you watch a movie or listen to a song.

Rhetoric and Rhetorical Strategies

Rhetoric is the art of ruling the minds of men.—Plato

OVERVIEW

Rhetoric is the art of persuasion, whether spoken or written. The AP English Language and Composition exam is a true measure of your ability to write persuasively, as well as to identify and analyze the rhetorical techniques good writers use. The purpose of this chapter is to give you an overview of the most common elements of rhetoric, so you can identify them in the texts you are given to analyze and use them to strengthen your own writing.

PERSUASION

To **persuade** is to convince someone else to believe something or to do something. The avenues one can use to persuade are many, from a simple letter or note to a speech in front of thousands of people. This chapter summarizes the main tools that writers and speakers use to persuade. Convincing your dad to let you use his car for a date is, perhaps, less difficult than convincing your principal that prom court is an antiquated idea based upon popularity and should be abolished.

An audience can be characterized by its perceived tendency to agree with you. We use the phrase "preaching to the choir" for situations when we're arguing a point of view that our audience already agrees with. Such arguments can be fun, but do not require much skill. The most difficult persuasive task is when we attempt to convince an audience hostile to our claim not only to accept it, but also to take action in defense of that claim. Always keep the audience in mind when considering the purpose and effect of the intended message.

THE RHETORICAL TRIANGLE

Aristotle defined qualities of argument centuries ago. We still use his language. Be sure you understand how these aspects of rhetoric apply both to texts you're analyzing on the exam as well as your own arguments in the free-response section.

- **Ethos**: The trustworthiness or credibility of the writer. You have to write what you know, what you believe, and support it well. Your essay will be voiceless and powerless if you don't believe in what you are saying.

  — An important element in ethos is **tone**. The tone of the prose must match the intent of the writer. For example, a condescending tone does not equal a willingness to foster positive change. You will not convince your audience if you talk down to it.

- **Logos**: Using reason and logic to persuade. You must have a point to argue and know how to do it. A good argument is based on solid facts to support a reasonable and well-founded claim.

- **Pathos**: Appeals to emotion or the emotional quality of the work.

  — Tone is critical here as well, especially for subtle appeals. Some writers make overt appeals to emotion, such as fear, doubt, etc.

THREE KINDS OF CLAIMS

A **claim** is what you are trying to prove. It is your proposition or thesis.

1. CLAIM OF FACT

When you make a **claim of fact**, you are stating something is true and you want your audience to believe you. Example: Daylight saving time benefits leisure industries.

About Facts

A **fact** is a statement that can be verified in a variety of ways:

- It is published in credible references;
- It can be known by experience or observation;
- It is measurable or quantifiable.

Facts can also change over time. For example, the fact that the United States is comprised of 13 states has not been true for awhile.

Facts may be true, but are not always true. For example: A high school diploma is necessary for success in life. This is generally true, but there are cases of highly successful people who did not earn a high school diploma.

Facts can be "qualified" using words such as "generally," "probably," or "typically." In this case, "qualified" means "not always."

2. CLAIM OF VALUE

When you make a **claim of value** you are making a judgment or evaluation. Example: Reality TV will rot your brain.

Ways to Evaluate:

- Right or wrong;
- Good or bad;
- Approve or disapprove;
- Beautiful or ugly;
- Worth your time or a waste of time.

Two Areas of Value:

1. aesthetics (what is pleasing, beautiful, artistic)
2. morality (what is moral, right, good)

Sometimes value judgments are actually matters of taste or preference. For example, you prefer straight-leg jeans and your friend prefers boot-cut jeans. In each case, the value lies within the person, not in the thing itself. There is nothing automatically better about either style, and presenting an argument about the superiority of boot-cut jeans is perhaps a waste of time. On the other hand, ads in fashion magazines are essentially arguments for exactly that; clothing manufacturers want you to value one style over another this year, so that you will buy what they are selling. Trends and fads are, to some degree, based on our need to feel beautiful and to fit in (belonging and esteem needs). What we approve of or disapprove of in fashion seems almost capricious—our likes are certainly not based on logic or reason. Don't worry. You will not be arguing about fashion on the exam, but you might be presented with a question a bit more weighty, such as whether or not something is moral or right.

Morality judgments can be tricky, as people's views of morality can be conditional and based on culture, religion, ethnic tradition, etc. However, there are universal truths that nearly all cultures uphold. Most societies believe that lying, stealing, cheating, and killing are wrong.

3. CLAIM OF POLICY

A **claim of policy** is when you argue that certain conditions or situations should exist or be changed. Example: All high school students should pass mandatory minimum proficiency tests before earning a diploma.

Argue a claim of policy if a problem exists for which a change in policy is warranted. You might need to refer to relevant values that support your opinion. Not everyone will agree that your proposal is the correct way to solve the problem, so you need to support your claim with appropriate data, examples, and testimony.

SUPPORTING YOUR CLAIMS

Two basic types of support:

1. evidence

2. basic appeals (appeals to needs and values)

1. **EVIDENCE**

   A. **Factual Evidence**

      Types of Factual Evidence:

      - Examples
      - Hypothetical Examples
      - Statistics
      - Expert Opinion

      Evaluating Factual Evidence:

      - Is it up-to-date?
      - Is it sufficient; is it enough?
      - Is it relevant?
      - Is it consistent with the audience's experience?

      Evaluating Statistics:

      - Are the statistics from a reliable source? Is the source objective or associated with a particular group or point of view that would create bias?
      - Are the terms clearly defined?
      - Are comparisons valid? Are you comparing things that can be compared?
      - Has any pertinent information been omitted?

   B. **Opinions** (experts, witnesses, qualified observers)

      Observers and experts interpret facts and their testimony or opinion can support claims of fact.

      Evaluating Opinions:

      - Is the source credible or otherwise qualified to give the opinion?
      - Does the source harbor any obvious biases?
      - Can the source's opinion be verified by fact?

2. **BASIC APPEALS**

A writer can appeal to readers'

- **needs** (see details below);

- sense of **tradition** (we've always done it this way);

- **ethics** (sense of fairness, right or wrong);

- **emotions** (pull at the heartstrings);

- **logic/reason** (suggest what is logical and support it with a reasoned argument).

There are also appeals to

- **authority** (stating facts, expert opinion, statistics);

- accepted or shared **values** (success, freedom, equality, etc.).

According to psychologist Abraham Maslow, human beings are motivated in their behavior based on their response to whether or not certain basic needs have been met. Maslow arranged his list of needs in a hierarchy. He believed that we needed to satisfy needs in a particular order, beginning with physiological and concluding with self-fulfillment.

- **Physiological Needs**: food, drink, air, health;

- **Safety Needs**: security, shelter, order;

- **Belonging Needs**: love from family and friends, belonging to a social group or community;

- **Esteem Needs**: recognition from others; self-esteem that comes from success and achievement;

- **Self-Actualization Needs**: the need to realize our potential, to become what we hope and dream we can become.

Test Tip

Many advertisements and arguments assume that our physiological needs are met, and sell to us based on other needs. Can you find ads that target safety needs, belonging needs, esteem needs? What about self-actualization needs? Your analysis of television commercials or print ads is actually an analysis of rhetorical strategies.

THE IMPORTANCE OF LANGUAGE

No doubt your English teachers have talked to you about how important word choice is for a writer. It's actually much more important than you realize. Words are powerful persuasion tools when the right person wields them for his or her purposes. In this section, I want to reiterate a few basic aspects of language about which you need to be aware, not only for your analyses of texts, but also to help you be a powerful "wielder of words" yourself.

Be aware that language can be used in many ways, ethical and not so ethical. It is important for you to adopt a skeptical stance regarding language. It's almost never a good idea to take words and phrases at face value. What else is there? What connotations exist? What equivocal meanings are apparent? Learn to read, as they say, "between the lines."

Terms and Definitions	Notes
Emotive language is that which expresses emotion or appeals to emotion in the reader.	Emotive language can be abusive, if the writer manipulates emotions for false claims or to gain power or control. Emotional appeals are very common in advertising, in political speeches, and in persuasive texts. It's important to recognize emotional appeals and to look at them for what they are instead of being swept up in the moment.
	A recent ad campaign for a particular smartphone tells consumers nothing about the quality of the product, what it can do, or why they should buy it. Instead, the advertisers present a variety of emotion-filled vignettes to draw in consumers. One of these narratives is about a wife telling her husband that after a long wait, she's finally pregnant and another has a son showing his father a picture of his newborn son. These obvious appeals to emotion are effective. Empathy connects us in a visceral way. Tears, whether joyful or compassionate, are powerful persuaders.

Continued →

Terms and Definitions	Notes
Connotation is the emotional or social meaning of a word or phrase.	Connotations have positive or negative associations and can change over time. Connotations are also culturally anchored. That is, a word can mean one thing in one culture but something else in another. Writers consciously choose certain words over others based on the emotional associations they make with readers. Consider the different connotative meanings in the following pairs of words: "criminal" versus "rat"; "woman" versus "chick"; "custodian" versus "janitor." In each pair, is there one word that is more positive? Why? Learn to look at why writers choose particular words to make their point. This will also help you use the right word for the job when you need to.
Euphemisms are words or phrases that are used instead of harsher or uglier words or phrases to lessen or soften the effect.	A common euphemism is to say "passed away" instead of "died," when we report someone's death. It is often quite difficult to learn that someone has died, so a gentle term, we think, makes the news easier to take. The main danger with euphemisms is that they're evasive, sometimes abstract, and generally too ambiguous for clear communication. If a euphemism is used to cover up a truth, then that is an abuse of language equal to a lie.

Terms and Definitions	Notes
Slanted language presents a particular view or is in line with a particular interest. In other words, it is biased or prejudiced language that favors a particular group or point of view.	A good example of slanted language can be heard in almost every current political campaign. Listen for the phrase "career politician." The connotation is negative. The speaker expects the audience to automatically think of any incumbent as a bad politician, simply because he or she has had the job for awhile. The term becomes almost a slogan that we should rally around, but why? Where's the evidence?
	Can you think of any other ways the term "career politician" is rhetorically unsound? Hint: Review your logical fallacies, Chapter 7.
	Journalists are cautioned to be objective and neutral in their reporting, but this is a difficult task for human beings. Instead, writers who want to be fair will strive to report both sides of an issue, or at least acknowledge that the other side exists. **Loaded words** sympathize with one side only.
	For example, to talk about an environmental rally by saying that more than a thousand tree-huggers showed up in their Birkenstocks to protest a new mine would be using slanted language. The loaded words "tree-huggers" and "Birkenstocks" pander to those who think that it's somehow wrong to want to protect the environment and those who do are crazy hippies (connotation of Birkenstocks). You can see how many people could be insulted by such slanted language.

Continued →

Terms and Definitions	Notes
Slang, colloquial expressions, and idioms **Slang** refers to informal language considered nonstandard, or not acceptable in formal situations. Examples of this are "cool," "sweet," or "stoked." **Colloquial expressions** are figures of speech that are regional and often anchored in time. Sometimes **colloquialisms** are simply one word. An example can be found with soft drinks, which can be called "soda" or "pop," depending on the region. An apartment may be called a "pad" or a "flat." **Idioms** are colloquial metaphors and are typically particular to a region. Two examples are: "Hotter 'n a fly on a griddle" or "Time to hit the hay."	These elements of vernacular can help one to bond with an audience, by speaking the language of the people. They also have an effect on an author's style. A memoir full of colloquial expressions has a down-home, honest feel to it. A serious, scholarly treatise would not include casual language, however. When you write your own persuasive essays for the exam, you will want to avoid casual language. Rather than try to memorize the subtle differences between these uses of language, simply remember casual versus formal or standard versus nonstandard.

Terms and Definitions	Notes
Clichés and Slogans A **cliché** is a phrase or expression that has been used so often that it has lost its value. A **slogan** is a phrase or statement meant to represent an idea, a movement, a campaign or even an organization. No doubt your school has a slogan. How does it represent you? Does it have meaning for you? When do words become just words?	Clichés have been around a long time and are often repeated because they express a truth or a shared value. However, to use clichés is a lazy shortcut. It is far better to express ideas with well-phrased original sentences. Maybe you've heard someone string together a slew of clichés. When the speech is over, you may have no idea what it was about. A slogan can also become a mindless phrase if it is repeated often enough or out of context. In *Animal Farm*, Orwell warns against the danger of slogans that are mindlessly repeated by the masses which sound like the bleating of sheep. Think about what it means when people say, for example, "Support the Troops." What does it mean? Are those self-stick ribbons that people put on their cars just slogans in disguise?
Picturesque language is language that appeals to the senses, otherwise known as description or **imagery**.	Images are powerful in rhetoric. As human beings, we can relate much more to things we can envision or perceive (even vicariously) through our senses. Imagery is highly emotive as well. Think about how visually oriented we are as a modern culture. Some say we live in an image culture. Abstract ideas are sometimes difficult to grasp, but if a writer creates an image that helps us to understand the abstraction, the point is more easily made.

Continued →

Terms and Definitions	Notes
Concrete versus abstract language **Concrete language** refers to real objects that we can sense or measure. Concrete passages are not difficult to imagine or perceive. **Abstract language** refers to things that are hard to define, or that can be defined in more than one way. Abstract ideas can mean one thing to me and another to you. An example of an abstraction is, "That's interesting," which means many things. What does "interesting" mean?	The basic problem with abstraction is that it is too vague. Ambiguity presents problems for the reader as well as the writer. Terms must be well-defined in order for an argument to be valid. If the reader has to keep asking what this or that means, it's not good.
Equivocation is found when the writer uses words that have more than one meaning in order to be intentionally ambiguous. Equivocation is an avoidance technique. A **double entendre** is a type of equivocation where one meaning is risqué or sexual. **Puns** also rely on double meanings for humor.	If you run into equivocal language, pay attention to both or all potential meanings of the words. Watch for any uses of ambiguous language. The most important question you can ask yourself as you read is, "What is missing or unstated here?"

Test Tip

A good crossword puzzle relies on double or equivocal meanings of words. Practice your word skills by doing the Sunday crossword from your local paper.

IMPLICIT VERSUS EXPLICIT

Implicit means implied. The idea or concept is alluded to or suggested. The "answer" is not directly found in the text but must be inferred or interpreted based on clues. **Explicit** is the opposite and means that an idea or concept is clearly or directly stated in the text. There is no need to infer. The use of the word "explicit" in media to refer to profane or vulgar text or images has created a misunderstanding of the word. "Explicit" does not mean profane or imply any negative association.

LOGICAL FALLACIES

A **fallacy** is a misuse of language or an error in argument that negates the validity of an argument. Please see Chapter 7 for a detailed view of logical fallacies.

PROPAGANDA

Propaganda is language or rhetoric used to persuade a mass audience, generally to convince them of a particular political, religious, or other ideology. Propaganda differs from other mass persuasive messages in that it is associated with a particular agenda and not a particular message. A variety of genres have been used to transmit propaganda including books, films, broadcast messages, and even pamphlets dropped from aircraft to townspeople on the ground.

While totalitarian regimes are most often associated with propaganda, the United States is also well-known for propaganda, such as "Duck and Cover" films for schoolchildren during the Cold War. The term "propaganda" is generally considered to be pejorative. Propaganda techniques are similar to logical fallacies, which pervert or distort the truth.

In Orwell's *1984*, Hate Week and the Two Minutes Hate activities are major components of the Party's propaganda machine, as each works against rational thought and further turns Oceania's citizens into "bleating sheep."

George Orwell's **Animal Farm** *is a simple, easy book to read that will help you grasp the concept of propaganda. Each of the propaganda techniques listed below is evident in the novel. In addition,* **Animal Farm** *is an example of satire (see Chapter 15). Orwell creates an allegory in order to criticize totalitarianism and the abuse of power. Animal and human characters in the novel have direct, real-life correlatives to key individuals from the Russian Revolution.*

PROPAGANDA TECHNIQUES

- **Appeal to fear**: Fear is one of the most effective methods of controlling others.

- **Appeal to authority**: Associated with fear, human beings seem reluctant to oppose authority. We're taught that we do not want to get in trouble. Also, we may find it easier to follow than to lead. We tend to blindly follow authority.

- **Unwarranted emotional appeals**: Even unrestrained joy (the mania of a crowd) can persuade and make people lose their reason.

- **Bandwagon technique**: Everyone else is doing it; why not you, too? If you think otherwise, you're not patriotic.

- **Glittering generalities**: Using abstract and undefined language to the extent that people want to believe it. Examples: freedom, glory.

- **Obtain disapproval**: Citizens band together to hate or stand against a common enemy.

- **Stereotyping**: It is much easier to disapprove of a group if we believe everyone in the group is the same. Example: All teenagers are lazy and selfish. (Don't you hate that?)

- **Scapegoating**: Find a person or a group to blame it all on.

- **Slogans:** A motto or phrase that is mindlessly repeated and has no particular meaning, but can bring people together in a common bond.

STYLISTIC DEVICES EFFECTIVE WRITERS USE

- Evocative or emotive language;
- Lists of relevant details;
- Figurative language, especially to get readers to see things in a fresh way;
- Imagery, appeals to senses and draws readers into the text;
- Repetition, used for emphasis;
- Parallel structure, used for emphasis;
- Irony, gets us to see the truth;
- Analogy, shows logical relationships.

MODES/FORMS OF RHETORIC

- Cause and effect;
- Problem and solution;
- Narrative;
- Description;
- Definition;
- Humor;
- Satire.

THE VERBS OF RHETORIC

1. **Analyze:** to break apart; to look at component parts of a text in order to understand an aspect of the whole.

2. **Characterize**: to depict something in a certain way; to give specific characteristics of someone or something.

3. **Cite:** to make reference to.

4. **Claim**: to make an assertion of something you intend to prove. There are also claims of value and claims of policy, all detailed earlier in this chapter.

5. **Clarify**: to draw distinctions, to make more evident, to lessen confusion.

6. **Compare:** to show how two things are alike or have similar qualities.

7. **Contrast:** to show how two things are not alike or have dissimilar qualities.

8. **Describe:** to use vivid language (such as imagery) to characterize or represent.

9. **Develop:** to enlarge or expand upon an idea.

10. **Discuss:** to consider in writing a variety of possible views (ways of interpretation) on a topic.

11. **Dramatize:** to give a story to a situation by adding vivid details, such as imagery, figurative language, etc.

12. **Elaborate:** to give more detail; to make an idea more complex.

13. **Emphasize:** to give added importance or weight to something.

14. **Establish:** to set a foundation for, to base a claim on an observation.

15. **Evaluate:** to assess in value or quality.

16. **Exemplify:** to give one or more examples.

17. **Explain:** to use details to clarify meaning.

18. **Illustrate:** to describe with anecdotes or examples.

19. **Imply:** to state indirectly; to have a logical consequence.

20. **Indicate:** to be a signal of; to state or express.

21. **Itemize:** to list individual items.

22. **Narrate:** to recount events, as in a story.

23. **Observe:** to take notice of, and thereby, it is implied, to draw conclusions.

24. **Offer a hypothesis:** to offer a theory or assumption to investigate or prove.

25. **Paraphrase:** to put into more common, less complex (or less technical) language.

26. **Predict:** to suggest the effects or result of an action or policy (or any idea that may evolve or change).

27. **Propose:** to suggest a plan or a solution to a problem.

28. **Provide an example:** see *exemplify*.

29. **Provide a history:** to provide a concise record of past events, policies, beliefs, etc.

30. **Rebuff:** to reject.

31. **Refute:** to prove something wrong.

32. **State a proposition:** similar to *offer a hypothesis*, a proposition is an idea worth considering.

33. **Suggest:** to offer a perspective, a solution, or a way of thinking about something for consideration.

34. **Support:** to give reasons and examples for a statement of fact or a claim.

35. **Synthesize:** combine various elements to produce a new concept or to make a point.

36. **Trace:** to follow the origins of an idea; similar to *providing a history*.

Logical Fallacies

He who establishes his argument by noise and command
shows that his reason is weak.—Michel de Montaigne

OVERVIEW

A **logical fallacy** is an error in reasoning or logic. When fallacies exist, some aspect of the argument is flawed, or it may be that the entire argument is rendered invalid. The purpose of this chapter is to list and explain the most common logical fallacies.

There are two reasons for you to be aware of these faults in logic. The first is that you are going to be reading a variety of arguments throughout the AP English Language exam, and being able to detect lapses in reason will help you view these arguments realistically. You are also going to be arguing your own point of view in one of the essays. It is important that you maintain control of your thesis and support it with solid, reliable reasoning. You will not want to commit any fallacies of your own.

Search the Web for "logical fallacies" and you will find dozens of credible sources that list and define fallacies. The list below is not meant to include all fallacies, only the most common.

COMMON LOGICAL FALLACIES

1. **Hasty Generalization:** A conclusion reached prematurely without sufficient evidence. Prejudices and stereotypes are types of generalizations. Words like "all," "every," "everyone," and "no" are associated with hasty generalizations. Example: All teenagers are lazy and uninterested in anything other than themselves. This

may also be called "jumping to conclusions." Example: Everyone is doing it, so it must be healthy.

2. **Faulty Use of Authority:** The arguer attempts to justify his claim by citing testimony or opinions of experts. Also, the arguer fails to acknowledge disagreements among experts or otherwise misrepresents the trustworthiness of sources. Example: Kobe Bryant believes that kids who watch too much television are not as smart as kids who play outside.

3. *Post Hoc, Ergo Propter Hoc* **(Doubtful Cause)** (Latin for *after this, therefore because of this*): This fallacy exists when the arguer suggests that because an event follows another event, it is therefore the cause of that event. Example: Everything was fine until we switched to daylight saving time. That's why the economy is in trouble.

4. *Ad Hominem* (Latin for *against the man*): When the writer attacks a person (personal character or reputation) instead of addressing the argument or the issue. This fallacy draws attention away from the real issues. Example: Don't vote for William Smith. He has been married three times.

5. **False Dilemma or Either-Or Fallacy:** This is when the arguer assumes that there are only two ways of looking at an issue. Example: America. Love it or leave it.

6. **Slippery Slope:** The arguer predicts that one thing will inevitably lead to another, and that one thing will be undesirable. This is a cause-and-effect error that relies on simplistic, erroneous connections. Example: If students study sex education in high school, they will become sexually promiscuous.

7. **Begging the Question:** The arguer makes an assertion as if she has already proven it. It lacks evidence. Example: Required courses such as freshman English are a waste of time. They should not be required.

8. **Straw Man:** In this diversionary tactic, the arguer attacks a view similar to, but not the same as, his opponent's view.

9. *Non Sequitur*: In Latin, this means *does not follow*. An arguer is guilty of *non sequitur* when he states: "Ms. Johnson is our new English teacher. She's young and should be good."

10. *Ad Populum*: An appeal to the prejudices of the masses that asserts: if many believe it, then it is so. The assumption here is that if everyone is going to agree with me, then I don't really need to support my claim with any evidence. Just because a lot of people believe something, that doesn't necessarily make it true. Example: Politicians often want whatever the American people want, as if everyone wants/believes the same thing.

11. **Bandwagon Effect or Jumping on the Bandwagon:** This fallacy is similar to *Ad Populum*, but relies on popularity or trendiness. The error in logic is obvious—just because it is popular, it isn't necessarily correct.

12. **Red Herring:** This fallacy exists when the arguer throws out an unrelated argument to divert the reader's/listener's attention.

13. **Appeal to Tradition:** This fallacy is apparent when the arguer suggests a course of action that is correct "because we've always done it this way." Just because something is traditionally true, that does not make it right or effective. Example: We arrange desks in a classroom in orderly rows. Any other way has not been proven effective.

14. **Faulty Emotional Appeals:** When the arguer seeks sensational or sentimental reactions in the audience; bases an argument on feelings (especially pity or fear), often to draw attention away from the real issues or to conceal another purpose. Example: If you don't study at least an hour every night, you won't get into college and you won't have a successful life.

15. **Guilt by Association:** Relies on prejudice instead of thought. When a person is negatively judged by the actions of those with whom he associates. Example: Senator Adams cannot be trusted. He played golf last year with Senator Jones, who has been indicted for campaign-finance fraud.

Test Tip

After you learn these fallacies, look for them in television commercials or in political ads. This will reinforce the fact that these fallacies exist and will help you remember the different types. It also will help you consider the "arguments" of commercials with a more critical eye.

The Writer's Tools:
Diction, Tone, Style, Imagery, and Figurative Language

Good writing is like a windowpane.—George Orwell

OVERVIEW

Writers have many tools to use when writing an essay, a speech, a letter, or any genre, and exactly how they use words is determined by many things: their purpose, the intended audience, and even the historical, social, and political context in which they write. There is much more to a writer's work than simply putting words together in a grammatically correct way.

One can find simple, persuasive texts in many places. On the side of a box of a popular breakfast cereal, we find a brief appeal to our desire to improve our environment. The writer has used statistics to support the company's claim that it is striving for sustainability. But, there is no imagery, no figurative language, and the words used are simple—we don't need a dictionary to help us understand what we're reading.

The short pieces you will be reading on the AP English Language exam will, of course, demand more of your reading and thinking skills than those required when reading a box of cereal, so it is important that you know the ways writers use words to achieve their goals.

This chapter is an overview of the basic tools writers use to manipulate and manage words, so that the resulting text is effective, arresting, and above all, persuasive.

▌DICTION

Diction is often defined as the "author's choice of words."

There are two ways to think of diction:

1. Specific effect of word choice: connotation and denotation
2. Overall style

DENOTATION

Denotation refers to the dictionary or precise meaning of a word. Authors' use of the right word for the passage can be key to their clarity of expression. Knowing a wide variety of words and their meanings is critical to being able to understand complex prose passages.

One of the main reasons students misread a passage is that they do not understand the vocabulary in the text. Unfortunately, you won't be able to consult a dictionary when you are taking the exam. Please see a list of potentially difficult vocabulary words in Chapter 12.

It is also important to be open-minded regarding word meanings. Be careful to not automatically attribute a common meaning to a word, especially when you are reading older texts, as meanings of words change over time. For example, the word "terrific" means "wonderful" or "great" in a contemporary context, but in the context in which it appears on one released exam, it means "terrifying." Another example is the word "awful," which means in its context "to be in awe of," but a careless reader might think it simply means "horrible." Considering the context in which words appear is critical to determining meaning.

To avoid misreading the material, especially when confronted with archaic language, determine word meanings from the broader context of the text. Archaic, obscure, or overly specific language will generally be defined in footnotes.

CONNOTATION

In analyzing word choice, you should also consider the connotation of specific word choice and the effect of those associations in the passage.

Connotation is the emotional sense of a word or the cultural meaning associated with a word. Connotations are generally positive or negative.

Jonathan Swift, in one section of *A Modest Proposal*, wants to suggest to his readers a connection between poor women and animals used for breeding, and so he refers to a newborn baby as "a child just dropped from its dam." Connotation and denotation are both important to Swift's purpose here. According to Webster's dictionary, a "dam" is a female parent of an animal. It's not "dame," which is a British term for a woman of rank, station, or authority, and therefore power. A "dam" is just the opposite. In this context, the connotation suggests lowliness, perhaps even filth, as in barnyard filth. A woman called a "dam" is not really considered human. All the connections to human motherhood are diminished in this one word. The connotation of the word "dropped" is important also. Human mothers do not drop their children in the birthing process. They are aided by doctors (or midwives) who help them, as much as possible, ease their child into the world. "Dropped" connotes mindlessness, as an animal that simply lets its body do its work. The overall effect of this language is to reduce the already wretched Irish poor to the same state as animals and therefore devalue them. If Swift can get his intended audience to accept this premise, the real proposal he has in store for them will seem to be a logical conclusion. There is so much meaning in just a few words.

Test Tip

When you read, if you begin to notice several words that fit together in connotative meaning, make a list of them in the margin (or circle them in the text). You are noticing a series of words that create a dominant impression. While this impression may not drive an essay's thesis, the list is probably a key to understanding it and is worth noting.

Tone and mood (detailed below) are critical elements of diction, particularly in establishing (or identifying) connotations. Writers choose words based on the emotional or social associations they conjure in readers. What's more, tone and mood are also key aspects of style. If you have a broad understanding of tone, in particular, and how it plays into a writer's purpose, it will help you answer a wide range of questions on the exam.

TONE

Tone is the attitude of the speaker toward another character, a place, an idea or a thing. In thinking of tone in this regard, it is important to pay attention to not only what a character or speaker does, but also to what he or she says. Sometimes we know more than the character does (dramatic irony) and this impacts our understanding of tone.

We also say that a passage or paragraph has a specific tone, which refers to its emotional quality. This quality comes from details like imagery, diction (a speaker's or narrator's speech, for example), even syntax, in which short, simple sentences seem more urgent and less reflective than more ornate sentence types.

Tone is created in a variety of ways. Diction and imagery are major influences on tone. This is because images evoke emotions and certain words have emotional connotations. When you recognize tone, you most likely "feel" it first. But you also have to have an intellectual understanding of what you feel.

The key to an analysis of tone is, first of all, to recognize it. You must acquaint yourself with typical tone descriptors (see the list at the end of this chapter), so that you aren't fumbling for a word to express what you think you see. The wider the variety of tone descriptors you are able to use, the better you'll be at providing a precise analysis. In other words, if you say a passage is "sad" instead of "melancholy" you may be limiting the precision of your analysis.

MOOD

Mood is related to tone. The term **mood** is sometimes used in association with setting. We can think of mood as the emotional quality of the setting.

While there is most likely a prominent or dominant tone in a passage, you should be aware of tone shifts. If the tone changes suddenly, it can signal an epiphany or some change in a speaker's or narrator's thinking. Tone shifts are critical markers in a passage. See the end of this chapter for a comprehensive list of words that can be used to describe tone.

OVERALL STYLE

Word choice impacts overall style also. One way to think of **style** is as the voice of the writer. Many decisions a writer makes—such as types and lengths of sentences (see more in Chapter 9 on syntax), types of words used (see diction), and the extent to which he or she uses imagery and figurative language—contribute to what we recognize as his or her style.

For example, Hemingway's style is characterized, in part, by short, simple sentence structure, while William Faulkner is known for excessively long sentences.

However, we also use the word "style" to mean something similar to tone.

Consider the difference in style of the two examples below:

a) She was like, pizza is so, like, fattening. (Casual, conversational)

b) She understood that pizza was excessively high in fat and calories. (Formal)

You will be expected to understand that style impacts other elements in a passage, such as characterization, the attitude of the speaker, and more. In the examples above, character "a" could be said to be less intelligent than character "b."

SOME TYPICAL STYLE DESCRIPTORS:

- **authoritative**: the voice is commanding and knowing
- **emotive**: the voice evokes emotion
- **didactic**: the voice is preachy, insistent
- **objective**: the voice is uncommitted, without judgment
- **ornate**: the voice is pretentious, flowery, or ostentatious
- **plain**: the voice is simple, straightforward, to the point
- **scholarly**: the voice is learned and authoritative, erudite
- **scientific**: the voice is precise and relies on the language of science (Latinate words)

See a more comprehensive list of style descriptors at the end of this chapter.

IMAGERY

Imagery is not just one of the most important elements of poetry, it also serves prose writers. **Imagery** is language that engages the senses and evokes emotion. We relate to imagery on a gut level, responding with our emotions. The more detailed the imagery, the more we can put ourselves into the writing.

TYPES OF IMAGERY

- **Visual:** what we can see
- **Auditory:** what we can hear
- **Tactile:** what we can touch
- **Olfactory:** what we can smell
- **Gustatory:** what we can taste
- **Kinesthetic:** sense of movement
- **Organic:** internal sense of being (well or ill)

These sensory perceptions created through language are vicarious (through the experience of the character or the narration). We might also consider these perceptions to be virtual. We don't actually experience them, but the emotions they evoke in us are real. The more vivid the imagery, the more real the emotion.

To become good at recognizing good imagery, make sure you are always looking for it. Stop when you recognize a particularly imagistic passage. Study it. What kind of imagery is it? How do you feel as you experience the passage? And, most importantly, what is the effect of this image?

EFFECTS OF IMAGERY:

- Helps establish tone
- Creates realistic settings
- Creates empathy in readers for characters
- Helps readers imagine themselves as part of a narrative

Test Tip

Engage your imagination in everything you read to practice this important cognitive reading skill. Visualize setting, characters, and action. Not only will this practice deepen your understanding of the work, but it will help you remember what you read.

FIGURATIVE LANGUAGE

When we read any text, we must read carefully and critically, and assume that not everything we read is meant to be taken literally. Writers use **figurative language**, language that is not literal, for various purposes. Many times, figurative language helps us understand complex ideas more clearly, especially if the writer connects to common things or ideas.

METAPHOR

A **metaphor** implies or states a comparison between two unlike things or individuals that helps us see them in a new or more meaningful way. **Similes** are also metaphors, but use the words "like" or "as" in making the comparison. "Life is like a river" is a simile.

Specific Types of Metaphor

- **Direct Metaphor**: the comparison is made directly using the word "is"; for example: Life is a river.

- **Indirect Metaphor**: "The river of life" also compares life to a river, but does so indirectly.

- **Extended Metaphor**: the comparison extends throughout the text (or part of a text) and is fully developed. The ultimate extended metaphor is allegory, which layers two narratives, a literal version with a figurative version. Allegory is more typically found in fiction, drama, and poetry, but is also a technique of satire.

- **Metonymy**: a metaphor in which one word or phrase is substituted for another with which it is closely associated (such as "hand" for "worker" or "crown" for "royalty").

- **Metaphysical Conceit**: an elaborate, intellectually ingenious metaphor (often extended) that shows the writer's realm of knowledge.

- **Analogy**: a comparison based on similarities; showing how two things are alike. An analogy differs from a basic metaphor in that a metaphor is typically completed in one statement or sentence, whereas an analogy can be a paragraph, such as an example to support a claim, or an entire essay as a pattern of exposition.

Comparison is one of our basic patterns of reasoning. We perceive the world and compare new things and experiences with what we already know to see how they are alike or different, and in this process, we make judgments and understand ideas.

OTHER TYPES OF FIGURATIVE LANGUAGE

- **Personification**: giving something non-human, human characteristics

- **Oxymoron**: juxtaposing two things apparently contradictory that still reinforce one idea. For example, jumbo shrimp, deafening silence

- **Hyperbole**: using exaggeration to extend reality. Hyperbole gets us to look more closely at what is actually true by giving us a sharp contrast.

- **Understatement**: this works in the opposite way from hyperbole. We use understatement when we say less than is appropriate for the situation or for our meaning.

STYLE AND TONE DESCRIPTORS

Many of the descriptors in the following lists come from questions about tone, style, attitude, and mood seen on released AP English Language exams. You will notice overlap, which is typical. Some tone/attitude words can be used to describe style equally as well. What you need to know is what these words mean.

Tone & Attitude

acerbic	fervent	remorseful
ambivalent	genial	respectful
appreciative	harsh	reverent
callous	indecisive	sanguine
capricious	indifferent	sarcastic
churlish	informal	scornful
civil	irate	self-aware
conciliatory	ironic	self-deprecating
condescending	jealous	self-effacing
contemplative	judicious	serious
critical	mocking	solemn
cynical	nostalgic	strident
defensive	optimistic	superficial
detached	petulant	suspicious
disapproving	prudent	sympathetic
disillusioned	reassuring	zealous
dismissive	reckless	
enthusiastic	reconciled	

Style

abstract	discursive	petulant
accusatory	disdainful	pompous
acerbic	disjointed	pretentious
allusive	earnest	quaint
ambivalent	eloquent	quizzical
apathetic	glib	reflective
bitter	gloomy	reverent
callous	haughty	ridiculing
candid	idiosyncratic	sarcastic
choleric	indignant	sardonic
churlish	informal	scornful
colloquial	jovial	self-deprecating
complex	judgmental	sincere
conciliatory	malicious	sinister
condescending	mocking	smug
contemplative	morose	solemn
contemptuous	objective	speculative
critical	obsequious	symbolic
cynical	optimistic	terse
derisive	ostentatious	urbane
descriptive	patronizing	vulgar
despairing	pedantic	
detached	pessimistic	

Syntax:
Sentence Construction and Word Order

I like the construction of sentences and the juxtaposition of words—not just how they sound or what they mean, but even what they look like.—Don DeLillo

OVERVIEW

Syntax refers, in general, to the order of words in a sentence that results in various sentence types used for a variety of rhetorical effects. We can also think of syntax as the rhythm of prose. Sentence variety creates interesting, fluent, readable prose. Aspects of syntax, such as repetition and placement of ideas, are used for emphasis.

A study of syntax is important for several reasons:

- Sentences impact the narrative pace of a passage, making it read fast or slow, which therefore impacts the idea/theme;

- Certain types of sentences are better at emphasizing ideas, making key notions, prominent through repetition, parallel structure, or juxtaposition.

- There are questions in the multiple-choice section of the exam that ask you to identify types of sentences.

WORD ORDER

In English, we have a common or typical word order in a sentence:

Subject ▶ Verb ▶ Object

Sometimes writers use **inverted syntax**, which is simply an atypical or unusual word order. There are several reasons why a writer would use inverted syntax:

- Inverted order makes us pay close attention.
- It creates emphasis.
- It slows down our reading of the text.

Typical/Normal Syntax	Inverted/Unusual Syntax
Stephen ate a blueberry muffin for breakfast.	A blueberry muffin Stephen ate for breakfast. *or* For breakfast ate Stephen a blueberry muffin.

When Robert Frost wrote, "Whose woods these are I think I know," he was no doubt using inverted syntax to satisfy his rhyme scheme, and writing "I think I know whose woods these are" was just not going to work for him. As a result, he created an unusual but highly memorable line.

It's not just poets who use inverted syntax. You will notice examples in prose as well. Again, the main reason is to draw attention to some aspect of the text worthy of an extended or second thought.

When you notice inverted syntax in a passage on the exam, mark it and make an annotation. Even if there is no question about it, you may have discovered an important marker worth further exploration.

SENTENCE TYPES AND ATTRIBUTES

Sentence Type	Attributes
Periodic	The most important idea comes at the end of the sentence. **Example:** Doctors were convinced they had destroyed the pernicious infection, but just when they thought he'd recover fully, Mario became savagely febrile and died.
Loose	The most important idea is revealed early and the sentence unfolds loosely after that. **Example:** After her chemotherapy failed, Margaret lay moribund in the hospice, glad for the kindness of nurses, thankful for each new morning that she was able to enjoy.
Parallel	A parallel sentence (sometimes called a balanced sentence) contains parts of equal grammatical structure or rhetorical value in a variety of combinations. Two examples of parallel structures: 1. The dog ate voraciously, joyously, and noisily. (The verb "ate" is modified by three multisyllabic adverbs, which seems somewhat lofty in style for such a mundane act as a dog eating.) 2. Joyce was worn down by the constant invasion of her co-workers, by their insistent stares, by their noisy whispers, by their unveiled disdain. She knew she had to find another job. (The parallel phrases are set off by commas; this also is an example of anaphora.)

Continued →

Sentence Type	Attributes
Repetition	Types of repetition in sentences: **Anaphora:** The repetition of the same word or words at the beginning of a series of phrases, clauses, or sentences. *Example:* The new paradigm was threatening, the new paradigm was bold, and the new paradigm made students angry as they struggled with the new dress code that would force them all to wear plaid jackets. **Epistrophe:** Ending a series of lines, phrases, clauses, or sentences with the same word or words. *Example:* Clara's eyes sparkled inscrutably in her wizened old face as her twenty-something boss told her that he no longer needed her, that he no longer had use for her, that he no longer would employ her. **Asyndeton:** Conjunctions are omitted between words, phrases, or clauses. *Example:* The only way the commoners could mitigate the Queen's rage was to lie humbly prostrate before her, to be temporarily subservient, to feign obedience for the moment. **Chiasmus:** Two corresponding pairs ordered in an ABBA pattern. *Example:* The Queen reveled in the villagers' adulation, but the villagers' adulation was false as they feared her peremptory decree that everyone should turn their surfeit of grain over to the court. **Polysyndeton:** The use of conjunctions (*and, but, or*) between words, phrases, or clauses. *Example:* The mountain climber felt immense trepidation as he faced his arduous climb up K2 but he knew the rewards would be great and the thrill exhilarating and the press conference flattering and he gained momentum from that renewed vigor.

Sentence Type	Attributes
Grammatical Sentence Types	**Simple:** One subject, one verb, modifiers, complements. Simple sentences are generally short, direct, and, in combination with more complex sentences, can be used for emphasis.
	Example: Puppies need a lot of care.
	Compound: Two independent clauses joined by a coordinating conjunction. Remember this mnemonic device: FANBOYS: **f**or, **a**nd, **n**or, **b**ut, **o**r, **y**et, **s**o.
	Example: The king's edict that adulterers would be punished by death caused a raucous din in the local taverns, for even the common folk knew that he had many indiscretions of his own for which to atone.
	Complex: Contains an independent clause and a (dependent) subordinate clause.
	Example: Since the nun's ascetic life provided her few material comforts, the wool shawl the novitiate knitted for her was a cherished treasure.
	Compound-complex: Contains two independent clauses and a dependent (subordinate) clause.
	Example: Even though Rafael's muse had sparked his fertile imagination, he nonetheless lost his drive to paint, so he eased his plight by driving a taxi.
Grammatical Sentence Purposes	1. Declarative sentence: Makes a statement.
	2. Imperative sentence: Gives a command.
	3. Interrogative sentence: Asks a question.
	4. Exclamatory sentence: Makes an emphatic or emotion-filled statement.

Copy several sentence pattern examples and rewrite them using as many vocabulary words as you can from Chapter 12. You'll reinforce your vocabulary and practice your sentence types at the same time.

MORE ASPECTS OF SYNTAX

1. **Climax**: The main idea or most important point in a sentence. The position of the climax may be varied for effect.

2. **Cadence**: The rhythm or "music" of a sentence that comes through parallel elements and repetition.

3. **Narrative Pace**: The pace or speed of a passage comes through the following elements:

   • Length of words;

   • Omission of words or punctuation;

   • Ellipsis (series of dots) indicates a portion is omitted;

   • Length of sentences;

   • Number of dependent/subordinate clauses;

   • Repetition of sounds.

Generally, the shorter the words (fewer syllables) and the shorter and simpler the sentences, the faster the pace. Conversely, the longer the words (more syllables) and the longer, more complex the sentences, the slower the pace.

REMEMBER THE THREE P's OF SYNTAX

1. **Prominence:** Prominence refers to the importance given to an idea in a sentence. Prominence is achieved both by placement and repetition. Sometimes an idea is isolated in a short sentence where it is given sole prominence. If a word is ever set off alone as a fragment, it is being given prominence that you'd best not ignore. Instead, ask the question, "Why is this word isolated?"

2. **Position:** Position means where the key idea is located. It will most often come at the beginning of the sentence (loose sentence) or at the end of the sentence (periodic sentence). But sometimes, writers use nonstandard syntax, or inverted word order, to draw attention to certain words or ideas.

3. **Pace:** Pace is when the speed of the text generally complements the author's purpose. While the following two examples are literature-based, they demonstrate the concept perfectly, and you may be familiar with each example. Quentin's section in Faulkner's *The Sound and The Fury* is presented primarily in stream of consciousness, with fast-paced narration that emphasizes the character's fragile state of mind. Another great example of how pace complements the writer's purpose is Maya Angelou's poem *Woman Work*. The first stanza in which she describes all the tasks to be done is meant to be read so fast that the reader actually feels tired after reading it. The rest of the poem is composed of four-line stanzas that read much, much slower. The images in these stanzas evoke peace, coolness, and rest.

Test Tip

Your own syntax is important in the essay section of the exam. See Chapter 10 for more on using sentence variety in your own writing.

Grammar Basics

*I never made a mistake in grammar but one in my life and
as soon as I done it I seen it.*—Carl Sandburg

The AP English Language exam is not exactly a grammar test. You aren't going to be asked to identify parts of speech or parts of sentences. However, you *are* going to be asked to show that you understand the relationship of a word to a word, of a word to a sentence, or of phrases or clauses to sentences and more. You will also need to be able to identify the antecedents of words or phrases. Furthermore, in the essay portion of the exam, you will be expected to demonstrate your ability to control the elements of grammar, mechanics, usage, and syntax in your own writing.

PRONOUNS AND ANTECEDENTS

Antecedent means that which comes before.

Generally speaking, you can think of an antecedent as any clause, phrase, or noun to which a pronoun or other part of speech refers. The AP English Language exam is going to expect you to make such referential connections.

Specifically, pronouns have antecedents. The antecedent of a pronoun is the noun to which the pronoun refers. In the sentence, "Jim suddenly realized **his** work on the project wasn't finished, which would make **him** late for the meeting to discuss **it**," the pronouns "his" and "him" refer to Jim, while the pronoun "it" refers to the project. One easy way to identify antecedents is to use the object of the pronoun in a question.

Example   The object of the pronoun "his" is "work." You next ask, "Whose work?" The clear answer would be Jim's.

This strategy seems ridiculous when we're looking at this silly little sentence, but what if the syntax of the sentence were much more complicated? Then what? Plus, you may be asked to find an antecedent to a pronoun that might be found one or two sentences earlier than the actual pronoun. You'll need to look and think carefully and not simply assume that the actual antecedent is the noun closest to the pronoun. You may be wrong!

The following excerpt from Michel de Montaigne's essay "Of Books" is a bit more complex than my previous example. Read it, and then answer the question that follows.

I have often observed that those of our times, who take upon them to write comedies (in imitation of the Italians, who are happy enough in that way of writing), take three or four plots of those of Plautus or Terence to make one of their own, and, crowd five or six of Boccaccio's novels into one single comedy. That which makes **them** so load themselves with matter is the diffidence they have of being able to support themselves with their own strength. They must find out something to lean to; and not having of their own stuff wherewith to entertain us, they bring in the story to supply the defect of language.

Question: What is the antecedent of the pronoun in bold? Find the answer at the end of this chapter.

When you're asked on the AP English Language exam to find an antecedent, it most likely is not going to be something simple. Use the strategy of asking the questions: Who? What? When? Where? Why? Think to look beyond the immediate sentence for your answer.

Pronouns and their antecedents need to agree in three ways: person, number, and gender.

- Person: first, second, or third person

- Number: singular or plural

- Gender: masculine, feminine, or neuter

THE GENDER ISSUE

In the old days, if one did not know the sex of the subject or if one was writing about people in general, one would always use masculine pronouns. Today, though, the once ubiquitous "he" is not so easily accepted. A contemporary essay that uses only masculine pronouns seems sexist. Some will try to rectify the situation by using a neutral blend. Awkwardly, they try to make "they," "them," and "their" replace masculine pronouns. The trouble with this strategy is that it breaks an important rule of pronouns and antecedents: it creates a situation where the pronoun no longer agrees with the noun in number.

For example:

- The old way: When a person is late for class, he must get an excuse from the office.

- The "they" way: When a person is late for class, they must get an excuse from the office.

- Another option: Use both "he" and "she": When a person is late for class, he or she must get an excuse from the office.

Problems:

- It is grammatically incorrect to use "they" (plural) to refer to a singular noun.

- It is awkward to keep writing "he/she" or "him/her" or the like.

Solution?

- It seems like a good strategy instead, to mix "he" and "she" throughout the piece of writing.

So . . .

When a person is late for class, he must get an excuse from the office. If the teacher is unwilling to accept her excuse, then the person must make up the time after school in detention.

When the gender of the subject is known, it's easy. We simply make sure that our pronoun matches the gender. Being aware of potential sexism in our writing is important. This is one small way to make sure we are inclusive and not exclusive.

PHRASES AND CLAUSES

While not sentences, phrases and clauses are important parts of sentences that serve a variety of functions. There is much more to the study of phrases and clauses than what is presented here. This section of the book will help you know and understand the basics.

1. PHRASES

A phrase is never a sentence. A **phrase** is a group of related words that does not contain a subject and a verb. There are several common types of phrases:

A. Appositive Phrase

An **appositive phrase** gives more information about the word (noun, subject) it follows and is set off by commas.

> **Example**   The band director, *a veteran of 31 years*, led his students to first place in the national competition.

B. Infinitive Phrase

An **infinitive phrase** consists of an infinitive—the root of the verb preceded by "to"—and the modifiers or complements associated with it. Infinitive phrases can function as adjectives, adverbs, or nouns.

> **Examples**   *To see the sun set* off the shores of Key West can be a spiritual experience. (This infinitive phrase serves as a noun or subject of the sentence.)
>
> Anita went to Harvard *to study criminal law*. (This infinitive phrase tells us why she went to Harvard, so it serves as an adverb.)

C. Prepositional Phrase

A **prepositional phrase** is a group of words that begins with a preposition that links to an object.

You can easily consult the Internet or a grammar handbook for a complete list of prepositions, but you are no doubt quite used to seeing them in what you read and perhaps even using them in your own writing.

Common Prepositions

at	over	before
on	under	up
in	into	down
above	among	beneath
beyond	after	

Examples of prepositional phrases:

Preposition	Object (of the preposition)
under	the *bed*
into	the *wild* (title of Jon Krakauer's book)
before	breakfast
after	an *understanding*

A stylistic aspect of some writers is to add information or emphasis with a string or series of prepositional phrases. Here is an example from Jonathan Swift's *A Modest Proposal*. As an exercise, underline all the prepositional phrases you see. What do you think the effect of this style is?

> I think it is agreed by all parties that this prodigious number of children in the arms, or on the backs, or at the heels of their mothers, and frequently of their fathers, is in the present deplorable state of the kingdom a very great additional grievance. . . .

WHY PREPOSITIONAL PHRASES MATTER

You may never have to identify the subject of a sentence on the AP English Language exam, but you can be certain that you will never find the subject of a sentence in a prepositional phrase. In fact, prepositional phrases are somewhat inert components of sentences. You could cross them all out and still end up with a grammatically viable independent clause (sentence). Knowing this may help you with those tricky referential questions. If you need to simplify the sentence, try crossing out all the prepositional phrases to leave the skeleton of the sentence visible. This strategy may help make a complicated sentence much easier to analyze.

Here is the same sentence from Swift with all the prepositional phrases, conjunctions, and modifiers crossed out. What is left is the skeleton.

> I think it is agreed by all parties that this prodigious **number** of children in the arms, or on the backs, or at the heels of their mothers, and frequently of their fathers, **is** in the present deplorable state of the kingdom a very great additional **grievance**. . . .

The most essential meaning can be boiled down to *number* (subject) *is* (verb) *grievance* (object). But, of course, Swift would not have been very convincing if he had written that way. He'd have come off sounding like the proverbial cave man. The point is that we can cross out prepositional phrases to more easily find these basic sentence elements.

Why is "children" not the subject? "Children" is in the prepositional phrase, "of children." The actual subject is "number." But of course, "of children" is necessary to the meaning of the sentence. Without it, we would ask, number of what?

Stylistically, Swift creates imagery in the string of prepositional phrases that shows children "clinging" to their parents, in an almost burdensome way. Their prodigious number feels, to a careful reader, more weighty.

2. CLAUSES

A **clause** is a group of related words that contains a subject and a verb. An independent clause can stand alone (see more on sentences). A dependent or subordinate clause is incomplete, and is used together with an independent clause to form a complete sentence. Dependent or subordinate clauses are also called **fragments**.

Dependent (or subordinate) clauses sometimes begin with a subordinating conjunction.

Common Subordinating Conjunctions

since	after	while
when	if	when
because		

Here are examples of dependent or subordinate clauses (so called because they are dependent on something else to make them complete sentences or they stand subordinate to the main sentence).

- *Since Sue first began to play the piano*, she understood it took practice to play well.

- John left the house early *when he knew the traffic would be bad*.

Both of these examples are embedded in sentences. When the dependent clause comes first, we set it off with a comma. When it comes second, we do not.

Because . . .

Do you remember a teacher saying we never start a sentence with "because"? He or she probably did not trust that you understood the difference between a dependent clause and an independent clause. It is actually not uncommon to see a sentence that begins with "because." "Because" is an important transitional marker in a sentence that shows cause and effect. Just don't forget that the dependent clause depends on something else to make it independent.

Example   Because the child could not identify all the letters in the alphabet, she was not allowed to move on to first grade.

However . . .

The transition "however" is not a subordinating conjunction. The use of the word "however" in the following example does not make it a dependent clause.

Example   However, Jane was still opposed to having her taxes done by her brother.

The previous example is an independent clause. It stands by itself as a sentence. Students who believe that words like "however" and "therefore" create dependent clauses will incorrectly link them to independent clauses with a comma and will create comma splice errors. (See the section on sentence faults for more about this.) "However" and other words are conjunctive adverbs (see list on next page). They are followed by commas.

Common Conjunctive Adverbs		
accordingly	however	nonetheless
also	incidentally	now
anyway	indeed	otherwise
besides	instead	similarly
certainly	likewise	still
consequently	meanwhile	then
finally	moreover	thereafter
further	namely	therefore
furthermore	nevertheless	thus
hence	next	undoubtedly

WHAT CONSTITUTES A SENTENCE?

A **sentence** must contain a subject, a verb (often referred to as a predicate), and express a complete thought or idea. "I am" is a sentence because it has a subject (I) and a verb (am) and expresses a complete thought (the subject understands him or herself to exist). We are almost always going to need more in a sentence than two words, however.

The subject of a sentence is typically a noun, but it can also be a pronoun, or even a phrase that serves as a noun. If you need to identify the subject of the sentence, the fastest way is to first find the verb and then ask the questions, who? or what?

What is the subject of this sentence?

After the swim meet, a bunch of players went to Cal's house for pizza.

Think it through.

> Well, the verb is "went," so I can ask "who went?" The answer is "a bunch of players." But, wait! I read that the subject can never be in a prepositional phrase, so if I cross out "of players," I am left with "bunch." I guess "bunch" must be the subject.

This example is simple, but I guarantee that if you are asked to find the subject of a sentence on the AP English Language exam, it won't be this easy. It is good to know this strategy.

BASIC SENTENCE STRUCTURES

There are four basic sentence structures. (Refer to Chapter 9 for more complex sentence types.)

1. **Simple:** Consists of a single independent clause.
   Example: Dad mowed the yard every Saturday.

2. **Compound:** Consists of two or more simple sentences joined by a comma and coordinating conjunction or by a semicolon.
   Example: Dad mowed the yard every Saturday, but on Sunday he refused to do any work.

3. **Complex:** Contains one or more dependent or subordinate clauses as well as one independent clause.
   Examples: (a) Since Margaret found the shortcut to work, she is never late.
   (b) When Bill cranks up the air conditioner, his wife complains since she is always too cold.

4. **Compound Complex:** Combines a compound sentence with a complex sentence.
   Example: Allison and Bill shared the day shift, but creating the schedule took compromise since Bill always wanted Friday afternoon off.

Work to eliminate sentence faults from your writing, especially if it's a known weakness. Part of your essay score is based on your ability to control the conventions of language.

BASIC SENTENCE FUNCTIONS

1. **Declarative:** Makes a statement (most of our sentences are declarative).
   Example: Tulip bulbs can be planted in the fall for a spring bloom.

2. **Interrogatory:** Asks a question.
   Example: What's wrong with you?

3. **Exclamatory:** Exclaims with urgency.
   Example: A tornado is coming!

4. **Imperative:** Commands.
   Example: Don't touch that!

COMMON SENTENCE FAULTS AND HOW TO CORRECT THEM

Professional writers sometimes intentionally use sentence fragments for emphasis or variety. However, in general, sentence fragments are not acceptable. When you write your essays for the AP English Language exam, you must know how to avoid sentence faults.

FRAGMENT

A **sentence fragment** is generally a dependent or subordinate clause left to stand on its own, which we know it can't. Phrases are also not independent. To fix fragments, they need to be attached to independent clauses.

Fragment	Sentence
Since time was running out.	Genevieve realized she needed to finish painting her bedroom since time was running out.
Longing for the next vacation.	Longing for the next vacation, Mario kept studying travel magazines.

FUSED OR RUN-ON SENTENCE

When two independent clauses are joined together, we call it a **fused** or **run-on sentence**.

COMMA SPLICE

A **comma splice** is two independent clauses joined by a comma.

Four Ways to Fix These Major Sentence Faults

	Fused or Run-on	Comma Splice
Wrong ▶	Arianna loved to get up early the air was so light and things were peaceful at 5:30 A.M. (Capital A.M. and P.M. is standard English convention. However, lowercase is Associated Press style.	Some people think it is difficult to grow roses, it just takes good soil, plenty of sunshine, and some basic care.
▼ Four ways to correct the error		
1. Add a period at the end of the sentence.	Arianna loved to get up early. The air was so light and things were peaceful at 5:30 a.m.	Some people think it is difficult to grow roses. It just takes good soil, plenty of sunshine, and some basic care.
2. Create a compound sentence by adding a comma and a coordinating conjunction. (See list below.)	Arianna loved to get up early, for the air was so light and things were peaceful at 5:30 a.m.	Some people think it is difficult to grow roses, but it just takes good soil, plenty of sunshine, and some basic care.

Continued →

3. Add a subordinating conjunction to turn an independent clause into a dependent clause.	Arianna loved to get up early because the air was so light and things were peaceful at 5:30 a.m.	While some people think it is difficult to grow roses, it just takes good soil, plenty of sunshine, and some basic care.
4. Add a semicolon, but only if the two halves have a strong logical connection: parallel in meaning or cause and effect.	Arianna loved to get up early; the air was so light and things were peaceful at 5:30 a.m.	Some people think it is difficult to grow roses; it just takes good soil, plenty of sunshine, and some basic care.

LIST OF COORDINATING CONJUNCTIONS

As we've said, the acronym FANBOYS will help you remember the seven coordinating conjunctions: for, and, nor, but, or, yet, so.

When you create a compound sentence, a comma must precede the coordinating conjunction.

To avoid making punctuation errors in your essays, rely on what you know. If you aren't an expert in using semicolons, don't use them. As for commas, when in doubt, leave them out. Students tend to stick commas in where they do not belong. Instead of worrying about punctuation, write clear sentences that say what you mean, but keep them somewhat lean. Learn the basic sentence structures and vary your use of them. If you stay with the familiar in your prose, you should be competent in your use of punctuation.

PUNCTUATION SIMPLIFIED

This short section is meant to help you avoid common punctuation errors by reminding you of a few basic rules. If punctuation is a real problem for you in your writing, consult a good grammar handbook and study the rules.

A. COMMAS

1. Use commas to separate items in a series of repeated parallel elements.
   Examples:
   Bring me the scissors, the paper, and the glue.

   "We shall fight on the beaches, we shall fight on the landing grounds, we shall fight in the fields and in the streets, we shall fight in the hills; we shall never surrender." —Winston Churchill.

2. Use commas to set off appositive phrases or non-essential phrases or clauses.
   Example:
   John, my uncle's second cousin, sells fresh produce every Saturday at the farmer's market in Westfield.

3. Use a comma after an introductory dependent clause, phrase, or word.
   Examples:
   After the rain stops, we should go for a walk.

   While the children play, let's make lemonade.

   Well, we should visit Aunt Mary soon.

4. Use a comma to separate two or more adjectives if they are not connected with a conjunction.
   Examples:
   The lush, verdant garden was inviting to visitors.

   The garden was lush and verdant and inviting to visitors.

5. A comma must never separate a subject from its verb.

B. QUOTATION MARKS

1. Set off quoted text with quotation marks and discrete words used to prove your point about diction.
   Example:
   The author's use of the words "riled," "annoyance," "steamed," and "vehemently," clearly point to the fact that the speaker is angry.

2. Use quotation marks to set off a direct quotation.
Example:
"I am tired of pizza," Mark said. "I want to cook something healthy instead."

3. Indirect quotations do not need quotation marks.
Example:
Mark said that he was tired of pizza and wanted to cook something healthy for a change.

4. Use single quotation marks for a quotation inside a quotation.
Example:
Senator Smith remarked, "The economic recovery is in sight, and as for this latest recession, all I can say is 'all's well that ends well.'"

5. In or out? Do the following punctuation marks go inside or outside quotation marks?

1. Commas? Inside

2. Periods? Inside

3. Semicolon? Outside

4. Question Mark? Inside if it belongs to the quotation. Outside if it doesn't belong to the quoted matter.

C.   COLONS AND SEMICOLONS

1. Use a colon to introduce a long quotation. In addition, a long quotation in an essay is generally indented.

2. A colon can precede a long explanation.

3. Use a colon to introduce a list.
Example:
For a great day at the beach, pack the following items: sunscreen, a blanket, a jug of water, and your sunglasses.

4. Use a semicolon to link two independent clauses of parallel or other logical connection, such as cause and effect.

D. APOSTROPHES

1. Use apostrophes to show omission.
   Examples: We're, they're, and o'er (over).

2. Use apostrophes to show possession:
   Examples: Mel's van, everyone's favorite.

3. Never use apostrophes to indicate plurals.
   Wrong ▶ There were too many banana's.

You can't really edit the world, but I was recently driving on a country road and saw a nice (professionally made) sign promoting the sale of "raspberry's." By this point in the book I'm sure you know that the sign should have promoted the sale of "raspberries."

E. MORE PUNCTUATION

1. Em dashes—generally the equivalent of two hyphens—are used to set off interrupters or appositive phrases in the same way commas can. Do not confuse an em dash with a hyphen.

2. Exclamation points!!!!!!! Just don't use them. The danger is that you will overuse or misuse them. If an exclamation point exists in the text you're quoting, that's different. But please avoid them in your own prose.

Test Tip

It's = it is. Always! In this case, the apostrophe does not show possession. To show something belongs to it, *omit the apostrophe. Example: That dog is chasing its own tail.*

COMMON USAGE ERRORS AND CONFUSED WORDS

I've seen some really smart students make these errors, so while I should not have to include this section, I feel I need to. Please be aware of these common errors and make sure you do not make them in your writing. These are the kinds of errors that drive English teachers (and no doubt AP readers) crazy!

accept, except	I accept this award. No one except Ryan may speak right now.
affect, effect	The effect (noun) of the sun's rays can be harmful. Turning in that paper late will affect (verb) your grade. [effect: a result; affect: a change]
a lot, allot	"A lot" is two words meaning "many;" "allot" means "to disperse." (Avoid using "a lot" because it sounds too casual.)
bring, take	Bring me my slippers then take the trash to the curb, please. Bring = come towards you; take = go away from you.
could have, not could of	should have, *not* should of; would have, *not* would of
fewer, less	There are fewer students in Forensics this year, so our meetings will take less time. Use "fewer" when referring to plural things; use "less" when referring to singular things.
good, well	You will do well today since you ate a good breakfast. "Good" is an adjective; "well" is almost always an adverb.
it's, its	Its fur is brown and it's in need of washing. "Its'" is a possessive pronoun. "It's" is a contraction for "it is."
knew, new	I knew you would ruin your new shoes. "New" is state of age; "knew" is past tense of "to know."
know, no	No, I don't know the capital of Rhode Island. "No" is a negative response. "To know" is to be aware of something.
lead, led (verb)	Lead on, Kyle, or do you prefer being led? "Lead" is present tense; "led" is past tense.
loose, lose	If you keep your hold on that leash so loose, you will lose the leash and the dog will run away. "Loose" is not tight. To "lose" is to have something disappear.

past, passed	In the past, people with manners would have asked for the potatoes to be passed instead of reaching over someone to get them. "Past" is a time before now. "Passed" is past tense of "to pass."
quiet, quite, quit	Be quiet or you will have to quit practicing with the band in our garage. Our neighbors are quite beside themselves because of the noise. "Quiet" is softer volume. "Quit" is to end something. "Quite" is a modifier.
than, then	If I knew then what I know now, I would have chosen this rather than that. "Than" is used to make a comparison. "Then" is a time transition or adverb.
their, there, they're	If they're going to play over there with their toys, then they are going to need to be careful. "They're" is a contraction for "they are." "There" shows where. "Their" is a possessive pronoun.
threw, through	She threw the ball through the air. "Threw" is past tense of "to throw." "Through" is a preposition showing where.
to, too, two	I too, have had two choices to make. "Too" means also, "two" is "one more than one," and "to" is a preposition.
waist, waste	Her waist was so small that we made a size 4 dress and the extra material went to waste. "Waist" is the middle of the body. "Waste" is to not use, to throw unnecessarily away.
weather, whether	The weather was so bad, we didn't know whether or not to go to the lake. "Weather" is rain, snow, and all that meteorological stuff, and "whether" is a transition used to show a choice.
which, witch	Which wicked witch in *The Wizard of Oz* did Dorothy's house fall on? (The WW of the East) "Which" is a relative pronoun used to refer to something. "Witch" is a sorceress.
who's, whose	Whose article won an award? Who's going to go pick it up? "Whose" is a pronoun. "Who's" is a contraction for "who is."

Continued ➞

| woman, women | A woman I know was voted Woman of the Year for her work in helping battered women. "Woman" with an "a" is singular, one woman; "women" with an "e" is plural, two or more women. |
| your, you're | I'm happy to announce that your team won, and now you're going to go to the next round in the Brain Brawl. "Your" is a possessive pronoun, and "you're" is a contraction for "you are." |

Answer to the antecedent question (page 94): "those of our times." Another way the AP English Language exam might ask you to look at the Montaigne passage is to question to whom "those of our times" might refer. With nothing else to base your answer on than the text given in this book, what would you say? If you said "writers," you'd be correct.

PART III:

ANALYTICAL READING AND THINKING

Engaged and
Active Reading

Tis the good reader that makes the good book.
—Ralph Waldo Emerson

OVERVIEW

In the multiple-choice section of the AP English Language exam, you will have 60 minutes to read five to six texts and answer approximately 55 questions related to those texts. There is also quite a bit to read in the essay section. The synthesis question will have six to eight resources that include a variety of genres: articles, excerpts from books, graphs, charts, or pictures. For another question, you will have a short persuasive document to read, analyze, and write about. If you don't understand what you've read, you will not be able to choose a correct response to a question or write intelligent essays.

Whatever the case, you will not have time for leisurely reading. You may only have time to read each text once, so you need to read carefully and with purpose.

ANALYZING YOUR READING HABITS

You know your reading habits need some improvement if any of the following is true for you:

- You find yourself thinking of something else about every other sentence;

- You have to reread a paragraph about five times to know what it means;

- You have to look up about every other word;

- You are bored by the passage and just skim through it, but then you have no idea what it is about;

- You sometimes characterize the text as "stupid," "dumb," "pointless," etc.

Some of the problems listed above have to do with **your attitude** about the reading. It is fair to say that not all the texts on the AP English Language exam will be to your liking, but it will be important for you to control your negative emotional response. Negative emotions will kill your motivation and will cloud your ability to think clearly. The fix? Approach each passage as something you can *mostly* understand. You aren't expected to be an expert on any of the passages.

A FEW STRATEGIES TO IMPROVE YOUR BASIC READING HABITS

If you find yourself rereading often, you may actually be reading too slowly, letting thoughts creep into your head. This is a matter of **concentration** and it is something you can control. Way before exam day, practice reading complex texts at a speed faster than your normal rate. Try to read not so fast so that you are skimming. Instead, read the passage quickly without reading every single word.

More strategies for improving your reading:

- Make a conscious effort to understand what you're doing as you read. As soon as you start to wander off mentally, toss out a mental lasso and pull yourself back. Work on keeping your focus.

- Visualize as you read. Picture the setting, the "characters," and the action of the passage as much as possible. Visualization will help you comprehend and remember what you read.

- If you start to get tired, drink water (not energy drinks) and remember to breathe. Do some neck exercises to get blood to your brain. You won't be able to get up and walk around during the exam, so try to get accustomed to reading and thinking for periods of an hour or more at a time.

- Practice reading while sitting at a desk or table, as this is most likely where you'll be for nearly four hours during the exam.

- Minimize distractions. DO NOT read with your ears plugged with ear buds listening to your MP3 player. You may say you can concentrate, but you are forcing your brain to think of two things at once, a practice that is stressful and counterproductive for exam prep. You will not be allowed to have any electronic devices with you for the exam, so get used to reading in relative silence.

- Practice controlling your emotions by choosing some tough texts to read. Read them, annotate them, and feel good about your progress. Start with Voltaire, Jonathan Swift, Ben Franklin, or Mark Twain. After these, Hunter S. Thompson might seem easy. A lot of older texts are online. You can download them to an e-reader, or read them online. It is best to have hard copies of texts, however, if you really want to practice annotating. You could search Project Gutenberg (*http://www.gutenberg.org*), for example, to find many of the authors listed in Chapter 4.

- Give yourself permission to skip words. You don't have to read every single word to know what's going on. This is not to say that you should skim—not at all, but if you think you have to look up every word, you will miss the "big picture." *Everything in its context* is a good mantra to keep.

- If there are questions to answer on the text (such as in the multiple-choice part of the exam), quickly skim some of the context of those questions. You won't have time to read all of the questions first, but if you know there is a question on rhetorical strategies, another on irony, etc., then you can look for those aspects of the text and mark them as you read.

- Learn how to annotate texts and then practice annotating. This may be the most important thing you can do to improve your reading skills for the AP English Language exam. Read more on this later in this chapter.

Empower yourself! A positive attitude will go a long way. Tell yourself you CAN DO THIS!! Think of each text on the exam as a noble, worthy opponent, but one that will not defeat you. Respect these literary opponents, recognize their strengths and special elements, but feel confident that you can read, understand, and respond to them. Never think you are too weak for any reading challenge.

ANNOTATING OR MARKING A TEXT

WHY DO IT?

When you read a difficult text, you're not reading for pleasure. You want to understand it deeply and, at least for the AP English Language exam, quickly. Difficult texts are not easy to know quickly, so marking the text as you read can help you grasp the key ideas and easily reconnect with your thinking upon a second look.

For example, if you immediately recognize the dominant tone, mark that down, and if the tone shifts in the last paragraph, note that as well. If a question follows the passage asking you to identify the tone, you'll probably be able to answer it without rereading the text.

HOW TO DO IT

Earlier in this book you were reminded of key literary and rhetorical devices to know so you can easily recognize them. Having a solid mental repertoire of these elements will make it much easier for you to spot significant details in texts.

Annotating—marking a text—means that as you read you are underlining key words, marking key phrases or ideas, and making margin notes of key ideas by paraphrasing them to show your deep understanding. This process facilitates active and engaged reading. If you are making notes while you read, if you are actively looking for what to mark, you will be less likely to drift off and begin thinking about something else.

WHEN TO START?

Start now, so you can train yourself. At first, practicing this skill may slow down your reading, but with time you'll be able to read more quickly and more deeply at the same time. Start to read always with a pen or pencil in hand, even if you're reading something like a magazine, just for practice.

SUGGESTED SYMBOLS OR MARKERS

Whether you use the suggested symbols below or create your own, it is important to keep your system simple (use only a few symbols) and stay consistent.

⬭	Circle unfamiliar words. You won't be allowed to use a dictionary on the AP English Language exam, but just circling unfamiliar words reminds you to try to understand them by using context clues. When you do have a dictionary available, it might be a good idea to look up a word if you cannot fully grasp its meaning from the context. Also, you can add these unfamiliar words to your list of words to know. See Chapter 9.
———————	Underline words in close proximity that share connotative or denotative associations; pair any underlined section with a textual note in the margin.
!	An exclamation point in the margin near a group of lines indicates a key idea; pair with brackets around specific text.
?	A question mark in the margin means "I don't understand." Noting questions prompts you to answer them later.
notes	Write brief notes in the margins to make your thinking visually accessible and easy to connect with upon a second look. Your notes can be about anything, but should be summaries of conclusions you've drawn about the text so far. Paraphrase key ideas in quick margin notes.

Continued →

[ ]	Use brackets around phrases or chunks of text (or enclose in a rectangle) to mark significant literary or rhetorical devices, such as appeals, imagery, figurative language, etc. Label the device in the margin. Make corresponding notes about what these might mean. Example: Don't just mark that the writer uses an ethical appeal, but make a note about shared values that make the appeal effective.

WHEN TO MARK A TEXT?

Mark now, as you are learning this skill—on nearly everything you read just to practice, but eventually only on texts you wish to study. It is really not something you'd use for pleasure reading, unless your pleasure is to read and understand difficult books. Then, yes, you would read with a pen in hand.

By all means mark your AP English Language and Composition exam, not only on the passages in the multiple-choice section, but also on the passages in the free-response section.

Mark in college—of course! You will have developed a reading skill that will help you read and study all kinds of texts in college, not just literary works.

WHAT TO LOOK FOR? THE SOAPSTONE STRATEGY

Use the acronym SOAPSTONE to find the basic elements of any nonfiction text:

- **S**   Speaker
- **O**   Occasion
- **A**   Audience
- **P**   Purpose
- **S**   Subject
- **T**   Tone

Review the fully developed SOAPSTONE graphic organizer in Chapter 4.

A NOTE ABOUT THE SUBJECT

The texts chosen for the exam convey interesting and important ideas. Try to avoid a simplistic statement regarding the subject. For example, a journal from an organic gardener is probably not simply about gardening. It may be about the ways plants can teach us about our environment. Look for ideas that are

- important (are of consequence)

- universal (important to most or all people)

- enduring (vital historically, vital now)

SAMPLE ANNOTATED TEXT

On the next page is an excerpt from Margaret Fuller's *Woman in the Nineteenth Century and Kindred Papers Relating to the Sphere, Condition and Duties, of Women.* I include this sample to show annotating skills in action. As you study this text, you may find ideas or elements that you would have marked or for which you would have made notes. If so, this shows you are thinking critically. Good for you!

Exercise: Write an essay for this text using the insights in the annotations. Use one of the following prompts to guide you:

1. The "good era" for women that Fuller imagines already exists in Miranda, a woman whose self-dependence is a model for other women. Analyze Miranda's own attitude toward her sense of self, especially as a model for others.

2. Who is Fuller's primary audience? What is it she wants that audience to know?

3. What, does Fuller argue, is the role of a parent in a daughter's sense of self?

4. Imagine the section that follows this one. What will Fuller focus on next and how will she support that argument?

from *Woman in the Nineteenth Century and Kindred Papers Relating to the Sphere, Condition and Duties, of Women*

by Margaret Fuller (1855)

Were thought and feeling once so far elevated that Man should esteem himself the brother and friend, but nowise the lord and tutor, of Woman,—were he really bound with her in equal worship,—arrangements as to function and employment would be of no consequence. What Woman needs is not as a woman to act or rule, but as a nature to grow, as an intellect to discern, as a soul to live freely and unimpeded, to unfold such powers as were given her when we left our "common home." If fewer talents were given her, yet if allowed the free and full employment of these, so that she may render back to the giver his own with usury, she will not complain; nay, I dare to say she will bless and rejoice in her earthly birth-place, her earthly lot. Let us consider what obstructions impede this good era, and what signs give reason to hope that it draws near.

I was talking on this subject with Miranda, a woman, who, if any in the world could, might speak without heat and bitterness of the position of her sex. Her father was a man who cherished no sentimental reverence for Woman, but a firm belief in the equality of the sexes. She was his eldest child, and came to him at an age when he needed a companion. From the time she could speak and go alone, he addressed her not as a plaything, but as a living mind. Among the few verses he ever wrote was a copy addressed to this child, when the first locks were cut from her head; and the reverence expressed on this occasion for that cherished head, he never belied. It was to him the temple of immortal

Handwritten margin notes:

Fuller's main claim is a claim of value: She believes women are to be equally free with men, to live, think, and grow according to their talents.

If man were so progressive/ enlightened to consider women as equals, we'd not need to discuss...

Man/ Woman— refers to the sex in general

mother's womb: each person comes to his/her life in the same way.

God/Interest

Author states her purpose: to consider what stands in the way of the ideal situation for women and to look at signs that the "good era" is close.

She's not angry that she's a woman

Miranda's story is Fuller's example that another reality for women can exist.

intellect. <u>He respected his child</u>, however, too much to be an indulgent parent. <u>He called on her for clear judgment, for courage, for honor and fidelity; in short, for such virtues as he knew.</u> In so far as he possessed the keys to the wonders of this universe, he allowed free use of them to her, and, by the incentive of a high expectation, he forbade, so far as possible, that <u>she should let the privilege lie idle.</u> *appeals to our self-actualization needs*

Miranda's father serves as an example of an ideal father. He believes
- *equality of sexes*
- *respects children's minds*
- *expects a female child to do all in life that any male child would be expected to do*

This section characterizes Miranda's relationships with both men and women.

Thus this child was early led to feel herself a child of the spirit. She took her place easily, not only in the world of organized being, but in the world of mind. A dignified sense of <u>self-dependence</u> was given as all her portion, and she found it a sure anchor. Herself securely anchored, her relations with others were established with equal security. <u>She was fortunate in a total absence of those charms which might have drawn to her bewildering flatteries,</u> and in a strong electric nature, <u>which repelled those</u> who did not belong to her, and <u>attracted those</u> who did. With men and women her relations were noble,—affectionate without passion, intellectual without coldness. The world was free to her, and she lived freely in it. Outward adversity came, and inward conflict; but that faith and self-respect had early been awakened which must always lead, at last, to an outward serenity and an inward peace.

Miranda emerges from childhood fully self reliant.

She's not beautiful, at least not in the ordinary way, which Fuller says is a benefit.

Her strong personality brought her together with others who were like her.

Despite having a progressive father + self-dependence, M.'s life is like everyone's: Includes conflict to adversity (Normal troubles)

hindrance, obstacle

Of Miranda I had always thought as an example, that the restraints upon the sex were [insuperable] only to those who think them so, or who noisily strive to break them. <u>She had taken a course of her own, and no man stood in her way.</u> Many of her acts had been unusual, but excited no uproar. Few helped, but none checked her; and the many men who knew her mind and her life, showed to her confidence as to a brother, gentleness as to a sister. And not only refined,

Being a woman is a problem only if you think it is.

Reinforces the idea that M. is self-reliant— she lives how she wants.

but very coarse men approved and aided one in whom they saw resolution and clearness of design. Her <u>mind was often the leading one,</u> always effective.

She was a clear voice + others listened to her. She's a role model for other women.

When I talked with her upon these matters, and had said very much what I have written, she smilingly replied; "And yet we must admit that <u>I have been fortunate, and this should not be.</u> My good father's early trust gave the first bias, and the rest followed, of course. It is true that I have had less outward aid, in after years, than most women; but that is of little consequence. Religion was early awakened in my soul,—a sense that what the soul is capable to ask it must attain, and that, though I might be aided and instructed by others, I must depend on myself as the only constant friend. This self-dependence, <u>which was honored in me</u>, is <u>deprecated</u> as a fault in most women. <u>They are taught</u> to learn their rule from without, not to unfold it from within.

→ My situation should not be unusual.

Too many women accept their subservient role; weakness is a learned role/behavior.

"This is the fault of Man, who is still vain, and wishes to be more important to Woman than, by right, he should be."

☆ M. is example that it (weakness) is <u>not a</u> female trait.

"Men have not shown this disposition toward you," I said.

ethical appeal

"No; because the position I early was enabled to take was one of self-reliance. And were <u>all women as sure of</u> their wants as I was, <u>the result would be the same.</u> But they are so overloaded with precepts by guardians, who think that nothing is so much to be dreaded for a woman as originality of thought or character, that their minds are impeded by doubts till they lose their chance of fair, free proportions. The difficulty is to get them to the point from which they shall naturally develop self-respect, and learn self-help.

if <u>all</u> women recognized their need to live freely to express themselves, they'd be like me, says M.

The goal must be to get women to recognize they are more powerful than they realize.

In a way, women allow men to rule them.

Men continue to "rule" women because they're vain and believe they're more important.

Enhancing Vocabulary

*One forgets words as one forgets names. One's vocabulary needs
constant fertilizing or it will die.*—Evelyn Waugh

OVERVIEW

I like what British writer Evelyn Waugh said about fertilizing our
vocabulary, as if it's something that grows like a flower garden. Plants
are tenacious and will strive to live despite our neglect of them, but if
we water and fertilize our garden, we will have abundant blossoms to
reward us. Our word vocabulary is like our garden. We must create the
rich soil (lots of words) that will give us, in an instant, the exact word for
our purpose. Think of this chapter's "Words to Know" list and the one
you create yourself as fertilizer for your vocabulary. A prominent goal for
you as you prepare for the exam is to strive to express yourself clearly and
precisely. The ability to choose the perfect word for the task is not to be
undervalued.

There are also two practical reasons for this chapter. One is that you
are expected to read and comprehend complex texts on the AP exam.
If you have a limited vocabulary, you will struggle with finding meaning.
While archaic or overly specific terms will be defined in footnotes, you are
expected to know a lot of words. AP readers also expect a certain level
of vocabulary in your essays. If you use sixth grade words, it *does* make
a difference in how your writing is perceived. I would never suggest that
you use "big" words just for the sake of using them, especially if you
are not quite comfortable with their meanings. However, since you are
expected to use college-level vocabulary, you should be comfortable with
more sophisticated word choices.

Test
Tip

> For fun, get a *Mad Libs* tablet and use some of the more difficult
> words below to create crazy little stories. They'll be silly, fun,
> and may make it easier for you to remember the words.

WORDS TO KNOW

The following words were taken from released AP exams. They were chosen for a variety of reasons: level of difficulty, archaic quality, obscure usage, or specific cultural connotation.

1. acuity (noun): sharpness, keenness

2. adept (adjective): having or showing knowledge and skill and aptitude

3. admonish (verb); admonition (noun): warn, scold, caution

4. ambiguous (adjective): unclear meaning, two possible interpretations

5. apocalyptic (adjective): involving or portending widespread devastation or ultimate doom

6. apocryphal (adjective): of questionable authenticity

7. appellation (noun): a name, title, or designation

8. archetype (noun); archetypal (adjective): an original model, pattern, or type (after an original model)

9. artifice (noun): pretense or ploy; clever or artful strategy

10. ascertain (verb): to determine; to find out

11. assiduous (adjective): diligent, persistent

12. baize (noun): a type of coarse woolen cloth, often green, usually used for covering card tables

13. base (adjective): inferior; dishonorable

14. bastion (noun): a well-fortified position

15. berate (verb): to rebuke, reprimand, or scold

16. bourgeoisie (noun): the middle class; in Marxist theory, the social group opposed to the proletariat (working class)

17. calumny (noun): slander; a false statement maliciously made to injure another's reputation

18. cant (noun): tedious talk; monotonous talk filled with platitudes

19. censure (verb): to reprimand; to excommunicate (expel, as from the priesthood)

20. charismatic (adjective): charming, compelling, appealing personality

21. chink (noun): crack or weakness in structure or armor

22. coarse (adjective): lacking refinement or rough grained in texture

23. confute (verb): to prove to be wrong or in error

24. connoisseur (noun): a person with expert knowledge or training, especially in the fine arts

25. corporeal (adjective): having physical substance, material form

26. decorous (adjective): well behaved, particularly according to social norms

27. decry (verb): express strong disapproval of

28. defer (verb); deference (noun): submit or yield to another's wish or opinion

29. deliquesce (verb): to disappear as if by melting

30. dilatory (adjective): inclined to waste time and lag behind

31. disparage (verb): to criticize someone or something in a way that shows you do not respect or value them

32. dogmatic (adjective): strict; inflexible expectations to adhere to a dogma (systemic belief, typically religious)

33. draught (noun): a current of unpleasantly cold air blowing through a room (archaic for draft)

34. dray (noun): a large low carriage with four wheels pulled by horses

35. dyspeptic (adjective); dyspepsia (noun): always angry or easily annoyed or having indigestion

36. elicit (verb): to call forth, draw out, or provoke; to bring or draw out

37. emit (verb): to send out a beam, noise, smell, or gas

38. enfranchised (adjective): empowered; the opposite is disenfranchised

39. engender (verb): to create

40. espionage (noun): spying; the discovering of secrets, especially political or military information, of another country or the proprietary information of a business

41. explicit (adjective): clear, precise; overtly stated

42. facile (adjective): easy, effortless

43. faux (adjective): false, fake

44. feign (verb): to pretend, to dissemble, to misrepresent

45. fester: to become infected, to suppurate; an infection (can be a noun or a verb)

46. festoon(ed) (verb): draped, decorated as for a parade or state event

47. fledgling (adjective): new and inexperienced

48. fobs (verb): employ trickery; pass off a fake as genuine

49. gainsay (verb): challenge, dispute

50. genuflect (verb), genuflections (noun): to bow as before a priest (obeisances, reverent gestures)

51. grandeur (noun): magnificent, splendid, vast beauty

52. grudging (adjective); grudgingly (adverb): done in an unwilling way; unwillingly

53. hack (noun): a reporter, artist, or writer whose work is not very good

54. husband(ed) (verb): to use something carefully so that you do not use all of it

55. illicit (adjective): contrary to accepted morality (especially sexual morality) or convention

56. illusory (adjective): not real, based on illusion

57. imbibe (verb): to drink, especially alcohol

58. impracticable (adjective): not possible, unusable

59. inexorable (adjective): without end, interminable

60. ingenuity (noun): cleverness; resourcefulness

61. introspection (noun): examination of and attention to your own ideas, thoughts, and feelings

62. kowtow (verb): to show too much respect to someone in authority, always obeying them and changing what you do in order to please them; what a toady does; sucking up

63. languid, languished, languor (noun): without energy; pleasant mental or physical tiredness or lack of activity

64. latent (adjective): potentially existing but not presently evident or realized

65. magnanimity (noun): great generosity of spirit or money

66. malevolent (adjective); malevolence (noun): ill will, maliciousness

67. mutton (noun): meat from a sheep

68. orthodoxy (noun): a belief or orientation agreeing with conventional standards

69. paramount (adjective): supreme or dominant

70. parochial (adjective): provincial; country-like, or of a parish (church community or region)

71. pathos (noun): poignancy; quality of emotion in a work of art or literature

72. pecuniary (adjective): relating to money; monetary

73. permeate (verb): pervade, penetrate, get into everything

74. pernicious (adjective): deadly, harmful, pestilent

75. pious (adjective); piety (noun): godly, reverent, holy (state of being pious)

76. plait (verb); plaits (noun): to braid; braids

77. porter (noun): a railroad employee who assists passengers

78. pragmatic (adjective): realistic, practical, expecting logical results

79. prattle (verb): idle talk, to go on and on meaninglessly

80. precipitate (verb); precipitous (adjective): to cause to happen, especially suddenly or prematurely; done hastily, without thought

81. precocious (adjective): characterized by or characteristic of exceptionally early development or maturity, especially mental development

82. prerogative (noun): privilege, right

83. profligate (adjective): wasteful, extravagant, prodigal

84. prostrate (adjective or verb): to lay face down on the ground in humility, submission, or adoration

85. prudent (adjective): careful and sensible; marked by sound judgment

86. qualm(s) (noun): an uncomfortable feeling of doubt about whether you are doing the right thing

87. randy (adjective): sexually aroused

88. recitation (noun): an event when one recites a literary work (usually) orally for an audience

89. reiterate (verb); reiteration (noun): to say or explain again

90. reputed (adjective): alleged, presumed

91. resonant (adjective); resonance (noun): strong and deep in tone or strongly reminiscent; evocative

92. rheumatism (noun): any painful disorder of the joints or muscles or connective tissues

93. sated (adjective); satiety (noun): satisfied; full

94. scant, scanty (adjective): barely sufficient

95. schizoid (adjective): of, relating to, or having a personality disorder marked by extreme shyness, flat affect, discomfort with others, and an inability to form close relationships; a person who is reclusive

96. seethe (verb): churn with anger or rage

97. self-abasement (noun): to put oneself down, to denigrate oneself

98. skirmish (noun): clash, battle, scuffle

99. sodden (adjective): drenched, soaked, sopping; expressionless, stupid, or dull, especially from drink

100. synergy (noun): interaction; parts working together

101. tawdry (adjective): cheap, gaudy, trashy, tacky

102. throes (noun): condition of agonizing struggle or trouble

103. timorous (adjective): fearful; shy; timid

104. torpor (noun): listlessness; languor, without energy, apathetic

105. torrent (noun): an overwhelming number or amount or a violently fast stream of water

106. transcendent (adjective); transcendence (noun): beyond ordinary; sublime

107. transient, transience: fleeting; not lasting

108. tremulous (adjective): quivering as from weakness or fear

109. turbid (adjective): churned up; cloudy, muddy, murky

110. unabashed (adjective): not embarrassed

111. unimpeachable (adjective): impossible to discredit, without fault

112. variegated (adjective): having streaks, marks, or patches of a different color or colors; varicolored:

113. veracity (noun): truthfulness

114. veritable (adjective): being truly so-called; real or genuine

115. vigilant (adjective); vigilance (noun): on guard, cautiously aware, continuous attention

116. vigilante (noun): one who takes or advocates the taking of law enforcement into one's own hands

117. vociferation (noun); vociferous (adjective): cry out loudly and vehemently, especially in protest

118. voluble (adjective); volubility (noun): talking easily, readily, and at length; fluent

119. weft (noun): the horizontal threads interlaced through the warp in a woven fabric

120. wholly (adjective): fully, completely

Test Tip *Make learning new words a game. When you learn a new word, commit to using it at least ten times in one day in a variety of contexts. Bonus: You might have fun annoying those around you!*

YOUR OWN LIST

Use this space to record new words and their definitions. Come back to this section often to reinforce your memory.

Word	Definition
1.	
2.	
3.	
4.	
5.	
6.	
7.	
8.	
9.	
10.	
11.	
12.	
13.	
14.	
15.	

GREEK AND LATIN ROOTS

At some point you will need to determine the meaning of unfamiliar words from context clues. If you have a working knowledge of some basic Greek and Latin prefixes and roots, you can often quickly decipher word meanings, particularly when words are scientific in nature. Perhaps you've learned many of these roots in a science or world language class. If so, concentrate on those in this list that are new to you. This list is by no means complete, but it does contain a good sampling of roots that will aid your decoding skills.

For fun, take note of the English examples below that contain more than one of the roots. *Autograph*, for example, means "self-write."

Root/Prefix	Meaning	English Examples
ab-, a-, abs-	away, from	abstain, absent
ante-	before	anteroom, antecedent, antebellum
anthrop-	human	anthropomorphic, misanthrope
anti-	against	antidote, antipathy
auto-	self	autobiography, autoimmune, autocratic
bell-	war	bellicose, belligerent
bene-	good	benevolent, beneficiary, beneficial
bi-	two	biennial, bisect, bicycle
bio-	life	biology, biosphere, biogenesis
cede-	go, yield, surrender	concede, recede
circum-	around	circumference, circumlocution
con-	with	conspire, connect
contra-	against	contraband, contrary, contrast
de-	down, from	devolve, decline, devoid
dic-, dict-, dit-	say, speak	diction, dictate
dis-, di-	apart, away	dissolve, dissuade, diverge, divest

Continued →

Root/Prefix	Meaning	English Examples
ex-, e-	out of, from	eject, emerge, extricate, example
fid-, fide-, feder-	faith, trust	confide, bona fide, fidelity
graph-, gram-	write, draw	graphic, telegram, autograph
hyper-	beyond, over	hyperbole, hyperactive
hypo-	under, less	hypodermic, hypocrite
inter-	among, between	interstate, intercede, introspection
intra-	within	intramural, intravenous
log-, logo-, -ology	reason, learning	logistics, catalog
loqu-, locut-	talk, speak	eloquent, colloquial, loquacious
mis-	ill, mistaken, wrong	misunderstood, misogyny
mal-	bad, evil	malnourished, malinger
morph-	shape, form	amorphic, metamorphosis
para-, par-	beside	paralegal, parameter
phil-	love	philosophy, philanthropic
post-	after, following	postpone, postgraduate
pre-	before	precursor, preface, premonition
pro-	forward, outward	project, protract
soph-	wisdom	sophomore, sophist
super-	above	superior, superimpose
tele-, tel-	far	television, telekinesis, telemarketer
trans-	across	transpose, transcontinental, transgender
vert-	turn	revert, convert, introvert
vid-, vis-	to see	visual, video, envision
viv-, vita-, vivi-	alive, life	vivacious, vitality, vivid
vol-	will, wish	malevolent, voluntary

The Value of Perspective:
Why Point of View Matters

*And this, our life, exempt from public haunt, finds tongues
in trees, books in the running brooks, sermons in stones,
and good in everything.*—William Shakespeare

OVERVIEW

There are two main ways to consider point of view: the point of view that you are to identify in the passage and your own point of view as you consider the passage and what it means. This chapter will help you realize the importance of both.

YOUR OWN POINT OF VIEW

An inherent disadvantage to youth is that it comes with a limited worldview. Most high school students have limited life experience. We cannot blame them for this, but as experience affects one's ability to conceive of complex literary themes, it is a matter worth addressing here. Plus, each of us, despite our age, can work to broaden our experience so we can have a fuller worldview.

In addition to your age, your point of view is influenced by:

- Your culture (ethnicity, religion, etc.);

- Your environment (urban, rural, specific region of the country);

- Your family values;

- Your economic status;

- Your actual life experiences such as travel, personal interactions with people who are different, even having been "in love."

These influences cause us to have particular biases. Everyone has biases. It is important for us to recognize that fact and understand that our point of view and our biases affect how we read. To be good critical readers, we must control and limit the effect of our biases.

CONSCIOUSLY AND PURPOSEFULLY ADD TO WHAT YOU KNOW ABOUT LIFE

One of the best ways to understand literature and its themes is to read. But sometimes we need to have experiences that help us understand what we read. To do this, consider expanding your knowledge of the world in the following ways:

- Engage in conversations with people from different cultures.

- Talk to older adults about their life experiences.

- Read opinions that seem directly counter to your own and carefully consider how these arguments are constructed. Mentally defend, challenge, or qualify such arguments.

- Add variety to your media preferences:
  - Read a variety of books and articles, both old and new;
  - Listen to different types of music;
  - View foreign films, with subtitles;
  - Read national and international newspapers;
  - Watch *The History Channel*, for fun;
  - Download lectures and philosophy podcasts. (iTunes U is a fantastic resource for free materials at a college level.)

BECOMING AN EMPATHETIC READER

Empathy is the ability to put yourself in someone else's place, to see things as he or she sees them. As readers, we must be empathetic if we are to truly understand the books we read. To do this means to actually put yourself in the place of the speaker, the narrator, or the character.

When you read, visualize yourself in the text. Make a little mind movie in which you walk through the setting, follow the characters, listen to them speak, and observe their actions. Allow yourself to see and hear what the speaker sees and hears. Even more importantly, allow yourself to feel what the speaker feels. This is empathy.

To be fair, it is much easier to empathize with the action of fictional characters in narratives. They are like us in a direct way. But the AP English Language exam does not ask you to analyze fictional characters. Instead you will be reading nonfiction prose, such as essays, diaries, memoirs, even letters. Such works typically feature one speaker writing about one topic. However, if you can't identify with this voice, you will have a difficult time discerning the main point of the essay. Even a purely expository essay will have some recognizable elements that help us visualize the text: setting (context of time and space), character (the speaker and any others necessary to the text), conflict (a problem to solve, an issue that begs exploration), even imagery (look for what you can perceive with your senses to help you fully experience the text).

In addition, many questions on the AP English Language exam ask you to determine the attitude or identify the point of view of a speaker. If you can become an empathetic reader, this task will be much easier for you.

The more you practice empathetic reading, the more you will develop a kind of "double vision," where you'll view the text from within and also from without as a critical reader who sees the parts as they relate to the whole.

In your double vision, you'll learn to appreciate how the writing conveys enduring and universal ideas through the perspective of a character, narrator, or speaker.

THE IMPORTANCE OF IRONY

AP readers say that students have difficulty recognizing irony in passages on the exam. And questions about irony are prevalent in the multiple-choice section. Recognizing irony is an aspect of seeing clearly. If something is not what it seems, perhaps there is something ironic. But more than that, you will need to determine the effect the ironic passage has in the text as a whole.

- **Dramatic irony** is a powerful tool authors employ to reveal thematic insight. Whenever you know something a character or speaker does not know, you should make note of the discrepancy in the margin of the text. As you follow your character around in your mind movie, pay attention to moments when you feel smarter or more aware than the character. What does that show you?

- A narrator's speech is not always meant to be taken literally. Watch for **verbal irony** when what the speaker says is different from what he or she really means. The voice may even be sarcastic. Look for the underlying truth and how that truth functions in the text.

- Lastly, watch for evidence of **situational irony**. This can be a discrepancy in the setting or situation that is not what you expect. For example, you would not expect a very wealthy widow to be eating cat food. What might that detail mean?

TONE AND POINT OF VIEW

Tone is an important tool in understanding a speaker's attitude. The author will create a specific tone that reinforces how the narrator or speaker feels about someone or something. When you are asked to determine the speaker's reaction to another person, an idea, or an event, look for the underlying emotions in the passage. Chapter 8 has a list of tone words to help you express what you see.

Shifts in tone are important to notice as they often signal an important change in idea. If the text is at first congenial but then evolves into bitterness and indignation like Swift's *A Modest Proposal,* you've got something worth examining closely.

REVIEWING MAIN POINTS OF VIEW

- **First Person:** The narrator tells his/her own story using first-person pronouns. This point of view is limited by what the narrator can know, see, or understand. First-person narrators cannot always be trusted to assess the situation honestly. They may be blind to their own faults, etc. Those who write autobiography or memoir do not always capture reality exactly, but no one expects them to do this. Look for places where first-person narrators are being self-deprecating. This may be honesty or irony.

- **Second Person:** The narrator uses second-person pronouns to make immediate connections with readers.

- **Third-Person Limited:** A third-person narrator tells another's story using third-person pronouns. A third-person limited narrator is similar to a first-person narrator in that the narrator can only see and know what his character can see and know.

- **Third-Person Omniscient:** This third-person narrator is godlike, seeing and knowing all without constraints of time or space, seeing even beyond earthly existence. Third-person narrators often digress into contemplative or philosophical forays. Third-person omniscient narrators will often voice the viewpoint of the author. This would be a rare point of view in nonfiction.

- **Objective:** An objective narrator tells a story in a similar way to that of a video recorder, simply revealing the sights and sounds it perceives (though not, of course, as strictly as that). You will recognize an objective narrator by the lack of emotion or personal interest in the subject.

Test Tip

Remember, you can't always trust a first-person narrator or speaker. As a careful and critical reader, you are expected to know what the narrator or speaker does not know.

SHIFTS IN POINT OF VIEW

A shift in point of view is something to examine closely. It is often a critical marker in understanding meaning or theme. Use the following list of questions as your guide:

1. Identify the shift. Where does it occur? From whose point of view to whose?

2. Why does the shift occur? What can the author accomplish with this new narrative point of view?

3. What changes are evident in narrative style, narrative voice, even syntax and diction?

4. What can you see that you did not see before? Something new, different, something opposite?

5. What limitations exist?

6. What does this new "viewer" know that the previous one did not? Or vice versa?

7. What is the overall effect of this shift?

As you consider your observations together, certain points will probably jump out as truly significant or insightful. Use one of these points to create a defensible claim for an essay.

POINT OF VIEW IN YOUR OWN ESSAYS

LITERARY-PRESENT TENSE

Characters or persons in a literary text live in the present time. To write about them, we use what is called the literary-present tense, in which we use present-tense verbs. We would write, for example, "Atticus *is* a great father to Scout and Jem," or "Oedipus *plugs* his ears with wax so he won't *hear* the Siren's song." While these examples are from fictional literature, literary-present tense is relevant when we write about nonfiction texts as well. You might write, "Swift argues that ...." or "Franklin writes, '. . . '"

TENSE

Because it's best that you use literary present tense verbs in your essay and when you cite source material, conflicts of tense can arise if the passage you cite is in past tense. However, when you use a direct or indirect citation, it is not always necessary to change the tense to conform. Purdue's Online Writing Lab advises you to "establish a primary tense for the main discourse, and use occasional shifts to other tenses to indicate changes in time frame."

You have probably been taught to mark any changes you make to a direct citation by presenting the change in [brackets]. In your essays on the exam, you probably won't need to do this. Instead, follow Purdue's guidance. See the following for an example of how blending tenses can be effective:

Woolf says that by the nineteenth century "it was the habit for men of letters to describe their minds in confessions and autobiographies." She is suggesting that these men were expressing the effect of their environment on their work as writers.

AUTHORITATIVE-THIRD PERSON

The essays you will write for the AP English Language exam are best written in third person, which gives you an authoritative voice. You will be taking a stance and supporting it. Whenever you write your own point of view, the tendency is to want to qualify your opinions by adding phrases such as "I think," "I feel," and "In my opinion." It is actually better to avoid such qualifiers.

Instead, write strong, confident claims that sound as if they are fact. It will be your task to provide evidence for your claims so your reader accepts your opinions, but don't intentionally limit your claims with qualifying phrases. Think of how you would respond to the example below. Which one of the pair seems stronger and more like a fact?

Qualified Claim	Authoritative Claim
In my opinion, Jefferson should have heeded Adams' advice and left the anti-slavery language in the Declaration of Independence. I feel it would have catapulted our country's sense of human rights ahead by hundreds of years.	Jefferson should have heeded Adams' advice and left the anti-slavery language in the Declaration of Independence. It would have catapulted our country's sense of human rights ahead by hundreds of years.

UNIVERSAL-FIRST PERSON

In general you will be using third person for all of your essays. However, there are times when first person seems perfectly correct for the point you want to make. We use universal-first person when we include ourselves in all the masses that understand universal truths or themes. We'll use "we" instead of "I" to show our alliance in a common understanding or purpose. It may be appropriate to use the universal-first person especially in your conclusion if you are extending your understanding of the theme as something we all know or should know.

The World of Ideas:
Philosophies, Concepts, and Literary Themes

You can never learn less, you can only learn more.
—R. Buckminster Fuller

OVERVIEW

Human beings are by nature curious. We want to know how our world works. For thousands of years, people have pondered the universe, both the world outside us and the inner world of the mind and soul. Typically, those who ask the big questions and expound upon them are called philosophers. The root definition of the word "philosopher" is lover of wisdom. In the same way, the writers you'll encounter on this exam are concerned with the big ideas of life.

The intent of this chapter is to give you a summary of some of these big ideas through time. It would be rare, for example, for you to have to know that Jeremy Bentham is a founder of Utilitarianism. But in a recent exam, there was a prose piece about Bentham. Since the exam judges your ability to read and comprehend complex texts, if you are aware of the major trends in philosophy and thinking over time, you might be more comfortable with them simply because you have more points of reference. So treat this chapter as a very brief primer in the history of ideas as well as a reminder of common literary themes.

THINKING: A FEW KEY TERMS

- **Aesthetics**: philosophy that deals with the nature and expression of beauty.

- *A priori*: *a priori* knowledge or justification does not depend on experience.

- *A posteriori*: *a posteriori* knowledge or justification is dependent upon experience or empirical evidence.

- **Axiomatic:** self-evident or unquestionable.

- **Empiricism:** knowledge comes from the **senses**, as we look, listen, smell, touch, and taste the various objects in our environment.

- **Epistemology:** the study of knowledge.

- **Ethics:** the study or philosophy of what is right or good.

- **Metaphysics:** the study of the nature of reality, including the relationship between mind and matter, substance and attribute, fact and value.

- **Ontological:** referring to the study of the nature of being, existence, reality.

- **Rationalism:** constructing knowledge of the external world, the self, the soul, God, ethics, and science out of the simplest, indubitable ideas possessed innately by the **mind**.

- **Skepticism:** we do not, or cannot, know anything, or at least we do not know as much as we think we do.

50 KEY "ISMS"

There are hundreds of terms that end in "ism" that represent political, literary, social, and religious views. This list is only meant to remind you of some of the more common "isms." To give you a simpler reference, these terms are given in alphabetical order, not chronological, and not according to any category.

1. **absurdism:** doctrine that we live in an irrational universe.

2. **agnosticism:** doctrine that we can know nothing beyond material phenomena.

3. **anarchism:** doctrine that all governments should be abolished.

4. **anthropomorphism:** attribution of human qualities to non-human things.

5. **antinomianism:** doctrine of the rejection of moral law.

6. **asceticism**: doctrine that physical (bodily) self-denial permits spiritual enlightenment.

7. **atheism**: belief that there is no god.

8. **atomism**: belief that the universe consists of small indivisible particles.

9. **bipartisanism**: the state of being composed of members of two parties or of two parties cooperating, as in government.

10. **capitalism**: doctrine that private ownership and free markets should govern economies.

11. **centrism**: adherence to a middle-of-the-road position, neither left nor right, as in politics.

12. **collectivism**: doctrine of communal control of means of production.

13. **Communism**: a theory or system in which all property is owned by all of the people equally, with its administration vested by them in the state or in the community.

14. **conservatism**: belief in maintaining political and social traditions.

15. **deism**: belief in a god but rejection of religion.

16. **determinism**: doctrine that events are predetermined by preceding events or laws.

17. **dualism**: doctrine that the universe is controlled by one good and one evil force.

18. **egalitarianism**: belief that humans ought to be equal in rights and privileges.

19. **egoism**: doctrine that the pursuit of self-interest is the highest good.

20. **empiricism**: doctrine that the experience of the senses is the only source of knowledge.

21. **existentialism**: doctrine of individual human responsibility in an unfathomable universe.

22. **Fascism**: a political philosophy that exalts nation and often race above the individual and that stands for a centralized autocratic government headed by a dictatorial leader, severe economic and social regimentation, and forcible suppression of opposition.

23. **fatalism**: doctrine that events are fixed and humans are powerless.

24. **feminism**: belief in the liberation of women in society to a social stature equal to that of men.

25. **gnosticism**: belief that freedom derives solely from knowledge.

26. **hedonism**: belief that pleasure is the highest good.

27. **humanism**: belief that human interests and mind are paramount.

28. **imperialism**: policy of forcefully extending a nation's authority by territorial gain or by the establishment of economic and political dominance over other nations.

29. **individualism**: belief that individual interests and rights are paramount.

30. **libertarianism**: doctrine that personal liberty is the highest value.

31. **Marxism**: the economic and political theories of Karl Marx and Friedrich Engels that hold that human actions and institutions are economically determined, and that class struggle is needed to create historical change, and that capitalism will ultimately be superseded by communism.

32. **materialism**: belief that matter is the only extant substance.

33. **monotheism**: belief in only one god.

34. **nihilism**: denial of all reality; extreme skepticism.

35. **objectivism**: a philosophical system founded by Ayn Rand, being one of several doctrines holding that all reality is objective and external to the mind and that knowledge is reliably based on observed objects and events.

36. **pantheism**: belief that the universe is God, that God is revealed in nature.

37. **polytheism**: belief in multiple deities.

38. **positivism**: doctrine that which is not observable is not knowable.

39. **pragmatism**: doctrine emphasizing practical value of philosophy.

40. **progressivism**: the principles and practices of those advocating progress, change, or reform, especially in political matters. When capitalized, the political and economic doctrines of the Progressive Party or Progressive Movement.

41. **radicalism**: the holding or following of principles advocating drastic political, economic, or social reforms.

42. **rationalism**: belief that reason is the fundamental source of knowledge.

43. **secularism**: the concept that government or other entities should exist separately from religion and/or religious beliefs.

44. **self-determinism**: doctrine that the actions of a self are self-originated.

45. **skepticism**: doctrine that true knowledge is always uncertain.

46. **socialism**: doctrine of centralized state control of wealth and property.

47. **solipsism**: theory that self-existence is the only certainty.

48. **stoicism**: belief in indifference to pleasure or pain.

49. **transcendentalism**: theory that emphasizes that which transcends perception.

50. **utilitarianism**: belief that utility of actions determines moral value and that the goal of human conduct is happiness.

POLITICAL CONTINUUM

What follows is a very basic map of the political continuum based on the wings in the British Parliament building. The purpose for including this graphic is to help you have a basic understanding of the often-used, but often-misunderstood, terms "left wing" and "right wing."

Left Wing	Right Wing
Liberal	Conservative
Solving problems using new methods, strong role of government	Solving problems using old methods, weak role of government
Progressive	Laissez Faire

Within the oval below we find concepts associated with democracy and outside the oval we find concepts associated with absolute rule (monarchies and dictatorships).*

AGL   J   E   H | D   FI   CBK

Examples

A. Karl Marx	B. Adolf Hitler	C. Mussolini	D. George W. Bush
E. Teddy Roosevelt	F. Calvin Coolidge	G. Stalin	H. John F. Kennedy
I. Ronald Reagan	J. Franklin D. Roosevelt	K. Osama bin Laden	L. Fidel Castro

*This graphic was created by Sheboygan Falls High School social studies teacher Lee McGlade.

COMMON LITERARY THEMES

Why study themes? At the heart of any piece of writing, whether a memoir or an essay on economics, is some underlying truth about human existence. In literature, we refer to these truths as "themes." Expanding your awareness of key themes might trigger a deeper grasp of a complex passage. Do take note: no author is going to tell readers directly that the point of the essay is to reaffirm that, for example, "power is a corrupting force." However, as an astute reader, you will be expected to draw that conclusion as you read.

THEMATIC STATEMENTS:

- All life is connected.

- Each life, no matter how small, matters.

- Life is too brief.

- Youth (innocence) and beauty don't last.

- We don't appreciate what we have until it's gone.

- Pride can blind us to the truth.

- Small acts of kindness and/or generosity can have a tremendous effect.

- Courage can reward those who push themselves.

- Sometimes we learn too late what we need to know.

- Social status, beauty, wealth, etc., do not matter.

- We learn through trial, hardship, or pain those lessons most valuable.

- The individual is sometimes in conflict with society.

- Individuals are often alienated and alone.

- Self-determination is a fierce inner force, but is often thwarted or delayed by outside forces.

- Fantasy is sometimes more real than everyday reality.

- Mortality (death) is inevitable.

- Human beings are sometimes too weak (or too blind) to do what is right.

- We often want what others have or we often want what we cannot have.

- Fear, jealousy, and greed are destructive emotions.

- We sometimes hurt those we love.

- People (of all cultures and of all times) are more alike than they are different.

- Nature does not care about people.

- Each of us is alone (often feeling small or frightened) in the world.

- Evil exists in the hearts of men (women).

- Power can be a corrupting force.

THEMATIC QUESTIONS:

- What is truth?

- What is beauty?

- What is real?

- What is justice?

- What is honor?

- What is love?

- What does it mean to live a good life?

- What does it mean to be a hero?

- What does it mean to have courage?

Chapter 16 analyzes free-response prompts from the last ten years and also includes a list of topics and themes.

Make a card listing your top ten literary themes and carry it with you. Pull it out to look at it often. Make these themes serve as the lens through which you view the world. You will start to hear these themes in songs, see them in movies, and recognize them on TV shows. More importantly, you will be better able to recognize them in the literature you read. The result of rehearsing themes is that when you read those complex passages on the exam, you will be better able to recognize them quickly.

A BRIEF HISTORY OF THOUGHT

The purpose of this section is to give you a broad overview of some of the main thinkers, writers, and philosophers who were influential in the history of thought as well as various philosophical frameworks or ideologies. Do not consider this outline to be all you need to know about philosophy. Instead consider it a place to get started. Choose several names from this list and do an Internet search. Learn what you can about what these people believed. Any extra effort here will expand your worldview and may even help you with a question or two on the exam.

Also, do not think that you must know all of these names and their ideas to do well on the exam. That is not the point of this list. This list is here to help you have a better sense of the history of thought in order to have a broader perspective of the world, both past and present.

Many descriptions below are from the *Internet Encyclopedia of Philosophy*. I have tried to represent the principal aspects of each person in a short space, but of course, what's here is by no means all there is to know about each person. The list is meant to send you *looking for more*, to pique your interest in a few thinkers so that you might learn about them on your own.

THE WORLD'S GREAT THINKERS

SIXTH CENTURY BCE

Philosopher	Works/Ideas/Concepts
Thales of Miletus, Greek	He investigated the origin of matter and is the founder of the school of natural philosophy.
Anaximander, Greek	He originated the world picture of the open universe, which replaced the closed universe of the celestial vault.
Pythagoras, Greek	He wrote nothing; he was a disciple of Anaximander. He believed men may be classified accordingly as lovers of wisdom, lovers of honor, and lovers of gain.
Buddha, Nepalese/ Indian; also known as Siddhārtha Gautama	The Buddha seeks a middle way between the extremes of dogmatism and skepticism, emphasizing personal experience, a pragmatic attitude, and the use of critical thinking toward all types of knowledge.
Confucius, Chinese	He believed in the "contagious" nature of moral force, by which moral rulers diffuse morality to their subjects, moral parents raise moral children, and so forth.
Heraclitus, Greek	He claims to announce an everlasting Word (Logos) according to which all things are one, in some sense. Opposites are necessary for life, but they are unified in a system of balanced exchanges.
Laozi (Lao-tzu), Chinese; early Daoist philosopher	*Tao Te Ching* Dao is the process of reality itself, as it happens in the natural flow of things. All this reflects the deep-seated Chinese belief that change is the most basic character of things.

FIFTH CENTURY BCE

Philosopher	Works/Ideas/Concepts
Anaxagoras, Greek	He gained notoriety for his materialistic views, particularly his contention that the sun was a fiery rock. First, he speculated that in the physical world everything contains a portion of everything else. His observation of how nutrition works in animals led him to conclude that in order for the food an animal eats to turn into bone, hair, flesh, and so forth, it must already contain all of those constituents within it.
Empedocles (of Acagras in Sicily)	He is credited with the invention of the four-element theory of matter (earth, air, fire, and water). Empedocles' worldview is of a cosmic cycle of eternal change, growth and decay, in which two personified cosmic forces, Love and Strife, engage in an eternal battle for supremacy.
Protagoras, Greek	Protagoras is known primarily for three claims: (1) that man is the measure of all things (which is often interpreted as a sort of radical relativism); (2) that he could make the "worse (or weaker) argument appear the better (or stronger)"; and (3) that one could not tell if the gods existed or not.
Socrates, Greek	Socrates tried to find the definitions of the virtues, such as courage and justice, by cross-examining people who professed to have knowledge of them. Thus, the *Socratic Method* is a method of learning through questioning.

FOURTH CENTURY BCE

Philosopher	Works/Ideas/Concepts
Democritus, Greek	Part of his atom theory suggested that the human soul consists of globular atoms of fire, which impart movement to the body.
Hippocrates, Greek	Health was defined as the balance of the four humors. Disease was defined as the imbalance of the humors. Four humors of the body: blood, phlegm, black bile, and yellow bile.

Philosopher	Works/Ideas/Concepts
Plato, Greek	The most famous student of Socrates, Plato wrote *Apology, Symposium, Republic*. He is known for the theory of Forms, according to which the world we know through the senses is only an imitation of the pure, eternal, and unchanging world of the Forms.
Zhuangzi (Chuang-Tzu), Chinese	Zhuangzi espoused a holistic philosophy of life, encouraging disengagement from the artificialities of socialization, and cultivation of our natural "ancestral" potencies and skills, in order to live a simple and natural, but full and flourishing, life.
Aristotle, Greek	Physics, Metaphysics, Poetics, Politics, Nicomachean Ethics The great classifier, Aristotle was the first to classify areas of human knowledge into distinct disciplines such as mathematics, biology, and ethics. He was the first to develop a formalized system for reasoning. Aristotle identified the highest good with intellectual virtue; that is, a moral person is one who cultivates certain virtues based on reasoning.

THIRD CENTURY BCE

Philosopher	Works/Ideas/Concepts
Epicurus, Greek	He taught that the point of all one's actions was to attain pleasure (conceived of as tranquility) for oneself, and that this could be done by limiting one's desires and by banishing the fear of the gods and of death.
Xunzi (Hsün Tzu), Chinese	He articulated a systematic version of Confucianism that encompasses ethics, metaphysics, political theory, philosophy of language, and a highly developed philosophy of education. Human nature lacks an innate moral compass, and left to itself falls into contention and disorder, which is why Xunzi characterizes human nature as bad. Ritual is thus an integral part of a stable society.

FIRST CENTURY BCE

Philosopher	Works/Ideas/Concepts
Cicero, Roman politician, orator, and philosopher	Strength of the Roman Republic depended upon the elite improving its character and placing commitments to individual virtue and social stability ahead of its desires for fame, wealth, and power.
Lucretius, Greek	Wrote *On the Nature of the Universe,* a collection of six books that explain the physical origin, structure, and destiny of the universe. Included are theories of the atomic structure of matter and the emergence and evolution of life forms—ideas that would eventually form a foundation and background for the development of Western science.

SECOND CENTURY

Philosopher	Works/Ideas/Concepts
Epictetus, Greek	The role of the Stoic teacher was to encourage his students to live the philosophic life, the end of which was eudaimonia ("happiness" or "flourishing"), to be secured by living the life of reason, which—for Stoics—meant living virtuously and living "according to nature."
Marcus Aurelius, Roman emperor and philosopher	*Meditations* Aurelius was a Stoic philosopher who followed Epictetus.

THIRD CENTURY

Philosopher	Works/Ideas/Concepts
Plotinus, Roman, born in Egypt	Thought to be the founder of Neoplatonism (resurgence and rethinking of Plato's philosophy), Plotinus developed a complex spiritual cosmology involving three foundational elements: the One, the Intelligence, and the Soul. It is from the productive unity of these three Beings that all existence emanates.

THE MIDDLE AGES: 400–1400

FOURTH CENTURY

Philosopher	Works/Ideas/Concepts
St. Augustine, from the area now known as Algeria	*Confessions* His ground-breaking philosophy infused Christian doctrine with Neoplatonism. Augustine adopts a subjective view of time and says that time is nothing in reality but exists only in the human mind's apprehension of reality.

ELEVENTH CENTURY

Philosopher	Works/Ideas/Concepts
Peter Abelard, French	Abelard formulated what is now recognized as a central nominalist tenet: only particulars exist. Abelard developed a theory of moral responsibility based on the agent's intentions. Moral goodness is defined as intending to show love of God and neighbor and being correct in that intention.

TWELFTH CENTURY

Philosopher	Works/Ideas/Concepts
Moses Maimonides, Spanish Medieval Jewish philosopher	*Guide for the Perplexed* The principle that inspired his philosophy was identical to the fundamental tenet of Scholasticism: there can be no contradiction between the truths that God has revealed, and the findings of the human mind in science and philosophy.

THIRTEENTH CENTURY

Philosopher	Works/Ideas/Concepts
St. Thomas Aquinas, Roman	*Summa Theologica* He was immensely influenced by Scholasticism and Aristotle and known for his synthesis of the two aforementioned traditions. Aquinas argues that God exists and is working through men.

THE RENAISSANCE (EUROPE): 1400–1600

SIXTEENTH CENTURY

Philosopher	Works/Ideas/Concepts
Niccolò Machiavelli, Italian philosopher and writer	*The Prince; The Art of War* He is considered one of the main founders of modern political science. Machiavelli studied the way people lived and aimed to inform leaders how they should rule and even how they themselves should live.
Thomas More, English lawyer, statesman, philosopher	*Utopia* (He coined the word *utopia*.) In Utopia, with communal ownership of land, private property does not exist, men and women are educated alike, and there is almost complete religious toleration.
John Calvin, French expatriate	*Institutes of the Christian Religion* Believes God is a wholly pure and good creator and humans, created by God, are corrupted and have no control over their own salvation.
Francis Bacon, English lawyer, statesman, essayist, historian, intellectual reformer, philosopher	*The Proficience and Advancement of Learning* He thought that knowledge is power, and when embodied in the form of new technical inventions and mechanical discoveries it is the force that drives history.
Thomas Hobbes, English philosopher	*Leviathan* His main concern is the problem of social and political order: how human beings can live together in peace and avoid the danger and fear of civil conflict.

THE BAROQUE PERIOD

SEVENTEENTH CENTURY

Philosopher	Works/Ideas/Concepts
René Descartes, French, called the Father of Modern Philosophy	*Meditations* He discovers that "I exist" is impossible to doubt and is, therefore, absolutely certain. Descartes is known for his phrase, "Cogito, ergo sum" or "I think, therefore I am."
Blaise Pascal, French	*Pensées* He offers a pragmatic reason for believing in God: even under the assumption that God's existence is unlikely, the potential benefits of believing are so vast as to make betting on theism rational. In other words, if we don't know whether God exists then we should play it safe rather than risk being sorry.
Baruch Spinoza, born Portugal (parents fled to escape the Inquisition)	*Ethics* In *Ethics*, Spinoza presents an ethical vision unfolding out of a monistic metaphysics in which God and Nature are identified. God is no longer the transcendent creator of the universe who rules it via providence, but Nature itself, understood as an infinite, necessary, and fully deterministic system of which humans are a part.
John Locke, British Empiricist philosopher	*Essay Concerning Human Understanding* Locke believed that although we can know little for certain and must rely on probabilities, it is our God-given obligation to obtain knowledge and not always to acquire our beliefs by accepting the word of authorities or common superstition.

EIGHTEENTH CENTURY

Philosopher	Works/Ideas/Concepts
Bishop George Berkeley, British (Irish) Empiricist	*A Treatise Concerning the Principles of Human Knowledge* He is best known for his motto, "esse is percipi," or "to be is to be perceived." He was an idealist, believing everything that exists is either a mind or depends for its existence upon a mind.
David Hume, British Idealist philosopher (born Scotland)	*The Philosophical Works of David Hume* He argued that it is unreasonable to believe testimonies of alleged miraculous events, and, accordingly, hints that we should reject religions that are founded on miracle testimonies.

THE FRENCH ENLIGHTENMENT (AGE OF REASON)

EIGHTEENTH CENTURY

Philosopher	Works/Ideas/Concepts
Jean-Jacques Rousseau, French philosopher	*Discourse on the Origin and Foundations of Inequality, The Confessions* Rousseau believed human beings are basically good by nature, but are corrupted by the complex historical events that resulted in present-day civil society.
Adam Smith, British (Scottish) Empiricist philosopher, thought to be leader of modern sociology	*The Theory of Moral Sentiments, The Wealth of Nations* Smith believed people derive pleasure from seeing the happiness of others because, by design, others concern us. Human beings are social. We care about others and their circumstances bring us pleasure or pain.
Immanuel Kant, German philosopher	*Critique of Pure Reason, Critique of Practical Reason, Critique of Judgment* A large part of Kant's work addresses the question "What can we know?" He argued against the Empiricists and said that the mind is not a blank slate that is written upon by the empirical world. On morality he said that one should act only according to that maxim by which you can at the same time will that it should become a universal law.

NINETEENTH CENTURY

Philosopher	Works/Ideas/Concepts
Jeremy Bentham, English philosopher and political radical	Known today for his moral philosophy, especially his principle of **utilitarianism**, which evaluates actions based upon their consequences. The relevant consequences, in particular, are the overall happiness created for everyone affected by the action.

ROMANTICISM

NINETEENTH CENTURY

Philosopher	Works/Ideas/Concepts
Georg Wilhelm Friedrich Hegel, German idealist philosopher	*The Philosophy of Right* Believed all knowledge was human knowledge. No knowledge is correct forever, but right or wrong in relation to a certain historical context.
John Stuart Mill, British philosopher	*A System of Logic, Principles of Political Economy, On Liberty, Utilitarianism, The Subjection of Women, Three Essays on Religion*, and his autobiography *On Liberty* puts forward the "harm principle" that "the only purpose for which power can be rightfully exercised over any member of a civilized community, against his will, is to prevent harm to others." In *The Subjection of Women*, he compares the legal status of women to the status of slaves and argues for equality in marriage and under the law.
Karl Marx, German philosopher and political economist	*Communist Manifesto, Das Kapital* Marx argued that capitalism would inevitably produce internal tensions that would lead to its destruction. Just as capitalism replaced feudalism, he believed socialism would, in its turn, replace capitalism, and lead to a stateless, classless society called pure communism.
Friedrich Nietzsche, German philosopher, essayist, and cultural critic	*Thus Spoke Zarathustra, Beyond Good and Evil* Nietzsche spoke of "the death of God," and foresaw the dissolution of traditional religion and metaphysics. Nietzsche claimed the exemplary human being must craft his/her own identity through self-realization and do so without relying on anything transcending that life—such as God or a soul.

TWENTIETH CENTURY

Philosopher	Works/Ideas/Concepts
Sigmund Freud, Austrian physiologist, medical doctor, psychologist and Father of Psychoanalysis	*The Standard Edition of the Complete Psychological Works of Sigmund Freud* Freud was arguably the first thinker to apply deterministic principles systematically to the sphere of the mental, and to hold that the broad spectrum of human behavior is explicable only in terms of the (usually hidden) mental processes or states which determine it, which suggests the view that freedom of the will is, if not completely an illusion, certainly more tightly circumscribed than is commonly believed.
John Dewey, American philosopher	*Democracy and Education, How We Think* Dewey believed inquiry should not be understood as a mind passively observing the world, but rather as a process which begins with cognitive dissonance that needs resolution. Father of Experiential Learning Theory.
Bertrand Russell, British philosopher, logician, mathematician, historian, agnostic, socialist, pacifist, and social critic	*The Problems of Philosophy, A History of Western Philosophy* He said, "Education is the key to the new world. Partly this is due to our need to understand nature, but equally important is our need to understand each other."
Ludwig Wittgenstein, Austrian philosopher	*Tractatus Logico-Philosophicus* Four main themes run through Wittgenstein's writings on ethics and religion: (1) goodness, value or meaning are not to be found in the world; (2) living the right way involves acceptance of or agreement with the world, or life, or God's will, or fate; (3) one who lives this way will see the world as a miracle; (4) there is no answer to the problem of life—the solution is the disappearance of the problem.
Martin Heidegger, German philosopher	*Being and Time* Heidegger claims that even though we seem to understand being, its meaning is still veiled in darkness. Therefore, we need to restate the question of the meaning of being.

Philosopher	Works/Ideas/Concepts
Jean-Paul Sartre, French existentialist philosopher	*Being and Nothingness* He defines two types of reality which lie beyond our conscious experience: the being of the object of consciousness and that of consciousness itself. The object of consciousness exists as "in-itself," that is, in an independent and non-relational way.
Simone de Beauvoir, French existentialist philosopher	In *The Second Sex*, she produced an articulate attack on the fact that throughout history women have been relegated to a sphere of "immanence" and the passive acceptance of roles assigned to them by society.
Ayn Rand, Russian American novelist and Objectivist philosopher	*Anthem, The Fountainhead, Atlas Shrugged, The Virtue of Selfishness* Self-interest rightly understood, according to Rand, is to see oneself as an end in oneself. That is to say that one's own life and happiness are one's highest values, and that one does not exist as a servant or slave to the interests of others. Nor do others exist as servants or slaves to one's own interests. Each person's own life and happiness is his ultimate end.

Irony and Satire:
Reading Between the Lines

Satire is focused bitterness.—Leo Rosten

OVERVIEW

The concepts of irony and satire, even though they are all around us, remain a struggle for many students. I think the reason for this is that irony and satire are not direct, but indirect. Meaning is not obvious, but subtle. As there are typically questions about irony and satirical passages on the exam, it is important to devote some extra time here to discuss them. This chapter will provide you with a good foundation to maximize your ability to both recognize and understand these concepts.

IRONY

While irony is a tool (the main tool) of satirists, it is, on its own, an important element in all literature. Yearly, there are questions on the exam about irony. Basically, *irony* is the term we use to indicate that uncomfortable space between appearances and reality. Irony gets us to pay attention, since it is a kind of cognitive dissonance that our brain wants swept up and made orderly. We want things to make sense or fit a constructed order. In general, irony lives in any technique meant to create contrast, such as hyperbole, understatement, oxymoron, and more. Be sure you are a master of the following types of irony and can easily spot them in the texts you read.

FOUR TYPES OF IRONY

1. **Verbal Irony**: what the speaker says is different from what he or she means. Sarcasm is a type of verbal irony, but it is harsh, even bitter, and typically expresses a veiled anger or resentment.

2. **Dramatic Irony**: the reader or listener knows something that the character or speaker does not know.

3. **Situational Irony**: a discrepancy between what is real and what is perceived. Situational irony refers to an occasion in which the outcome is significantly different from what is expected or considered appropriate.

4. **Socratic Irony**: Socrates taught his students by pretending to be ignorant about the subjects his students were discussing in order to get them to think on their own. Related to this playing "devil's advocate" is the situation in which an arguer ironically takes a position he or she does not actually hold in order to push an argument to its limits.

Test Tip *Start an irony journal. When ironic situations or comments "pop up" in your everyday life, make a list of them. Actively collecting examples of irony will force you to pay attention to it and will, as a result, sharpen your irony radar!*

SATIRE

Satire is language or writing (even if the mode is visual) with a specific purpose. The purpose of **satire** is to point out the inadequacies, vices, and corruptions in people, institutions, and cultures with the intent of bringing about change. Satire is often wryly funny, sometimes even knee-slapping funny, but sometimes the satirist hits a raw nerve, and we may be too uncomfortable to laugh at what is clearly no laughing matter. The satirist is a person in tune with what ought to be, and he or she may see what others cannot see or are too timid to express: the truth. The ultimate goal of a satirist is to bring about positive change for the betterment of all.

As ordinary citizens, we expect that people in power, especially if we bestow that power upon them, will not abuse it and will not exploit, undermine, or cheat us in the execution of their duties. We also know that human beings are innately flawed, which provides a rich field for satirists, whose job it is to point out people and institutions that break our explicit or implicit social contract.

THE SOCIAL CONTRACT

To be good at analyzing satire, it is important that we understand that human beings have, in general, a social contract with each other. Satirists point out a break or departure from this social contract. To understand this social contract, think in terms of humanity's norms. A **norm** is a universally agreed upon standard of behavior. In this social contract, we also include rules (laws). The commandment "Thou shalt not kill" is a good example of a long-standing rule that most people in all cultures agree is an important rule by which to live. Three aspects of norms and rules determine the extent to which we universally value them in our social contract. The chart below illustrates these aspects of "universality."

Qualities of Universality ▶	Long-standing	Most reasonable people agree that it is just/fair	Accepted in many cultures
"Thou shalt not kill."	✓	✓	✓
Stealing is wrong	✓	✓	✓
Lying is wrong	✓	✓	✓
You should not wear white shoes after Labor Day*.			
Women must not express their opinions in public.			

*Ask your grandmother about this one. ☺

Test Tip *Create your own list of universal truths that you believe are central to our universal social contract.*

Why not simply be a muckraker, or a whistle-blower? It is sometimes politically or personally dangerous to stand up to powerful figures, whether they are institutions or individuals. Surely you've heard stories of whistle-blowers losing their jobs, *or worse*. Since satire is inherently ambiguous, there is safety in the gray areas. All satirical techniques allow the satirist to say two or more things at the same time. Satirists mainly insinuate instead of attack directly. This aspect of satire provides relative safety for the satirist, but can also present difficulty for AP English students. We must read carefully and learn to read what's implied or insinuated. This can sometimes be very difficult to do, which is why you need to practice the skills shown in this chapter.

For example, while Stephen Colbert's targets may be corrupt politicians, *we* are his audience. His goal is for *us* to snap out of our lethargy and become aware and eventually act. He wants us to stand up for what we know is right. Jonathan Swift could not have solved the problems of the Irish poor by himself, but he expected the landowners and the politicians to begin acting in honorable ways. *A Modest Proposal* is outrageous, but its intent is to shame those who abandoned the poor.

Most satirists are also, to some extent, entertainers. Even Geoffrey Chaucer's portrayal of the cheating Miller in *The Reeve's Tale* is initially laugh-out-loud funny. When we examine the story more closely, we see all kinds of human foibles there and good lessons for us all.

It is also a fact of human nature that we don't respond to the dictates of a know-it-all. We shun the arrogance of those who tell us what to do. But when a satirist first astonishes us or makes us laugh and gives us an oblique picture of ourselves in a mirror, we somehow are more willing to accept our faults.

STYLES AND TYPES OF SATIRE

Two Styles

1. **Direct** satire (also called Formal): directly stated by the satirist

2. **Indirect** satire: communicated through characters in a narrative

Two Types

1. **Juvenalian Satire**: Named after Juvenal, a Roman poet active in the late first and early second century; author of the *Satires*. This type of satire is bitter, angry, contemptuous, and full of moral indignation. If you do not laugh but instead react with outrageous surprise, you are probably reading Juvenalian satire.

2. **Horatian Satire**: Named after Horace, Roman poet who lived 65–8 BCE It is characterized by gentle, urbane comedy that corrects through sympathetic laughter.

TYPICAL SATIRICAL TARGETS

Powerful People	Institutions	Events/ Conditions	Human Nature
Politicians	Congress	Oil Spills	Cowardice
Religious Leaders	Churches	Wars	Greed
Teachers	Broadcast Networks	Social Trends/ Fads	Hypocrisy
Police Officers	Corporations	Neglect of Duty	Incontinence (inability to control desires)
Parents	Sports Teams		Arrogance
Celebrities			Ignorance

SATIRICAL TECHNIQUES AND DEVICES

Lists of satirical techniques will vary from source to source. The list below is meant to give you a broad view. As with any list of literary terms, there is some overlap. Various sources use different terms for similar concepts. The Quick Guide (following the list) is a more summarized approach. If you are short on time, rely on the Quick Guide, but also familiarize yourself with this list as well.

1. **Allegory/Parable:** An **allegory** is a narrative with a literal and a symbolic meaning. By using allegory, writers can disguise their satirical targets as a character. A **parable** is a story that teaches a lesson. Parables are sometimes cautionary tales such as narratives that warn what might happen if behavior does not change.

2. **Ambiguity:** Inherent in most of these techniques, ambiguity is simply when the meaning of something is unclear and it may mean more than one thing.

3. **Exaggeration:** To enlarge, increase, or represent something beyond normal bounds so that it becomes ridiculous and its faults can be seen. *Caricature* is the exaggeration of a physical feature or trait. Cartoons, especially political cartoons, provide extensive examples

of caricature. *Burlesque* is the ridiculous exaggeration of language. An example is when a character who should use formal, intelligent language speaks like a fool or a character who is portrayed as uneducated uses highly sophisticated, intelligent language. To enlarge, increase, or represent something beyond normal bounds so that it becomes ridiculous and its faults can be seen.

4. **Diminution:** Taking a real-life situation and reducing it to make it ridiculous and showcase its faults. Also, **Reduction**.

5. **Distortion:** Taking something out of its ordinary surroundings sometimes reveals its idiocy or inadequacies.

6. **Farce:** Similar to burlesque, a farce is a narrative in which the ridiculous characters in the situation are exaggerated and the outcomes of the plot are absurd. It is essentially a comedy.

7. **Incongruity:** To present things that are out of place or absurd in relation to their surroundings. Particular techniques include oxymoron, metaphor, and irony.

8. **Innuendo:** An implied remark that disparages another's reputation.

9. **Invective:** A direct insult. A longer version of invective is a **diatribe** (we'd call it a rant).

10. **Knaves and Fools:** These clowns of satire are exaggerations of our follies. Taken to the extreme, their ridiculous behavior still rings true, and we see in them something of ourselves. Knaves and fools are key elements of farce.

11. **Malapropism:** Absurd or humorous misuse of a word, especially by confusion with one of similar sound. Example: "Republicans understand the importance of bondage between a mother and child." (Dan Quayle)

12. **Oxymoron:** Words or phrases used together that present a paradox. Examples are "wax fruit," and "electric candles."

13. **Parody:** To imitate the techniques and/or style of some person, place, or thing, mimicking the techniques and/or style in order to ridicule the original. For parody to be successful, the reader must know the original text that is being ridiculed.

14. **Reduction:** To belittle the satirical target, reducing power or stature. Caricature is one way to reduce status, since it makes the target look ridiculous or silly.

15. **Reversal:** To present the opposite of the normal order. Reversal can focus on the order of events, such as serving dessert before the main dish or having breakfast for dinner. Additionally, reversal can focus on hierarchical order—for instance, when a young child makes all the decisions for a family or when an administrative assistant dictates what the company president decides and does. To present the opposite of the normal order (e.g., the order of events, hierarchical order).

16. **Understatement:** The opposite of exaggeration, understatement does basically the same thing. By contrast, it draws attention to the truth.

SATIRE: QUICK GUIDE

I created this quick guide for students to take with them since it is more portable than a book. During our satire unit, I encourage students to see through the lenses of a satirist, which means everything they encounter should be viewed as fodder for its potential to be satirized. Learning the tools a satirist uses means more than just memorizing a few terms. It means that you must recognize irony and exaggeration when you see it and decide if the writer has a barb in mind.

SATIRE: Quick Guide

What is it? A satirist points out, usually through humor, what is wrong in people and institutions. In any analysis of satire, we look for three things: Target, Purpose, Techniques. You want to know what is being mocked or ridiculed in order to know what the satirist wants us to know and do.

1. What is the satirical target?

   - A person? A company/corporation? An idea? A social trend/convention?

2. What is the satirical purpose?

   - Force a recognition of common sense. "Let's get real, people."

   - Urge a change in policy. "This is not how it should be done."

   - Create an understanding that something is wrong/illegal/immoral or should be.

Continued →

3. How is the satire achieved? What techniques are used? There are more than these nine, but these are often cited as the main ones.

- **Exaggeration**
  Hyperbole/overstatement, or plain exaggeration is used to take something to the extreme. The contrast gets us to see the reality.

- **Understatement**
  The opposite of exaggeration, understatement does basically the same thing. By contrast, it draws attention to the truth.

- **Distortion**
  Taking something out of its ordinary surroundings sometimes reveals its idiocy or inadequacies. Distortion unmasks an idea.

- **Irony**
  Plain old irony points out discrepancies that perhaps should be obvious, but might take the satirist to show us.

- **Oxymoron**
  A good example is "deafening silence." An extremely loud noise would be deafening and silence is the absence of any noise. When the words don't fit, the meaning becomes obvious.

- **Innuendo**
  Innuendo is an indirect attack or insinuation. It's useful when the target is dangerous or powerful. Intention can always be denied.

- **Reversal**
  To present the opposite of the normal order, which is a type of distortion, but reversal gets us to look at what should be by way of the contrast.

- **Reduction**
  Look for caricatures or other ways to knock the corrupt and powerful off their self-made pedestals. Does a sneaky politician look clownish in a cartoon? That's reduction.

- **Ambiguity**
  While many aspects of satire are ambiguous, some statements are directly so. Look for fuzzy statements that can mean more than one thing.

4. Put in your own words what it is that the satirist wants us to **know** or **do**.

Note: In addition to common satirical techniques, any piece of satire may also employ typical rhetorical strategies. Be sure to know all of those as well as the list of appeals. See Chapter 6.

GENERAL GUIDE FOR ANALYZING SATIRE

I created the following guide for my students to help them analyze several texts that we study together in our satire unit. My students sometimes work independently, but also with partners, especially if a text is complex. If you have a study team, you might want to consider sharing this guide with them. In your group, read and study some of the texts listed in the chart at the end of this chapter.

General Guide for Analyzing Satire

Title of work: _____   Author: _____

1. What is the main satiric target (social institution, social convention/norm, etc.)?

2. Who are the specific representatives of the target (individuals or groups)?

3. Which aspects of our social "agreement" are flawed?

4. What change does the author want to see?

5. Find and label in your text examples of specific satirical techniques. (See the list above.) Then, choose two and, in the space below, explain their effectiveness.

6. How are wit and humor employed? Give specific examples.

7. Is this work a sample of Juvenalian or Horatian satire, and how do you know?

8. How well does the author achieve his/her purpose? Do you think the message is clear or too ambiguous? Explain.

(Copy and use to analyze a variety of satirical texts.)

RESOURCE GUIDE

Some academics say satire is dead, but it may just be that good satire is harder to find. The list below should give you a good start in finding new and old satire to study. If you find the genre difficult, please do spend some time with this. It will pay off in the end. This list of works is not meant to suggest the full range of literary or cultural satire, but rather to remind you of what is out there that is generally easy to access.

Do not limit yourself to what is listed here. Instead, be open to satirical possibilities anywhere. If you're laughing and the writer or commentator is making fun of someone who did something not quite right, that's satire. Analyze it. Think it through. You'll become an expert in no time.

Cautionary note: It is easy to get caught up in the humor when you watch some of these shows or read some of the articles, but keep your analytical head about you. Always work on identifying the satirical target and what techniques are used to blast away at the stupidity, hypocrisy, or corruption.

Photocopy several copies of the General Guide for Analyzing Satire (see previous page), and study some examples from the current media. Do the same with a text from a classic satirist such as Jonathan Swift or Mark Twain.

Current Examples		Classic Satirists
Television/ Movies	**Books/Newspaper/Internet**	**Classic Satirists**
The Daily Show	*The Onion* (an article from the Onion was featured in the free-response section of the 2005 exam). *The Onion* was originally a print paper. They have published several books as well.	Geoffrey Chaucer: *Canterbury Tales*
Family Guy, Seth MacFarlane	Andy Borowitz, "The Borowitz Report," The New Yorker.	Jonathan Swift: *A Modest Proposal*, *Gulliver's Travels*
Saturday Night Live	*The Heckler* (satirical look at Chicago sports)	Voltaire: *Candide*
The Simpsons, Matt Groening	Garry Trudeau's comic strip, *Doonesbury* (first published in daily papers in 1970)	Benjamin Franklin: *Rules by Which a Great Empire May Be Reduced to a Small One* (public domain)
South Park, Matt Stone and Trey Parker	Dave Barry: variety of titles	Mark Twain: *The Adventures of Huckleberry Finn*, *Advice to Youth* (earlier AP prompt)
This is Spinal Tap, *Best in Show*, *Waiting for Guffman*, Christopher Guest	David and Amy Sedaris: variety of titles	
	Joseph Heller: *Catch 22*	

SAMPLE WORK WITH ANNOTATIONS

The following is a speech by Mark Twain called *Advice to Youth* (1882).

Primary Satirical Target: Hypocritical adults (parents) who tell children one thing but live the opposite.

Being told I would be expected to talk here, I inquired what sort of talk I ought to make. They said it should be something suitable to youth— something <u>didactic, instructive,</u> or something in the nature of good advice. Very well. I have a few things in my mind which I have often longed to say for the instruction of the young; for it is in <u>one's tender early years</u> that such things <u>will best take root</u> and be most enduring and most valuable. First, then, I will say to you my young friends—and I say it <u>beseechingly, urgingly—</u>

Tone — initially sincere

Genre: speech

The young are impressionable

My message is very important! (It actually is — the real message.)

Series of maxims/moral truths

1) Always obey your parents, when they are present. This is the best policy in the long run, because if you don't, they will make you. Most parents think they know better than you do, and you can generally make more by humoring that superstition than you can by acting on your own better judgment.

First indication that he may not always be serious, or mean what he says.

2) Be respectful to your superiors, if you have any, also to strangers, and sometimes to others. If a person offends you, and you are in doubt as to whether it was intentional or not, do not resort to extreme measures; simply watch your chance <u>and hit him with</u> a brick. <u>That will be sufficient.</u> If you shall find that he had not intended any offense, come out frankly and confess yourself in the wrong when you struck him; acknowledge it like a man and say you didn't mean to. Yes, always avoid violence; in this age of charity and kindliness, the time has gone by for such things. Leave dynamite to the low and unrefined.

Reversal: Such behavior is not at all socially acceptable. Exaggerated example of how people sometimes act poorly and then say "Sorry, didn't mean it."

3) Go to bed early, get up early—this is wise. Some authorities say get up with the sun; some say get up with one thing, others with another. But a lark is really the best thing to get up with. It gives you a splendid reputation with everybody to know that you get up with the lark; and if you get the right kind of lark, and work at him right, you can easily train him to get up at half past nine, every time—it's no trick at all.

Ambiguity→"Lark"
Lark is an early bird but also a whim. Getting up early is a relative virtue, but maybe getting up each day w/a sense of newness + adventure is good.

tongue-in-cheek

Now as to the matter of lying. You want to be very careful about lying; otherwise you are nearly sure to get caught. Once caught, you can never again be in the eyes to the good and the pure, what you were before. Many a young person has injured himself permanently through a single clumsy and ill finished lie, the result of carelessness born of incomplete training. Some authorities hold that the young ought not to lie at all. That of course, is putting it rather stronger than necessary; still while I cannot go quite so far as that, I do maintain, and I believe I am right, that the young ought to be temperate in the use of this great art until practice and experience shall give them that confidence, elegance, and precision which alone can make the accomplishment graceful and profitable. Patience, diligence, painstaking attention to detail—these are requirements; these in time, will make the student perfect; upon these only, may he rely as the sure foundation for future eminence. Think what tedious years of study, thought, practice, experience, went to the equipment of that peerless old master who was able to impose upon the whole world the lofty and sounding maxim that "Truth is mighty and will prevail"—the most majestic compound fracture of fact which any of woman born has yet achieved. For the history of our race, and each individual's experience, are sewn

⚹1

⚹ Yes — careful, but not in a traditional way.

If you're going to lie well, it takes practice.

The typical view of all adults/parents.

⚹2 These are actually good traits.

⚹2

This maxim is in itself a lie. Good ex. of hypocrisy.

nice phrase, a complicated lie

Society doesn't really value the truth.

thick with evidences that a truth is not hard to
kill, and that a lie well told is immortal.

Lying is so common that some lies become immortal.

There is in Boston a monument of the man who
discovered anesthesia; many people are aware,
in these latter days, that man didn't discover it
at all, but stole the discovery from another man.
Is this truth mighty, and will it prevail? Ah no,
my hearers, the monument is made of hardy
material, but the lie it tells will outlast it a million
years. An awkward, feeble, leaky lie is a thing
which you ought to make it your unceasing
study to avoid; such a lie as that has no more
real permanence than an average truth. Why,
you might as well tell the truth at once and be
done with it. A feeble, stupid, preposterous lie
will not live two years—except it be a slander
upon somebody. It is indestructible, then of
course, but that is no merit of yours. A final
word: begin your practice of this gracious and
beautiful art early—begin now. If I had begun
earlier, I could have learned how.

Example of an immortal lie.

This seems like a cynical truth.

Irony — Emphasizes his earnestness. He's not able to lie. But of course, he writes fiction.

Never handle firearms carelessly. The sorrow and
suffering that have been caused through the
innocent but heedless handling of firearms by
the young! Only four days ago, right in the next
farm house to the one where I am spending
the summer, a grandmother, old and gray and
sweet, one of the loveliest spirits in the land, was
sitting at her work, when her young grandson
crept in and got down an old, battered, rusty
gun which had not been touched for many
years and was supposed not to be loaded, and
pointed it at her, laughing and threatening
to shoot. In her fright she ran screaming and
pleading toward the door on the other side of
the room; but as she passed him he placed the
gun almost against her very breast and pulled
the trigger! He had supposed it was not loaded.

And he was right—it wasn't. So there wasn't any harm done. It is the only case of that kind I ever heard of. Therefore, just the same, don't you meddle with old unloaded firearms; they are the most deadly and unerring things that have ever been created by man. You don't have to take any pains at all with them; you don't have to have a rest, you don't have to have any sights on the gun, you don't have to take aim, even. No, you just pick out a relative and bang away, and you are sure to get him. A youth who can't hit a cathedral at thirty yards with a Gatling gun in three quarters of an hour, can take up an old empty musket and bag his grandmother every time, at a hundred. Think what Waterloo would have been if one of the armies had been boys armed with old muskets supposed not to be loaded, and the other army had been composed of their female relations. The very thought of it make one shudder.

irony — real guns/ weapons are "the most deadly . . . ever created by man."

Distortion — A wild youth with a gun is ridiculous — but compared to reality — harmless. Guns in real life are not unloaded + they kill for real.

*(left margin, vertical)* Reversal — But war isn't silly stuff.

There are many sorts of books; but good ones are the sort for the young to read. remember that. They are a great, an inestimable, and unspeakable means of improvement. Therefore be careful in your selection, my young friends; be very careful; confine yourselves exclusively to Robertson's Sermons, Baxter's Saint's Rest, The Innocents Abroad, and works of that kind.

Biblical allusion

But I have said enough, I hope you will treasure up the instructions which I have given you, and make them a guide to your feet and a light to your understanding. Build your character thoughtfully and painstakingly upon these precepts, and by and by, when you have got it built, you will be surprised and gratified to see how nicely and sharply it resembles everybody else's. Cynical tone.

Didactic texts that are most likely worthless. He's mocking himself by including his own book. Learn from life, not books!

Appeal to identity + esteem needs; we want to find our own way + not follow.

Twain's main point: If you want to be like all the other adults in the world, learn to lie + use violence to solve your conflicts.

PART IV:

RESEARCH AND WRITING

Free-Response Questions

*I do insist on making what I hope is sense so there's always
a coherent narrative or argument that the
reader can follow.* —Howard Nemerov

OVERVIEW

The purpose of this chapter is to explain the types of free-response
questions that have appeared on previous AP English Language exams.
While each of the three questions requires distinct skills, they all require
you to do your best rhetorical reading and writing. All three questions
require you to develop and defend an argument.

GENERAL TYPES OF FREE-RESPONSE QUESTIONS

QUESTION 1 SYNTHESIS

You will be presented with an issue to consider. There will be five to
seven sources, at least one of which is likely to be a visual text. You are to
develop your own claim and support it with evidence from at least three
sources. See the detailed explanation of this question in Chapter 18.

QUESTION 2 RHETORICAL ANALYSIS

A. You are given a prose passage to read and analyze. In general, you
will be asked to explain how the author uses rhetorical strategies to
achieve his or her purpose. You will not be given a list of strategies,
but are expected to discover these on your own. (See Chapter 6.)

B. You are given a prose passage to read and write about. In general, you will be asked to defend, challenge (or refute), or qualify the author's position.

C. You will be given two short texts that share elements: topic, style, purpose, etc., and be asked to compare and contrast them, while also analyzing the writer's or speaker's purpose and strategies.

QUESTION 3 PERSUASIVE

A. You are given a short quotation or a very brief passage that presents a debatable issue. You are asked to develop your own position on the issue and defend it. Your evidence for this essay comes from your own knowledge, reading, and experience.

B. You are given a premise and you will choose your own relevant issue to argue. Your support for this essay comes from your own knowledge, reading, and experience.

ABOUT PROMPTS IN GENERAL

An essay prompt does several things:

1. Asks you to carefully read a specific text(s), quotation, or question.

2. Gives you a specific task to accomplish (see examples later in this chapter).

3. Directly tells you to write a well-organized essay.

4. Instructs you to defend your claim with specific evidence.

Test Tip

It is critically important for you to know exactly what a prompt is asking for and respond appropriately. You will earn a very low score if you fail to do what the prompt asks you to do or if you substitute a simpler task for the one presented to you.

ANALYZING ESSAY PROMPTS: STEPS FOR SUCCESS

1. **Analyze your prompt**. Underline key words in the prompt, especially verbs that state your task, but also underline any hints about a topic or perspective.

    ➤ Sample prompt from a previous exam with keywords, verbs, and hints underlined:

    > *In his 2004 book, <u>Status Anxiety</u>, Alain de Botton argues that the chief aim of humorists is not merely to entertain but "to convey with impunity messages that might be dangerous or impossible to state directly." Because <u>society allows humorists to say things that other people cannot or will not say</u>, de Botton sees humorists as serving a vital function in society.*

    > *<u>Think</u> about the implications of de Botton's view of the role of humorists (cartoonists, stand-up comics, satirical writers, hosts of television programs, etc.). Then write an essay that <u>defends, challenges, or qualifies</u> de Botton's claim about the <u>vital role of humorists</u>. <u>Use specific, appropriate evidence</u> to develop your position.*

2. **Paraphrase your task**. This step is crucial to your understanding. You don't have to actually write out your paraphrase, but say it in your head. By phrasing, in your own words, what you believe your task to be, you will understand it better and will remember it more as you write, which will help you stay focused. You can also reword the prompt using first person, stating what you need to do. See the example below.

    ➤ Paraphrase for prompt above:

    > *Alain de Botton says that humorists (comedians, cartoonists, television hosts) do more than entertain us. He thinks we allow them to say things no one else can say, which gives them an important voice in society. I need to think about what this means, and decide if I agree with de Botton or not (or somewhere in between), then develop my claim in my essay.*

3. **Use the prompt as your guide**. When you know what you're supposed to do, you can read a passage or source materials more efficiently and more intelligently.

➤ Annotate any supplied texts as you read, with the prompt in mind.

➤ Create a mini-outline that contains your main claim (thesis) and your key points. This is your "answer" to the prompt. It must fit the expectations presented in the prompt.

4. **Review the prompt** as often as necessary to make sure you aren't digressing or losing focus.

If you get in the habit of using the prompt-analysis strategy given above on all your practice essays, it will become an automatic skill for you by exam time and you'll barely be conscious of the process. That's efficiency!

DEFEND, CHALLENGE, QUALIFY

You are sometimes asked to defend, challenge, or qualify an author's purpose or point of view in a passage. It is important to know what these terms mean.

Defend (sometimes **support** is used to mean the same thing)	Defending someone else's point of view means that you agree with it. You will create your own argument that uses evidence from the text as well as from your own knowledge and experience to support your claim that the author is correct.
Challenge (sometimes **refute** is used to mean the same thing)	Challenging or refuting someone else's point of view means that you disagree with it. You will create your own argument that uses evidence from the text as well as from your own knowledge and experience to support your claim that the author is incorrect.
Qualify	Qualifying someone else's point of view means that you agree with some parts of his or her argument but disagree with other parts. Or, it could mean that while you think the author is generally correct, you want to point out some exceptions or some qualifications that exist. You will create your own argument that uses evidence from the text as well as from your own knowledge and experience to support your claim that the author is not exactly correct.

SAMPLE PROMPTS

PROMPT FOR FREE-RESPONSE QUESTION 1: SYNTHESIS

The prompt for the synthesis question does not vary all that much from year to year. The example prompts below are taken from previous AP English Language exams and are representative of prompts you are likely to see on your exam. This free-response question is called "synthesis" because you are expected to bring together (synthesize) evidence from various sources as you build your argument. You will read more about this concept in Chapter 19.

You will always be expected to develop your own point of view or your own claim, which you will defend with evidence from at least three of the supplied sources.

Content Task	Key Elements
Write an essay in which you develop a position on the effect of _____. Synthesize at least three of the sources for support.	Cause and effect
Develop a position on whether or not _____. Synthesize at least three of the sources for support.	Evaluation
In an essay that synthesizes at least three of the sources, develop a position about what issues should be considered most important in making decisions about _____.	Evaluation
In an essay, argue the extent to which _____ should support _____. Synthesize at least three of the sources for support.	Evaluation
Evaluate the most important factors that [one] should consider before _____.	Evaluation
Develop a position on _____.	Policy
Then synthesize at least three of the sources into an essay that evaluates _____ and offers a recommendation about _____.	Evaluation

PROMPT FOR FREE-RESPONSE QUESTION 2: RHETORICAL ANALYSIS

The example prompts below come from previous exams and are representative of prompts you are likely to see on your exam. The genres listed are most often excerpts, though some shorter texts are provided in full. Consult Chapter 20 for more information on this free-response question.

Content Task	Key Elements	Genre (basis for question)*
Analyze how the author's style conveys the complexity of his or her response to _____.	Style, author's attitude/point of view	Essay
Analyze the methods the author uses to persuade _____.	Rhetorical strategies	Speech
Analyze the strategies used in the article to satirize _____.	Satirical techniques	Article, satire
Evaluate the pros and cons of the author's argument.	Evaluation	Book
Analyze the rhetorical strategies the author uses to develop his or her position	Rhetorical strategies	Essay
Analyze the strategies the author uses to develop his or her perspective.	Rhetorical strategies	Article
Analyze how the author uses rhetorical strategies to characterize _____.	Rhetorical strategies, characterization	Book
In the two passages below, the author satirizes _____. Write an essay in which you analyze how the author's satire illustrates _____.	Satire; compare/contrast	Two articles by same author

---

* Nearly all will be excerpts, and not full texts.

Content Task	Key Elements	Genre (basis for question)*
Write an essay in which you analyze the rhetorical strategies the author uses to develop his or her argument.	Rhetorical strategies	Article
Analyze how the author uses rhetorical strategies in the letter to argue against _____.	Rhetorical strategies	Letter
Decide if you agree with the author's point of view. Explain your position with an essay that uses specific evidence for support.	Defend, refute, qualify	Premise of a book
Read the following excerpt from the letter and write an essay that analyzes how the author uses rhetorical strategies to argue against _____.	Rhetorical strategies	Letter
Analyze the strategies the author uses to characterize _____.	Rhetorical strategies; characterization	Memoir
Analyze how _____ prepares her audience for her message.	Analysis of rhetoric	Introduction to a speech
Analyze rhetorical strategies _____ uses to advise _____.	Rhetorical strategies	Letter

* Nearly all will be excerpts, and not full texts.

PROMPT FOR FREE-RESPONSE QUESTION 3: PERSUASIVE

The example prompts below give you an historical view of prompts for question 3. This prompt allows you to showcase your broad knowledge that you've acquired from reading. Nearly all of your evidence will come from memory of books, articles, and other texts you have read. To some degree, you can provide personal anecdotal evidence as well. This will be discussed more fully in Chapter 21.

Content Task	Key Elements	Basis for Question
Write an essay in which you support, refute, or qualify the author's claim that _____. Use appropriate evidence to develop your argument.	Defend, challenge, or qualify	Excerpt from essay
Compare and contrast how each writer describes _____ and conveys the effect of the subject on the writer as observer.	Compare/ contrast; author's perspective	Two descriptive essays
Evaluate the pros and cons of the author's argument. Use appropriate evidence as you examine each side and indicate which position you find more persuasive.	Evaluate, judge, analyze effectiveness	Article
Write an essay in which you analyze the strategies used to satirize _____.	Rhetorical strategies/Satire	Article
Take a position on the value of the idea presented and support your view with appropriate evidence.	Create a claim and defend it.	Question
Develop a position with evidence from your reading, observation and/or experience.	Create a claim and defend it.	Short quotation from a newspaper columnist

Content Task	Key Elements	Basis for Question
Evaluate the pros and cons of _____ and indicate why you find one position more persuasive than the other.	Judgment; analyze effectiveness	Presentation of a two-sided issue
Consider this quotation about _____. Then write an essay that defends, challenges, or qualifies the writer's assertion about _____. Support your argument with appropriate evidence from your reading, observation, or experience.	Defends, challenges, or qualifies	Quotation
Write an essay in which you support, refute, or qualify the author's assertions about _____. Support your argument with appropriate evidence.	Defend, challenge, or qualify	Passage from a book
Write an essay that defends, challenges, or qualifies the author's claim about _____. Use specific and appropriate evidence to develop your position.	Defend, challenge, or qualify	Quotation from a book
Analyze the strategies the speaker uses to _____.	Rhetorical strategies	Excerpt from a speech
Using appropriate evidence, write a carefully reasoned essay in which you defend, challenge or qualify the author's perspective.	Defend, challenge, or qualify	Excerpt from a book

Continued →

Content Task	Key Elements	Basis for Question
Write to _____, explaining what you mean by _____ and argue for or against _____. (Take note, that in this prompt, you are to write a letter, and not structure your response as a typical essay.)	Defend or challenge	Excerpt
Write an essay that defends, challenges, or qualifies the author's claim about the vital role of _____. Use specific, appropriate evidence to develop your position.	Defend, challenge, or qualify.	Idea from a book
Write an essay in which you develop a position on the establishment of _____. Support your argument with appropriate evidence.	Create and support a claim.	Reference to an online article

Start reading a lot of opinion pieces: columns, editorials (and editorial cartoons), and essays on a wide variety of topics, and for each one, determine the author's thesis and what rhetorical strategies the author uses to achieve his or her purpose. Start examining everything you read through this critical lens. You can also read through the "defend, challenge, qualify" lens. Think about your own perspective in addition to the one the author presents.

ANALYSIS OF THEMES AND TOPICS

The following is a list of themes and topics from past free-response prompts. Topics were culled from the standard exam and exam B. As you read through this list, you will notice some obvious repetition, which may mean that these topics are favorites of the College Board, that these themes are essential human themes, or even that the most prominent themes may reappear on future exams. The purpose of this list is to show you what issues students have been presented with in the past. You could also use this list to guide your reading. If you are fairly uninformed on a particular topic, you could make it a point to read more about it prior to exam day.

- Value of technology in education
- Slavery
- Function of humor and humorists in society
- Daylight saving time
- Midwestern values
- Effects of consumer culture
- Individual and conformity
- Free speech
- Effect of television on society
- Environment
- Effect of adversity on one's character
- Value of penny coin
- Scientific research method
- Corporate advertising/sponsorship in schools
- National school curriculum
- Anti-intellectualism
- Effect of dissent in America
- Effect of advertising on society
- Emigration
- Ethics of rewarding charitable acts in schools
- What museum artifacts represent
- Value of muckrakers/whistle-blowers
- Race
- How fads reflect American values
- Effect of money in society
- Value/effect of personal opinion/commentary in society

- Compulsory voting
- Effect of reading on independent thought
- Consumerism and advertising
- Poverty
- Race
- The Mississippi River
- Value of trial-and-error thinking
- Cultural differences
- Common sense and personal values
- Protecting the environment
- Morality
- Cultural norms
- Effect of entertainment on society
- Admiration of birds in flight
- Race
- Emigration
- Individual and society
- Plagiarism in schools
- Effects of Civil War from Lincoln's point of view
- Childhood memories
- Abuse of power
- Appreciation for natural world/beauty
- Man versus machine/technology
- Self-awareness
- Limitations of viewing the world through photographic images
- Dress code
- Value of polite speech for society
- Value of public libraries

- Locavore movement
- Role of journalism in national discourse
- Value of college
- Technology versus nature
- Child labor
- Genetically modified food

See Chapter 4 for lists of authors and texts to consider reading before your exam.

Essay Basics:
Creating Excellence Through Structure, Style, and Voice

*If the writing is honest it cannot be separated from the [one]
who wrote it.*—Tennessee Williams

OVERVIEW

You are not going to have to write the most brilliant essays ever
written to do well on the AP English Language and Composition
exam, but you *are* going to have to show that you understand the task
presented to you, that you can formulate logical, defensible arguments,
and that you can write well-organized, insightful essays. Having said
that, your essays for the exam are considered drafts and AP readers are
instructed to award points for what students do well. This chapter aims
to acquaint you with what you need to know to write the best essays
you can.

You will be writing three essays in two hours, which gives you
approximately 40 minutes for each essay. While you have the option of
using your two hours in any manner that works best for you, it is clearly
not a lot of time. Therefore, it is important to work efficiently and not
waste time.

You are given 15 minutes of reading time, but you do not have to wait
until the end of that time to begin writing. You may begin planning and
writing as soon as you feel ready.

See Chapter 16 for a list of the essay types and an analysis of essay
prompts from released exams.

TYPICAL PROBLEMS

If you could ask an AP reader to list some typical mistakes students make in writing their essays, the AP reader might mention the following:

- No discernible thesis (therefore, no controlling idea).
- Failure to analyze (the writer summarizes or paraphrases instead).
- Failure to move from "what" to "how" and "why."
- Failure to support generalizations or claims with evidence from the text.
- Poorly developed ideas, perhaps repeating one or two ideas over and over.
- Inability to integrate and embed quotations from the supplied text or sources in sentences.
- Wordy introductions, mostly a restatement of the prompt.
- "Boring" conclusions that simply restate the thesis or prompt.
- Loosely constructed paragraphs that are not unified.
- Reliance upon five-paragraph essay, but without real analysis (organization without content is not an essay).
- Imprecise use of language. Never use big words to impress. Instead, use the exact right word for the job. See Chapter 12 for more on vocabulary.
- Failure to synthesize sources.

GENERAL QUALITIES OF A GOOD ESSAY

- It is far better to write a relatively short essay with a defensible thesis and a few insightful claims supported with textual evidence than to have a longer essay that is about nothing. If you don't understand the prompt or the text, your essay will be about nothing.

- An essay is not a list of separate ideas clumped together.

- An essay is not a summary of the text or sources—it is an **argument** that you control. A generalization without support is not an argument.

- You need a thesis that responds accurately to the task given in the prompt.

- A good essay is well organized, even if it is a draft. It should have discernible parts: introduction, body, and conclusion.

A STANDARD OF EXCELLENCE

According to the College Board, "The best papers come from writers who thought deeply and insightfully about the questions; understood that they were writing to an educated, sophisticated audience; made their thinking and reasoning lucid and transparent; and developed their claims with evidence, reasoning, and details drawn from their reading, observation, and experience."

HOW DO YOU GET THERE?

First of all, you have to care about the essays. You are writing about ideas, not answering questions. Your level of commitment will show in your work. Secondly, you have to work diligently to attain this level of excellence, which cannot start the week before the exam. There truly can be no cram session for better writing. Writing is a process that takes time, but fortunately, you've been practicing your writing skills since kindergarten.

Lastly, you have to believe you are up to the challenge. If you do not have confidence, all is lost. This book is meant to help you discover just what you need to do your best work on the exam.

VISUAL GUIDE TO EXCELLENCE

SCORE RANGE

1–2 <————————————————————————————> 8–9

Little to no support for claims	Abundant support
Evidence not explained	Evidence clearly and concisely explained
Casual, simplistic word choice	Sophisticated vocabulary
Simple	Complex
Imprecise/Sloppy	Precise/Careful
Simplistic sentences	Varied, complex sentences used for effect
Error-laden	Control of conventions and prose
Off task	Focused on precise understanding of task
Writer lacks commitment	Writer cares about work, goal, audience

THE WRITING PROCESS

There is no time on exam day for the full-blown writing process: pre-writing, drafting, revision, etc. But that doesn't mean that prior to exam day you should ignore these basic steps of composition. You will be or should be writing many practice essays prior to May. For each one, it is good practice to revise your work. If you are writing essays for a class, your teacher may encourage you to revise. If so, perfect. If not, do it anyway.

Revision is beneficial in a number of ways:

- You are better able to see your strengths and weaknesses.

- Revision makes you a more flexible writer. If you are willing to concede that your word choice could have been better, or that a sentence is wordy, or that your third paragraph is disorganized, then you are much more open to alternative options. Stubborn students who say things such as, "Well, that's how I wrote it," and then refuse to see a different way will also not develop the reflective processes of mind needed on exam day.

- Revision trains your brain. If your teacher scored your last essay in the middle range, how can you make it better? What can you do to earn a score of 8? Training your brain to think of these strategies will help you remember them on exam day. Not only that, but you will be writing better essays overall.

Use your peers as revision partners by reading and critiquing one another's work. Be sure you are measuring an essay using a standard rubric, either one given by your teacher or the scoring guidelines for a particular essay found at the College Board website.

STAND IN A DIFFERENT PLACE

Learning to judge the qualities of your own writing fairly and objectively is not easy. One strategy you can employ is to put the work away for a while, at most a day or two, but at least an hour. When you return to it, you will be "standing" in a different place. We always benefit from seeing a thing in a new way. We see things that were not there before. This new view of your own work should reveal weaknesses, such as omitted words, clumsy phrasing, incomplete arguments, and more.

Before you write the first word for any of the three essays on your exam, create a brief plan. Try to jot down a mini-outline in the margin, noting your thesis and several supporting points. Any quick references to evidence you use and rhetorical strategies you employ will also help keep you from "winging it," which will likely not be an effective approach.

Even though time is limited on exam day, if you find you have ten minutes or so at the end of Part Two, use it to take one more look at the essay about which you felt the least confident. This second look, or second perspective, may show you some minor error(s) that you can easily fix, which will surely have a positive impact on your score.

ELEMENTS OF A GOOD INTRODUCTION

- You must acknowledge the task given in the prompt in your introduction.

- Give the writer's name and the title of the work (watch spelling on both).

- Avoid long exposition or discursive prose meant to engage the reader. You don't have time for this. Instead, create an introduction that is precise and allows you to jump quickly into your argument.

- Include a thesis that reveals your insightful understanding of the key ideas in the text.

MORE ON THESIS STATEMENTS

A **thesis statement** is the sentence where you state your main claim or what you intend to prove in your essay. If you don't have something to argue, you don't have a thesis. While reading, you must have come to some conclusion about the text(s), something you believe about the text(s) that you can defend and support. Your thesis comes from that. If you have a good thesis statement, it will serve as your guide.

YOUR THESIS STATEMENT:

- Is generally found at the end of the introduction (the last sentence, typically);

- Should be specific, covering only what you will discuss and can support in your essay;

- May change slightly as you write, so you may have to adjust the specific wording of your thesis statement. If this is the case (if you find this occurs to you often) write your introduction last. If you do this, be sure you save space for it.

- Reflects your rhetorical purpose (see Chapter 6);

- Is arguable: someone may dispute or disagree with you;

- Is supportable: you can actually defend the thesis with evidence from the supplied text, sources (synthesis essay), your knowledge, reading, experience, or observations.

SIMPLE THESIS STATEMENT FORMULA

Claim + Reason = Thesis

HOOKS OR LEADS: DRAWING YOUR READER INTO YOUR WRITING

Journalists grab their readers' attention quickly with engaging leads. They use a variety of strategies that you can adopt in your own writing. The following list of leads is meant to get you to think consciously about how to begin your essays. If you need some variety, some oomph in your introductions, consider playing around with some of these leads.

One way to play is to revise any argumentative essay that you have written. Rewrite the introduction several times using some of these lead strategies. Whatever you decide, you must have a reason for choosing a particular lead style. If your choice seems arbitrary and unrelated to your purpose, it will count against you.

7 TYPES OF LEADS/HOOKS

1. **Factual**: Begin with a startling or arresting statistic or fact;

2. **Quotation**: Start with a controversial or thought-provoking quotation;

3. **Imagistic**: Set the scene or describe the situation;

4. **Narrative**: Begin with a short anecdote or story that relates to the main claim;

5. **Question**: A thought-provoking question gets your reader thinking. Caution: using a question implies that you will use second-person voice, but you should avoid the "did you ever" kinds of questions. Maintain your third-person authoritative voice even in questions. Example: Are seat belts ever harmful to passengers?

6. **Ironic**: Start with an ironic situation or statement;

7. **Dialectic**: Begin with a short dialogue, such as a witty repartee between two hypothetical speakers/characters. The dialogue could also be serious.

EXAMPLE INTRODUCTION

The following generic introduction was written for a prompt on a past AP English Language exam, which asked students to develop a position on "the ethics of offering incentives for charitable acts." While this introduction is much longer than desirable, it shows one way to integrate an engaging lead and still incorporate all necessary aspects of a good introduction.

The two students huddled at lunch, their heads nearly touching as they discussed a brilliant new opportunity to earn an A in English for the semester. "Are you sure it will work?" Joe asked Matt. "Look," Matt said as he punched numbers into the calculator, "at five extra credit points for each pound of food we bring in . . . ." Joe's eyes brightened as he envisioned his weak B changing before his eyes, all with no real effort on his part. "Sweet," he said. In her desire to encourage her students' social consciousness, their English teacher offered extra credit for their donations to the annual fall food drive. The result will no doubt mean more food for the hungry (an incidental but important side effect), but Joe, Matt, and their peers will be no more socially responsible than they were before the food drive. Their focus is not about what they can do to help others; it is about their desire to help themselves. The teacher's actions, while seemingly right, are actually detrimental, as she may unwittingly be promoting a new level of selfishness in her students.

> **Lead**: Combination narrative/dialogue, presents a hypothetical situation that gets the reader thinking and sets up the claim.
>
> **Thesis**: The teacher's actions, while seemingly right, are actually detrimental, as she may unwittingly be promoting a new level of selfishness in her students.
>
> **Summary of Thesis Formula**: Claim (The teacher's actions are detrimental) + Reason (promoting selfishness in her students) = Thesis

See the rest of this essay at the end of this chapter.

DEVELOPING THE BODY OF THE ESSAY

The body of your essay is where you argue your thesis. You will need to make several points or claims that prove your thesis. A good *formula* for developing the ideas in your argument is the CSE formula:

1. State a <u>C</u>laim (this may be your topic sentence in a paragraph);

2. <u>S</u>upport it with evidence from the text;

3. <u>E</u>xplain your reasoning, especially showing how or why.

MORE ON EXPLAINING YOUR REASONING

Sometimes, you will think that your ideas are clearly stated, when they're actually only **implicit** (implied). You need to make your ideas **explicit**, meaning you need to show exactly how and/or why what you say is so. Make connections. Make your ideas transparent. One of the biggest problems in student essays is that they contain too many implied ideas.

If you (or your reader) can still ask the following questions about your essay, you have not fully explained what you mean:

- Why?

- What is important or significant about this idea?

- What does this have to do with the claim?

ORGANIZATION AND LENGTH

There is no set number of paragraphs expected for your AP essays. You should let the essay develop organically from what you know. AVOID using the five-paragraph formula. It is too constrictive, and it forces you to think about the formula instead of your ideas. You may have three body paragraphs, or you may have four, five, or even six. Your paragraphs do not have to be the same length, either. If you make your point in three sentences and need to move on to the next paragraph, then do it. The next point you make may need seven sentences. Let your argument determine how you write.

Regardless of the number of paragraphs in your essay, remember that a paragraph is a coherent collection of sentences that support one main idea. The sentences belong together. A topic sentence sets the purpose for the paragraph. Some paragraphs may be extensions of topics set up in the preceding paragraph. If this is the case, make the transition clear to your reader with transitional phrases such as, "Another example of __," or "One more way to think about __ is ___."

WRITING A CONCLUSION THAT INSPIRES: HOW TO END YOUR ESSAY WELL

Avoid generic summary conclusions that simply restate the thesis. They're boring, and they rob you of the opportunity to go beyond your analysis of a text to relate your personal insight. While your conclusion should not be personal, your particular insight **does** come from you and sometimes the conclusion is where your voice is most strong. Still, remember to stay focused on the text.

CONCLUSION TIPS

- Never introduce a new claim in the conclusion. Claims must be supported with evidence. Your conclusion is not the place to continue your argument. It is the place to wrap up your argument.

- You generally should not cite the text in the conclusion.

- A good conclusion should remind readers of the most important concepts of your essay.

- A good conclusion makes the essay feel finished.

- Avoid overused phrases like "in conclusion," "to sum up," or the like. Instead, make a smooth transition to the end of an essay.

CONCLUSION STRATEGIES

- Restate the central idea or argument. Phrase the idea differently than you did in your introduction.

- Make suggestions: possible solutions to a problem, a new way of thinking about something, a plan of action, etc.

- Reiterate the topic's significance: explain how an issue or idea affects people or will affect people.
- Use a rhetorical device:
  - relevant quotation;
  - anecdote;
  - metaphor;
  - ironic statement;
  - reference to historical event.

"BUT WHAT IF I RUN OUT OF TIME?"

It is possible that you will not have time to write a conclusion. Of course it is best if you can end with something, even a sentence or two, but in the event that the proctor is standing over you with his hand out, your essay will have to stand without its ending. Do not fret too much. The introduction and the body are the most crucial parts and should show your insightful analysis. It is possible to score well without a true conclusion.

COMMON TRANSITIONS

Learn and use transitional words and phrases in your writing. If you do, you will be less likely to write confusing or foggy prose.

Transitions not only lead your reader through your thinking, they help you organize your argument. Find transitions for comparing and contrasting later in this chapter.

Purpose ⇩			
Show Location	above	below	by
	away	beneath	beside
	against	between	outside
	along	off	over
	amid	of	across
	among	down	under
	around	in front of	onto
	from	inside	on top of
	back	near	into
	behind	beyond	throughout

Continued ➡

Purpose ⇩			
Show Time	about third prior to next week next second tomorrow yesterday then	first today tomorrow as soon as during meanwhile afterward immediately before	until later after at till soon in the meantime
Emphasize a Point	again in fact indeed	with this in mind for this reason to emphasize	truly to repeat
To Conclude or Summarize	as a result thus in summary consequently	due to all in all accordingly to sum up	in short therefore finally in conclusion
To Add Information	again besides for example together with and next	additionally another furthermore finally in addition further	along with as well for instance also likewise moreover

ABOUT ERRORS

The essays you write for the AP exam are meant to show off your lucid thinking and your ability to write well. However, even the most brilliant writers do not write perfect drafts the first time. And 40 minutes is not nearly enough time for you to go through the stages of the writing process. It is expected that your essay is a draft, not a polished final copy. Some "cross-outs" are to be expected and will not necessarily detract from your score.

BUT. . . your essay can't be so messy and disorganized that it is impossible to read. The best strategy for avoiding disorganization is to plan your main points before you write. Create a mini-outline first.

The kinds of errors that I'm referring to here are when you write, for example, "Their are." You would obviously cross that out and neatly write "there" above or near the crossed-out word.

Sometimes you find you want to rewrite an entire sentence. If you have finished all three essays and you are going back to reread the one you think is your weakest, you may want to do some minor revisions. "Minor" is the key word. If your essay starts to look like a Jackson Pollock painting, you're in trouble. It seems wise to show some revision effort with a change here or there. It shows that you care and that you recognize that you can improve your own prose. Just don't overdo it here.

> *The best way to train yourself to be able to write a complete AP essay in 40 minutes is to practice again and again. It is not an effortless goal, but your diligence will reward you.*

INTEGRATING OR EMBEDDING TEXTUAL EVIDENCE

Weaving textual evidence into an essay is a skill that you can practice and learn to do well. You should study good models. Reading a newspaper can help you. Journalists are experts at integrating quotations into their text. They must attribute quotations to their sources also. While they're not quoting literary texts, they follow similar guidelines for embedding their quotations as you do. Chapter 18 provides a fuller explanation of this skill, particularly as employed for Question 1.

1. Learn these rules for integrating your textual support:

    *   Use partial quotations; it will be rare that you need an entire sentence from a text. Use only the part that helps you prove your point.

    *   You need to supply context for the full or partial quotation. This means to set it up somehow, or transition into the quotation with your claim.

    *   As a general rule, don't begin the sentence with the quotation.

    *   Use quotation marks around anything you take from the text, even isolated words.

- If your essay is mostly quotations from the text, you are probably summarizing, which is one of the worst things you can do. Don't over quote!

- When you weave in the cited text, you must end up with a grammatically correct sentence. If you have to change tense or wording, use [brackets] around the parts you change.

- The quotation or cited text is not self-evident; you must still explain it. Why did you include the quotation? What does it show or prove?

2. Some model phrases to consider:

- The writer or speaker argues, claims that, suggests, etc. _____.

- His description of _____ shows how _____.

- _____ reads quickly, even frantically. This narrative pace suggests that something _____.

- When *author* writes that _____ she shows how _____.

- The imagery in paragraph four contrasts with the imagery in paragraph one. _____ suggests _____, while _____ is clearly meant to _____.

- *Speaker's name* relates the process by which she learned about _____ from her observations of ____. She writes _____.

Notice the use of strong verbs, particularly in the first model phrase. Review the verbs of rhetoric in Chapter 6 to familiarize yourself with more verbs to use in your own arguments.

Test Tip

When you read student essay samples from the AP Central website, look specifically at how the writers of top-scoring essays incorporate evidence from the text to prove their point.

USE PRECISE LANGUAGE: CONFIDENTLY SAY WHAT YOU MEAN

- **Use Higher-Level Vocabulary**

  I have admonished you to not toss in showy "big" words that you don't know. However, you should show that you have a sophisticated vocabulary. Begin to use the words you are learning (see Chapter 12). If you never use a "big" word, your prose may sound simplistic. AP readers are looking for your ability to use a college-level vocabulary.

- **Use Strong Verbs**

  Avoid using being verbs or linking verbs, as they do not express action. Instead choose strong, vivid action verbs. Your writing will be more powerful and clear. Your writing also will be more visual. When we write with linking and being verbs, we rely too much upon adjectives. Adjectives can be vague or ambiguous. See the samples below.

Being/Linking Verbs

is	been	should have been
am	being	would have been
was	have been	feels
were	had been	seems
are	shall be	
be	will be	

How do you know if it's an action verb? If you can do it (act it out), it is an action verb. I can act out "dance," but I cannot act out "was."

Check your own writing for strong verb use. Choose any essay and highlight all the linking/being verbs you have used. Then, revise the essay and replace those highlighted verbs with action verbs. Notice the difference in the quality of your essay.

EXAMPLES:

Weak	Strong
Sylvia was clumsy.	Sylvia tripped over the smallest pebble.
The images are interesting.	The images in the first paragraph evoke pity for the narrator.
The simile is effective.	The simile conjures images of wickedness.

WORDS AND PHRASES TO AVOID

Some words are inherently ambiguous. Others are simply meaningless. Others are clichés or overused expressions that are out of place in a scholarly essay. It is best always to avoid words and phrases that promote imprecision.

- "Very," "really," "completely," etc. Superlatives added to adjectives are generally not needed.

- "Interesting." We all know that saying "that's interesting" can mean so many different things that it can actually mean nothing. Avoid all ambiguous language. See Chapter 7 for details about effective use of language.

- "This," "that," and "it" can be ambiguity traps. It's best not to use them. For example: "That is why he never told even his closest friends about it." What is *that*? Furthermore, what is *it*?

- "Like," as in "the character was so like suffocated by his mother's dreams for him." Watch out for slang or colloquial language when writing. You are writing, not speaking.

- "Talks about" as in "This passage talks about." Passages do not talk. Instead say, "The author writes, shows, reveals," etc.

- "Wonderful," "skillfully," "fantastic," when meant to compliment the writer. Do not "suck up" to the writer. This gains you no points. Praising the prose is not analyzing the prose.

NEVER, NEVER . . .

- Begin a sentence with a pronoun.

- Begin a paragraph with a pronoun.

- Use ambiguous pronouns: this, that, those, it, etc.

- Write in the same manner as you speak. That is, do not use a conversational style that screams out, "I am not serious."

- Use words you do not understand. If you misuse a word, you will lose credibility.

- Use more words than necessary to make your point.

AVOID CLICHÉS, TRITE EXPRESSIONS, AND REDUNDANT PHRASES

If you've heard it before, it may be a cliché. Clichés are empty expressions that may have been clever at one time, but now simply distract from your writing. If you rely on clichés, you are avoiding your job as a writer, which is to use precise language to say what you mean.

A Few Common Clichés:

- A close call

- A fish out of water

- At wit's end

- Bird's-eye view

- Coming down the pike

- Fall on deaf ears

- Never a dull moment

- Nerve-wracking

- Nipped in the bud

- Out of the box

- What goes around comes around.

Redundant Phrases

Redundant Phrase	Replace with
at this point in time	at this point; at this time
cancel out	cancel
complete opposite	opposite
each and every	every
evolve over time	evolve
join together	join
look back in retrospect	in retrospect
nostalgia for the past	nostalgia
overexaggerate	exaggerate
past experience	experience
past history	history
plan ahead	plan
the reason why	the reason
this day and age	in our time; presently
ultimate goal	goal

ACTIVE AND PASSIVE VOICE

Being aware of the difference between active and passive voice is important. If you've ever run a grammar check in Microsoft Word on a document you've written, you may have been told that you have too many passive sentences. Typically, it is better to write in active voice rather than passive. Passive voice can seem weak, indecisive, or tentative. Active voice is much more authoritative sounding.

An active verb is one in which the subject is the doer. With a passive verb, the subject is not the doer, but is the object, receiver, or effect of the action. When you add forms of "be" to a verb, you change the verb to passive, such as "is," "are," "was," "were," etc.

EXAMPLES

Passive	Active
The cookies were baked by Susan.	Susan baked the cookies.
The movie was chosen by Arthur.	Arthur chose the movie.
Invitations to her party were sent by Beth.	Beth sent invitations to her party.

VALUE OF PASSIVE VOICE

If the subject is less important than the object, passive construction may be an advantage.

Active	Passive
The farmer gathered these eggs yesterday.	These eggs were gathered yesterday.
The boss hired a new computer tech today.	A new computer tech was hired today.

YOUR OWN SYNTAX

You must be able to write effective and fluent sentences for effective prose. You can use syntactical patterns, which is what the writers whose work is featured on the exam use. Study the patterns (Chapter 9) and learn the value of each. Practice writing various types over time. For example, during one week, just write simple sentences. During the next week, write compound sentences, and so on. End up being able to use anaphora or polysyndeton without even thinking about how to do it, just knowing why you want to.

The best way to get better at sentence crafting is by recognizing it in the texts you read and emulating the patterns and effects you see.

To practice writing better sentences, use the following activity:

COPY-CHANGE ACTIVITY

Find and copy a highly effective paragraph from a text and study it. Learn the sentence patterns. Label the sentence types you see. Then, rewrite the paragraph with a new topic. Change the nouns and verbs to fit the new topic, but don't change their placement. Replicate phrases, clauses, and punctuation exactly. Learn by imitating.

EXPOSITORY PATTERNS

Develop your paragraphs using a variety of rhetorical or expository patterns. Use what seems appropriate for the text. In other words, you can't force something that doesn't work. Here are a few basic ways that you can argue your point. See more expository patterns in Chapter 6.

- **Exemplification**: Use examples from the text to prove your point. Of course, you will want to choose the best examples for your purpose.

- **Process Analysis**: If you recognize a process (how something works or operates) in a text, you can identify it and analyze its elements.

- **Cause and Effect Analysis:** Show why something happens, the series of events leading to or causing a concluding event.

- **Compare and Contrast**: Often, you will be asked to do this as your main task (such as compare two texts), but even if you aren't, you may have a reason to show similarities and differences.

COMPARE/CONTRAST

There is a good chance that you will be asked to write an essay comparing the elements of two texts. Therefore, the following guide is meant to help you understand the basics of compare/contrast essays. *Compare* means to show similarities. *Contrast* means pointing out differences.

The texts you will be presented with have some obvious similarities; otherwise, they would not be paired. What will differ will be the ways the authors treat the subjects. For example, the speaker's attitude toward the subject may be completely different. It will be important for you to understand both overt and subtle similarities and differences. As you read, annotate each text and make marginal notes listing what you find.

COMPARE/CONTRAST TRANSITIONAL WORDS AND PHRASES

To compare:

In the same way	Also
Likewise	Like
Similarly	

To contrast:

Conversely	On the contrary
However	On the other hand
Rather	

INTRODUCTION

Mention both texts and be sure your thesis suggests the main ways the two texts are similar. Do not say, "Jones' journal is similar to Smith's in some ways, but there are also some main differences." Instead say, "Even though both writers characterize women as intelligent and nurturing, Jones' view deprecates women when he says 'they are emotionally weak and incapable of managing tough business situations.' "

ORGANIZING THE BODY OF THE ESSAY

Main Methods

1. Whole to Whole:
   - Discuss the important aspects of one text, then the other. You may lose track of your main points if you're not careful.
2. Show all similarities, then all differences:
   - Can seem less integrated, less fluent.
3. Subject by subject (point by point):
   - For example: tone in each speech or text, imagery in each poem.

SAMPLE ESSAY

Now let's examine a completed essay that was introduced earlier in this chapter when students were asked to develop a position on "the ethics of offering incentives for charitable acts."

Note that this essay was not scored by an AP reader and that it is longer than would be typical in order to show all components.

The two students huddled at lunch, their heads nearly touching as they discussed a brilliant new opportunity to earn an A in English for the semester. "Are you sure it will work?" Joe asked Matt. "Look," Matt said as he punched numbers into the calculator. "at five extra credit points for each pound of food we bring in. . ." Joe's eyes brightened as he envisioned his weak B changing before his eyes, all with no real effort on his part. "Sweet," he said. In her desire to encourage her students' social consciousness, their English teacher offered extra credit for their donations to the annual fall food drive. The result will no doubt mean more food for the hungry (an incidental but important side effect), but Joe, Matt, and their peers will be no more socially responsible than they were before the food drive. Their focus is not on what they can do to help others; it is on their desire to help themselves. The teacher's actions, while seemingly right, are actually detrimental, as she may unwittingly be promoting a new level of selfishness in her students.[1]

The need to provide for others less fortunate than we are is ingrained in our common sense of self.[2] We are taught as young children in churches, in schools and at home that there are others who don't have what we do. The story of the Good Samaritan teaches that we must always help others when we see they are in need. Some states even have Good Samaritan laws that protect passersby who intervene from liability in case something goes wrong. Boy Scouts, postal workers, and other community organizations annually sponsor food drives for the hungry. Even

---

[1] An analysis of this introduction can be found earlier in this chapter in the section on introductions.

[2] Topic sentence/claim

in our own homes, moms admonish us to finish all the food on our plate, because we don't throw food away when others in the world are starving.[3] In general, we deem charitable acts to be good, even noble.

And yet,[4] while no reward for giving should be necessary, we live in a culture that actively promotes reward for giving.[5] It seems we[6] are a society that needs to be prodded to do what is right. When public radio and television stations conduct their pledge drives, they offer gifts in return: coffee mugs, tote bags, or t-shirts.[7] Take your coffee mug to work and you can subtly let everyone know that you support public broadcasting. Some charities entice giving up front by sending address labels or personalized stationery, like note pads or greeting cards, hoping to "guilt" people into giving. They're saying, "Hey, we gave you this nice gift, so don't you want to thank us with your donation?" Even those pseudo-documentary infomercials for "adopting" a needy child in a third-world country promise a reward for one's generosity. If you sponsor a child, you will receive letters from him or her that let you know how things are going. Perhaps the letter serves more to keep the organization honest than as a reward,[8] but if you slap that letter on the refrigerator with the free magnet you got from the March of Dimes,[9] then you remind yourself daily what a good person you are, and that is also, of course, a reward.

Even bigger gifts to communities, like endowments that provide money for a new hospital wing, a state-of-the-art technology center for the local community college, or a new auditorium for the high school are rewarded by naming the facility after the benefactor.[10] Gala parties are thrown to honor and publicly thank the donor, whose real reward is a kind of eternity that only money

---

[3] Series of examples in support.

[4] Transition signaling a contrasting idea.

[5] Claim

[6] Universal first person—the writer includes herself as a member of this society.

[7] Begins a series of examples from real life to support the claim.

[8] Acknowledges an alternative point of view.

[9] Notice the writer's cynical tone here. The tone reinforces the idea that it is wrong to need a reward for doing what is right.

[10] This short paragraph gives more examples, but they are grouped separately because they share a common quality: all are examples of large philanthropic gifts.

can buy. By contrast, those rare anonymous gifts make the news simply because they're so unusual.

The culture of reward for giving is unfortunately prevalent in schools.[11] In my school, student council sponsors a food drive every year around Thanksgiving time.[12] They entice students by awarding a pizza party to the first-hour class with the most donations. Matt and Joe are my hypothetical classmates. My English teacher wanted us to win. She told us how important it was for us to replenish the food pantry, especially with the economy in such bad shape. Too many people were out of work and it was hard for parents, especially single parents, to feed their kids. She should have stopped with her appeal to our sense of what is right. Where she went wrong was in following society's model by offering a tangible reward for doing what we should do anyway.[13] Maybe she even wanted the esteem of her peers. After all, if we won, it would show that she could persuade us and get us to work together.

It may seem benign to give a student extra credit for bringing in ten cans of corn, but it's not.[14] The end goal may have been reached. The food pantry is full again. Fewer people will go hungry, but the negative results must not be ignored. Students who manipulate the system for a grade are cheats. An A not earned through intellect and effort is worthless. A transcript with that A on it is a lie. A system that allows, or even worse, promotes extra credit for charity is hypocritical. In such a system, grades mean nothing.[15] In this situation, students give not because they should, but because they will benefit. They act selfishly instead of selflessly, and no one can blame them. The system encourages selfishness.

To truly be good people, we should give from the heart because it is the right thing to do. We should not need others to praise us. We should not need public accolades, whether they are our name on a building or a simple sticker saying "I gave blood." At most, our reward

---

[11] Claim

[12] Example from personal experience.

[13] Transition sentence that sets up the claim in the next paragraph.

[14] Claim

[15] Series of statements that show the effect of rewarding charity.

must come from within, from the satisfaction we get from doing what is right. We may nurture our esteem without proclaiming it to anyone, and that is how it should be.[16]

Parents can teach this concept to their children and teachers must reinforce it as well. Adults must begin to work against the reward model prevalent in the media and begin to reinforce a different narrative, appealing to nobility and morality and not to our own desires or needs.[17] For example,[18] my friend's parents decided to stop the crazy cycle of gift giving one Christmas. The idea was that the family would buy no presents for each other. And what's more, each one was to give something, either time, or a gift, to someone else who needed it more. In the end, the family did both. They worked together on Christmas Day to serve a turkey dinner to the homeless. And when they did their Christmas shopping, it was to buy toys and warm clothes for someone they would never meet. My friend wasn't too excited about it at first. In fact, all she did when she first found out about the plan was complain about how unfair it was. I was on her side, too, initially. But[19] then I listened to all of her "I wants," and she started to sound so selfish and petty. When we got together after Christmas, however, she sounded much different. She told me how the people she met at the homeless shelter affected her and how she felt like she could not do enough to help them. Her stories were moving, and I was even a little jealous of her experience.[20] She never once mentioned that she didn't get a single present from her parents for Christmas. That didn't matter anymore.

My friend didn't go around school bragging about how great she was now, for helping the homeless. I don't think she told anyone but me. But how are we to learn what noble charity means if we are not exposed to stories like hers? I do not believe that people are

---

[16] This transitional paragraph sets up the premise for the solution. This paragraph explains the concept the writer wishes us to believe and act upon.

[17] Call to action. The writer states specifically what must be done.

[18] The writer includes an anecdote that illustrates how the desired change might occur.

[19] Don't overlook simple transitions. "But" introduces a contrasting idea.

[20] The effect of the story is to draw the reader into a scenario, but the writer shows how he is also affected. This empathy helps establish the writer's credibility.

innately selfless. We need to be taught.[21] What if[22] the consumer machine included stories like this? I know our economy would crumble if people just stopped buying and consuming, but if we could also follow a less selfish model just because it is right,[23] we could have it all and still give to those who don't. In such a world, we would not need to entice charitable giving with silly or even harmful rewards,[24] and we would be better people as a result.

Test Tip

Footnote and analyze your own essay. Find an engaging prompt (in school or online) and write the essay. Then assign a code for things like thesis, topic sentence, evidence, explanation, etc. Insert a superscript number in your essay to those corresponding elements. In your analysis, also look for examples of appeals as well as times you used a sentence pattern or repetition device for effect. Circle all your "being" verbs. Can you change them to more active verbs? Learning to judge the quality of your own work is one of the most important ways you can prepare yourself for the exam.

MORE COMMENTS ON THE SAMPLE ESSAY

POINT OF VIEW

Notice how the writer uses first, third and even second person interchangeably as the document dictates. The writer maintains authority, but effectively engages the reader by putting him or her in the situation. The first-person point of view in this essay is also effective. The risk in sharing examples from personal experience is that they are unique and limited to the individual, but this writer's examples seem likely to be shared by most high school students.

---

[21] Final claim, but this is not a new idea presented in the conclusion. Instead, the writer restates an earlier claim in order to reinforce it here.

[22] Using "what if" statements allows the writer to suggest what could be if the desired change occurred. As readers, we are asked to imagine an ideal situation.

[23] Ethical appeal.

[24] Reiterating the main thesis: rewards for giving are not ethical.

LANGUAGE

Underline words in this essay that seem beyond what a typical high school student would use in everyday speech. What effect does scholarly diction have on the reader? Which words in particular help the writer create a more effective argument?

EXPOSITORY PATTERN

This is a problem-solution essay that argues for society in general, but parents and teachers specifically, to teach children that it is good to be charitable and that charitable acts do not require external rewards. The first part of the essay illuminates the problem and gives many examples to support the writer's main premise. The second part of the essay uses an anecdote, the story about the writer's friend, in support of a solution.

APPEALS

The writer uses ethical and emotional appeals as well as appeals to readers' esteem needs.

Test Tip

Go one step further. Instead of merely studying the sample essay above, write your own essay in response. Defend, refute, or challenge this writer's point of view. If you have a study group, suggest that each of you do the same. Then share your essays and talk about what you have learned.

Citing and Documenting Sources Effectively

Weave, don't plop.—Dawn Hogue

OVERVIEW

There are three distinct essays on this exam and each requires a different approach regarding your source material. The synthesis essay looks much like a typical research paper and will require you to document your use of supplied sources. The second question requires you to cite the provided text in your analysis. Finally, your evidence for your argument for the persuasive essay comes primarily from your reading, knowledge and experience, all of which are sources stored in your memory. You will mention titles, authors and ideas in books, but it will, of course, be impossible to quote text directly in this case. You may also make reference to the supplied quotation or short excerpt used in the prompt for question three. This chapter aims to give you a summary of the basic skills and techniques you will need to manage your evidence in your essays on the exam.

Not only will you be expected to cite and document sources correctly, you will also be asked several questions about documentation in the multiple-choice section of the exam. These questions are not meant to prove your knowledge of APA or MLA styles (see below), but rather are meant to test your general understanding of how and why authors reference, cite, and document sources.

ABOUT STYLE GUIDES

The examples in this chapter use MLA style (Modern Language Association), which is generally preferred in English and humanities courses. APA (American Psychological Association) has its own style rules.

APA is the dominant style used in the social sciences. There are also Turabian and Chicago styles.

When you are in college, you will be directed by your professor to use one style or another. No one memorizes the rules for any given style. You will probably own one or more style guides in your life and rely upon them when needed. The AP English Language and Composition exam is not a test of your "style savvy." It is a test of your writing and thinking ability. However, there is a presumption that your teacher has given you some general instruction in using one or more style guides. If you have no concept of what a style guide is or what it means, this chapter gives you a brief primer in MLA. There are numerous websites available to give you a more in-depth look if you need it. An excellent resource for MLA and APA is Purdue University's OWL (Online Writing Lab).

DOCUMENTING SOURCES

When we embed quotations, summaries or paraphrases from various sources in our own work, we must document the source, which simply means to show from where the information originates. Plagiarism is a failure to document source material.

PARENTHETICAL REFERENCES

In each of the examples below, notice the punctuation and follow the model. The source used for illustration here is fictional. It is important to note that you will rarely need to make a page number reference on the exam. However, the practice essays you do in your high school or college courses will require page numbers.

1. The directions for the synthesis question tell you that you can simply refer to each source by its designation: Source A, for example.

   The availability of newspapers online helps "democratize society because anyone with Internet can access not only the local paper, but also national and international papers" (Source A).

If you mention Source A in your sentence, you won't need to add it in parentheses. Example: According to Source A, the availability of. . . .

2. Another method is to include the author's last name and page number, if available, in parentheses at the end of the sentence or section that uses the citation.

> The availability of newspapers online helps "democratize society because anyone with Internet can access not only the local paper, but also national and international papers" (Sanders 219).

3. Use the author's name in the sentence and give only the page number.

> Sanders says that the availability of newspapers online helps "democratize society because anyone with Internet can access not only the local paper, but also national and international papers" (219).

4. Another option is to give the author and the title in your sentence.

> In "The Demise of Dailies: An Honest Look," Sanders says that the availability of newspapers online helps "democratize society because anyone with Internet can access not only the local paper, but also national and international papers" (219).

5. For your exam essays, you'll be citing short texts without page numbers. To help you document your evidence, line numbers will be provided. These line numbers are specifically helpful for the rhetorical analysis essay. Here's an example.

> Sanders argues that online newspapers help "democratize society because anyone with Internet" has access to news from a variety of sources (Line 24).

Once you've shown that you are referencing line numbers in parentheses by using the word "line" or "lines," you can omit those words and simple include the numbers themselves.

6. Very likely, excerpts from longer passages will be noted by lines, which you can reference by replacing the page number with the line number.

Take a look at the sample essay for the Synthesis Question in Chapter 19 to see how the writer cites and documents sources.

While you would be expected in ordinary circumstances to use MLA, APA, Chicago, or another style according to your instructor's needs, time given for the exam simply prohibits truly accurate adherence to any style. AP readers are far more interested in your ideas and how well you express and support them than in your uncanny knowledge of APA style. While the guide above can be helpful, if it's easier to simply cite the source by its letter, do so. You will not be penalized.

DIRECT AND INDIRECT REFERENCES

Typically essay directions on the exam will instruct you to use both direct and indirect references or citations. What this means is that you are expected to vary the ways that you cite a resource. The hope is that you will not rely too much on direct quotations. A direct reference is simply a direct quotation, text taken word for word from a source and shown to be such by use of quotation marks. An indirect reference is a paraphrase, where you cite the writer's idea, but in your own phrasing, which is sometimes also shorter than the original. Being able to use both types of references shows your skill as a writer.

CLARIFYING TERMINOLOGY

When I refer to "quotation," I mean any text taken from a source to use as evidence in an argument, whether a single word, a short phrase, or a complete sentence. To indicate a direct quotation (replicated exactly as shown in the original text), quotation marks are used.

Some students have expressed confusion about using quotations, as they have inferred this means they must search the source for something already in quotation marks. But this is not what we mean when we say "quote the text."

QUOTING SOURCES

The following is a quick guide to the different ways you can quote a source. The sources used for illustration here are fictional.

1. Weave the quoted passage into your own sentence. The following example is a **partial quotation**.

   Sanders says that the availability of newspapers online helps "democratize society because anyone with Internet can access not only the local paper, but also national and international papers" (219).

2. **Introduce the quotation** with a sentence and a colon.

   Anyone wanting to explore various points of view can easily do so by reading a variety of newspapers online: "Easy access to national and international newspapers online gives ordinary citizens, especially those in rural or remote areas a portal to world views" (Sanders, 220).

3. Use a **long quotation** by introducing it with your own sentence. A long quotation is one that is four or more lines long. There are specific style rules (MLA) for long quotations. Since it is indented ten spaces or one inch from the left margin, there is no need to use quotation marks. The text should be double-spaced. In this case, the final period goes before the parenthetical reference.

   In "Celebrating the Death of Newspapers," Roger Sanders argues that the loss of tangible newsprint papers is not the lamentable situation that some claim it is:

   There are, of course, some legitimate reasons to be sorrowful at this time of transition. No more will the gritty presses roll in pre-dawn hours inking papers to be sold on the street just a short time later. The industry and ingenuity that made newspapers a critical part of America in the last 400 years, however, is not dead. Instead it is something new, something for the future, and we must see the possibilities that lie within these changes that will make us even stronger as a nation. (195)

You would not use such a long quotation in an essay you write for your exam. An in-class essay might be different, however.

MAKE IT GRAMMATICALLY CORRECT

If you are using a direct quotation that does not fit grammatically into your prose, you may need to change a word or two. For example, you might have a situation in which using a quotation as it is results in a subject/agreement error. In such a case, make the change but recognize it by putting the changed word in [brackets].

Whenever you weave in a quotation, paraphrase, or summary, the end result must be a complete, correct sentence. Review Chapter 10 on grammar basics. The longer and more complicated a sentence is, the more you run the risk of inadvertently writing a fragment or a comma splice.

It is very important for you to practice integrating source material into your own writing. You want to achieve fluency. Study good models to see how effortlessly an excellent writer weaves in quotations, paraphrases, and summaries. The true danger in simply plopping in a quotation like a glob of mashed potatoes on your plate is that you may lose control of your writing. The essay is yours; it is your argument. Use direct and indirect references as evidence for your ideas. Your essay should not be a string of someone else's words, no matter how lovely.

SUMMARIZING AND PARAPHRASING SOURCES

Surely you already know that a summary is a shorter version of a passage and a paraphrase is similar in that it may also be shorter than the original, but in a paraphrase you've put the text into your own words. These are tools we've been taught to use in our writing since we were in grade school. In the context of this exam, it is important for you to remember that a summary or paraphrase is also a method of citing a resource in support of your argument.

Both are indirect references, which means your evidence from the text is not "word for word" as in a direct reference. Besides imbuing your essay with a stronger sense of your voice, summaries and paraphrases are important for other reasons.

A summary is obviously used when the breadth of the information is too great to represent in a small space or the information is not portable. It might be necessary, for example, to summarize the main point of a graphic (such as a chart or other diagram) to make the information usable as evidence. Sometimes a paragraph is simply too long and needs to be compressed. When you write a summary, be careful not to interpret. Instead, shorten the work with precision, keeping the exact argument intact. You may even use some words and phrases from the original, but you will need to write your own statement. The trick to a good summary is finding the key facts and represent them exactly in your version.

When you write a paraphrase, you are doing so for two reasons. One reason is that the text you want to cite is complicated, perhaps too technical for your needs or the wording too sophisticated for your reader. In this case, you must read carefully to make sure you understand the original enough to reword it.

The second reason to paraphrase is to create a sentence or phrase that fits your essay and writing style. You want to create an idea that is a fluent companion to what you've written. Still, a paraphrase is not a different idea—you are not changing the writer's intentions or the facts.

Summaries and paraphrases require some skill. It's much easier to quote a source word for word. This is exactly why the AP exam expects you to mix it up and use a combination of direct and indirect references. If you need practice, then you should practice. This is an easy goal to achieve.

Test Tip

When you are reviewing your sources for the synthesis essay, you may encounter a text that is too difficult to paraphrase. If so, you risk not understanding it and might use the information incorrectly. Avoid that source as evidence. You are expected to cite only three to four of the sources, so leaving something out isn't going to be a problem. However, remember that the point of choosing three to four sources from the group is to test your ability to support your point with the appropriate evidence. Do take some time to read and comprehend to the best of your ability each of the provided sources, so that you <u>do</u> have a choice.

PRIMARY AND SECONDARY SOURCES

Know the difference between primary and secondary sources. A **primary source** is created by the person with the vision, insight, or story to tell. A **secondary source** is a synthesis of primary sources or an analysis or interpretation of information garnered from primary sources.

Primary	Secondary
autobiographies, diaries, email, interviews, letters, minutes, news film footage, official records, photographs, raw research data, and speeches works of art, music, literature, etc., an original creation	literary criticism analyzing a play, poem, novel, or short story magazine or newspaper articles about events or people, commentary or analysis textbooks

GENERAL GUIDELINES

- Cite only what's needed, not more, not less. If you only need a phrase from a quotation, cite only that.

- On the other hand, if you need only a phrase, it may be best to paraphrase instead of using a direct quotation. Remember, you still must document a paraphrase. In general, use direct quotations when you cannot say something better (more eloquently or more succinctly) than the original.

- Use a paraphrase when an idea needs clarification or when integrating the original phrasing will be an awkward fit for your prose. If you have to [bracket] more than one word in a direct quotation, you may be much better off paraphrasing.

- In any paragraph, end with your own sentence, not a quotation. The essay is yours, so it is your voice that must dominate. Even in the conclusion, if you use an engaging quotation, end with one more sentence of your own prose that puts your cherry on the top.

TERMS TO KNOW

There are typically several questions in Part I of the exam that focus on the methods and techniques of documentation and citation. This brief list simply defines some key terms for you.

1. **Bibliography**: a list of sources consulted.

2. **Citation**: a reference used in evidence; also to document a source used in an essay.

3. **Direct quotation**: using another's words or a passage from a text as written, word for word. Direct quotations may be whole or partial. Whole means that an entire sentence or group of sentences is used. Partial means that only part of the text is used, whatever is most pertinent to the writer's needs.

4. **Endnotes**: notes, cross-references, or other pertinent information indicated in the text with superscript numbers showing that corresponding notes can be viewed at the end of the text.

5. **Footnotes**: notes, cross-references, or other pertinent information indicated in the text with superscript numbers showing that a corresponding note can be viewed at the bottom of the page.

6. **Paraphrase**: to put a source note into your own words.

7. **Parenthetical documentation**: inclusion of documentation information, such as an author's last name or a page number, in parentheses near its inclusion in the text.

8. **Plagiarism**: to intentionally or unintentionally use someone else's work or words without citing or crediting him or her; intellectual dishonesty.

9. **Summary**: essentially a shortened version of an original text.

10. **Works cited**: a list of sources cited in the paper.

Free-Response Question 1:
The Synthesis Essay

*The use of criticism, in periodical writing, is to sift,
not to stamp a work.*—Margaret Fuller

OVERVIEW

The first prompt you'll encounter in the free-response section of the exam is the synthesis question. This question tests your ability to argue a point that is supported by references, which are provided for you. By the time you are a junior or senior in high school, you have most likely had at least one, if not several, experiences writing a traditional research paper. This part of the exam is not much different from that.

Consider what the word *synthesis* means for a moment. According to a scoring guidelines document from the College Board, "Synthesis refers to combining sources and the writer's position to form a cohesive, supported argument and accurately citing all sources." So, you will be reading and analyzing documents, formulating your own argument, and pulling it all together.

The College Board tries to present you with topics for this essay that are relevant to your own life and experiences. That makes it a whole lot easier for you to care about the topic, which may help you write a better essay. For example, a recent Synthesis Question asked students to consider whether or not personal digital technologies (tablets, smartphones, MP3 players, computers, even television) have an adverse affect on our lives.

WHAT IS A SYNTHESIS ESSAY?

Think of a synthesis essay as a short research paper. You are given resources to use in support of a thesis that you develop after you read the prompt and the resources. This section will describe the process of writing this essay.

To begin with, when you open your green booklet for Part Two of the exam, you will have 15 minutes to read and consider a collection of resources: excerpts from articles, books, and journals, photographs, charts and graphs, illustrations, or cartoons. There will always be one or two visual texts for you to "read." You will typically have six to eight resources to study. As you read each of these, even the graphics, you must make notations—*annotate them*. See Chapter 11 for more on engaged and active reading.

Test Tip

Probably by the time you are reading the third or fourth resource, you are going to see commonalities. You will want to make note of them, such as "A, D, and E all support the idea that _____." This will help you to know which sources to use, but could also help you decide on your own point of view.

Before you read the supplied resources, however, you need to understand the prompt. You will be given a clear, precise prompt. As with all of your essays for this exam, you must read it carefully, and understand the subject and your task.

Remember that the introduction to each source is also useful information. All information given to you is given for a reason.

For this part of the exam, you are given a 15-minute reading period. It may take you the entire fifteen minutes to read, quickly annotate, and assess the sources. But if you are ready to move on after twelve minutes, move on. There is no restriction against doing so.

Write your thesis, which will be a clear but brief (generally one sentence) statement that expresses your opinion and shows your reader what you will be arguing. You should use the prompt to create your original thesis. Be sure you can support your thesis with the supplied references. By the time you actually write the thesis, you probably will have thought about your main supporting points.

The next quick step is to outline these points somewhere on your planning page (blank space in your green packet). Actually write it out instead of trying to keep it in your head. Testing situations are stressful, and stress produces cortisol, a brain chemical that can have a detrimental effect on short-term memory.

You will need to use three (or four) of the resources to defend your position in this essay. You are directed to make both direct and indirect references. See more on this below. DO NOT cite all of the sources, thinking it will make your paper stronger. It won't. First of all, not all of the resources will support your point of view. The true danger in citing too many sources is that you will be simply summarizing them and not using them to support your argument.

Keep in mind that you are expected to synthesize. You must blend evidence from more than one source to defend or prove an assertion. This should happen in more than one of your body paragraphs.

The rest is just writing! Of course, this implies a lot of things:

- Clear, precise word choice;

- Concise, but fully developed sentences and paragraphs;

- Logical organization and progression of ideas;

- Correct use of source material to support your argument, both direct and indirect references;

- Correctly citing the sources you use.

Test Tip

Make a mini-outline in the margin and try to stick to it. Don't think, however, that you can't veer off at the last minute if you happen to suddenly think of the perfect point to make. The outline, if it is a summary of your main points, as it should be, will help you keep your argument on track. It will also keep you from lapsing into summary, or worse, an irrelevant digression.

SUMMARIZING, EXPLAINING, AND ARGUING: WHAT IS THE DIFFERENCE AND WHY DOES IT MATTER?

To do well on this essay, you MUST take a position and argue it. This is not a paper in which you simply explain what the writers are saying. It is also not meant as a test of your ability to summarize the contents of the resources. Often, however, this is what students fall back on since it is quick and easy.

HOW TO KNOW IF YOU ARE . . .

Summarizing	Your paper will sound very much like the three or four resources you've chosen. You will be retelling what you learned from an article, excerpt, or a chart. Your reader will not be able to tell what you think. In a way, you are acting like a copying machine.
Explaining	Your paper will sound like you are trying to get your reader to understand the various resources. You are showing what you have learned, but you do not have a point of view. You may even cite parts of an article to show what you mean, but all you are doing is illuminating someone else's ideas. You are acting like a tutor or museum tour guide.
Arguing	Your thesis sets up your own position, one with which someone else might disagree. You have taken a stance. Your essay will have several (three or four) reasons why what you say is true. Your reader will be able to find these points easily. You are a critical thinker and persuasive writer. You are acting as an influential leader who hopes to change the minds of his or her readers.

The chart above shows the different aspects of an overall approach to the essay. You would never just summarize all of the sources and present that as an argument, nor would you just explain all of the sources. However, within your argument, you might summarize a section of Source A, or you might need to explain the ethical appeal of a photograph given as Source D.

COMMON PROBLEMS

The following list is a summary of the main problems AP readers see in students' synthesis essays.

- Not taking a clear position or wavering between positions.
- Substituting a thesis-oriented expository essay for an argumentative essay.
- Being reluctant to engage in verbal combat because "everyone's entitled to his or her own opinion," so there's nothing to argue about.
- Slipping out of focus, digressing into a tangential topic that does not aid the writer's argument.
- Misreading sources.
- Alluding to sources instead of citing them.
- Lacking development or organization.
- Providing a weak link between argument and sources.
- Displaying an immature control of writing, syntax, and mechanics.
- Offering vague generalizations.
- Simply summarizing the sources.

STRATEGIES FOR SUCCESS

Here is your quick guide for success on this part of the free-response section:

- Carefully read and understand the prompt. Stay focused on the question.
- Make sure your thesis contains a point of view—that is, your argument or what YOU think. Your claim must be one that you can defend with the documents you are given.
- Create a mini-outline in the margin, with your thesis leading the way. Come up with at least three main points to support your thesis. For each of those, list or note what evidence you will use from the resources to prove your claim. Don't forget to combine (synthesize) evidence from multiple sources.

A STUDY METHOD USING ONLINE SAMPLES

This is a strategy that I use in my own classroom to teach my students about the synthesis essay. They report that it really helps them get prepared in a minimum amount of time. For this method, you can use any two sample student essays from the AP Central site. It is a good idea to have two in which you can see differences, so choose one that earned a high score, such as an 8 or 9, and one that earned a more moderate score, such as a 5 or 6.

You are on your honor to follow the intentions of this method and do as instructed so that the process reveals insights to you. The purpose of this assignment is not only to give you an idea of a good synthesis essay, but also to provide you with practice in writing and scoring your own. It does take time (and ink from your printer), but your resources will be well spent.

This table is a visual guide to accompany the information that follows.

Free-Response Questions			
Questions	**Scoring**	**Samples and Commentary**	**Scoring Distributions**
Free-Response Questions [Click on this link to get the set of questions.]	Scoring Guidelines	Sample Responses Q1 [These are the ones you want for this exercise.]	Scoring Distributions
	Student Performance Q&A	Sample Responses Q2	
	Scoring Statistics	Sample Responses Q3	

ACCESSING THE MATERIALS YOU NEED

Go to *https://apcentral.collegeboard.org/courses/ap-english-language-and-composition/exam*. You will find a table that contains information that looks like what is shown above.

1. First, click on the "All Questions" link. Choose the most recent year's questions first. Make sure there are corresponding samples and commentary for that year. You will open a PDF document that looks exactly like the one used for the exam in that year. Print out one of these documents and set it aside without reading it.

2. Next, click on the link for "Sample Responses Q1." If you have a lot of ink, print the entire document, which should give you scoring guidelines (the grading rubric), three sample student essays, and the scoring commentary (the AP readers' comments about the essays for this prompt). If this document is complete, it will be about 12–14 pages long.

3. Once this document is printed, choose the first and the last essay. Save the middle one for later.

4. Fold the scoring commentary in half and set it aside. Do not read it.

5. Next, if it was not included in the document you printed, click on the link for "Scoring Guidelines," and print that. Set it aside without reading it.

USING THE DOCUMENTS

Analyzing Two Essays

You will read and score two sample essays using the scoring guidelines. You get to pretend to be an AP reader. But before you score the essays, you must read the prompt and all the resources that you received in the first packet you printed. You need to know the information available to the students. After you've done that, complete the assignment below.

This activity can be done independently or with a partner. I have my students work in teams because I like the think-aloud process that ensues. What one student may miss, another may see. If you have a study partner, why not do this activity with him or her?

Reading, Scoring, and Justifying Sample Synthesis Essays

Directions: Read one essay at a time. The essays are labeled with a letter or number combination for identification, such as 1A. After you read the essay, give it a score (use the Scoring Guidelines for your rubric). Then you need to justify that score, which means write why you think you would give it a 7 or a 3. Make specific reference to elements in the sample essay that corresponds with the scoring guidelines. Once you've done this, move on to the next essay. Read and score it, then justify that score. Finally, it's time for the big reveal. You can unfold the scoring commentary to see what the real AP Readers said. Put the actual score in the blank, and read the commentary (their justification). Then, comment on how you matched up with the actual score. Did you get it right? Did you come close? This means you have a good understanding of what it takes to write a solid, high-scoring essay or what to avoid so you don't earn a low score.

Essay #1

Identification number _____   Score _____

Justify your score:

Actual Score: _____

Comments on Compatibility:

Essay #2

Identification number _____   Score _____

Justify your score:

Actual Score: _____

Comments on Compatibility:

WRITING YOUR OWN ESSAY

Now is the time for you, as a self-motivated student, to see what you can do. Take that same prompt (or another, if this one is too familiar to you now), and write your own essay. Be sure to follow all the guidelines presented in this chapter.

If you are overflowing with confidence, try a new and unfamiliar prompt (get it at the same website). If you are tentative and need training wheels, go ahead and write your own essay using the prompt and resources you just examined. Be careful that you are not merely borrowing that successful student's thinking. By starting in a familiar place, you should feel like you have some support. Do try a different prompt eventually, though.

Finally, you need to score your own essay using the official scoring guidelines for that prompt. This is the tough part. Can you be objective? If you can honestly judge your own strengths and weaknesses using the scoring guidelines, you will learn a lot about what you still need to learn for this essay. This is also a great time for you to engage that study partner. You and your partner can exchange essays. The view will be more objective, and the best part is the conversation you will have afterward, which will only strengthen your skills.

SAMPLE PROMPT AND STUDENT ESSAY

Below you will find a sample synthesis prompt and a sample essay that responds to the prompt. You can use this material in a couple of ways:

1. You could simply read the material to understand the component parts of a synthesis prompt and a corresponding essay.

2. Without reading the sample essay, you could use this section as an opportunity to write your own synthesis essay, taking care to put into practice what you've learned. After you've written your own essay, compare it with the sample essay and see how your attempt measures up.

However you decide to use these materials, the prompt and sources replicate what you will find on your exam.

SAMPLE PROMPT

QUESTION 1

(Suggested time: 40 minutes.)

As technology has advanced, the curricula in American schools have changed. Schools increasingly use technology as a means of educating students today. Not only are schools focusing more on teaching computer skills, they also are including the use of such technology as video games, iPods, and podcasts as part of ordinary class work. Not surprisingly, school districts vary widely in their ability to provide technological aids for all students. Yet incorporating new technologies into the average classroom remains a priority for school districts across the country. What is the effect of this changing approach to education? Is it a clear improvement over traditional education, or is it merely a compromise?

Carefully read the following six sources, including the introductory information for each source. Then synthesize information from at least three of the sources and incorporate it into a coherent, well-developed essay taking a clear position that defends, refutes, or qualifies the claim that schools that are embracing the new technological approach to education are effectively teaching students the skills they need in today's world.

Make sure your argument is central; use the sources to illustrate and support your reasoning. Avoid merely summarizing the sources. Indicate clearly which sources you are drawing from, whether through direct quotation, paraphrase, or summary. You may cite the sources as Source A, Source B, etc., or by using the descriptions in parentheses.

Source A (Empire High School)

Source B (U.S. Department of Education)

Source C (Cartoon)

Source D (Johnson)

Source E (Miller)

Source F (National Education Association)

SOURCE A

"Arizona High School Chooses Laptops Over Textbooks." *VOANews.com.* Voice of America, 20 Oct. 2005. Web. 15 Oct. 2010.

The following passage is excerpted from an article about a new educational approach adopted by Empire High School in Vail, Arizona.

A new high school opened in Vail, Arizona, this past July with all the resources you would expect to find in classrooms these days—except textbooks. Instead, every student received an Apple laptop computer . . . making Empire High School a pioneer in the growing use of technology in American education.

. . . a committee visited classrooms that were making partial use of laptops, and came away with two distinct impressions. "One was that students in schools where laptops were being used were clearly more engaged," Mr. Baker says. "And the other impression was that we felt we could do more with laptops. Because we had the opportunity here of opening a new school, we could make them an integral part of what we do, and actually change the way we do things. And we sort of forced that issue by not buying any textbooks."

Teachers helped plan the school's wireless curriculum, often experimenting with different ideas in classrooms where they taught before. . . .

Michael Frank teaches a first-year biology course, where students use their laptops to access instructions for their lab work, organize data, and graph the results. . . . "[Students] will be putting together all the results from this experiment in a PowerPoint presentation for the class later. . . . And I know I can just give them an address for a website that has information and they can go look at it there. A lot of times with science, we use it because you can get immediate access to the most recent information. You don't have to wait 5 or 6 years for it to get into a textbook. So there's much more access to just a huge amount of data about things."

. . . There was a surprise once classes got under way as well. . . . "We thought the kids would be better at computing than they actually are. Being able to drive your Xbox or your iPod is not the same thing as being able to take a computer, use it, create a document, save it with a file name, put it in a particular location and retrieve it. And that has been a real challenge."

But administrators say the system is working well overall, and students seem to agree. . . .

Calvin Baker also stresses that he is not trying to make Empire High a technology school. And he says quality education still has to be about things like hard work, self-discipline and outstanding teaching — with laptops becoming a natural part of the classroom, just as they have become a natural part of workplaces across America.

SOURCE B

"Archived: Educational Technology Fact Sheet." *Ed.Gov.* U.S. Department of Education, 29 Mar. 2006. Web. 15 Oct. 2010.

The following information is excerpted from the Department of Education's "Educational Fact Sheet" regarding the availability of technology to students in the United States. Today's technology allows distance learning courses; in these courses, students work on their own from home or another off-site location, communicating with teachers and other students by using such technology as email, video conferencing, and instant messaging.

Statistics:

- In 2003, the ratio of students to computers in all public schools was 4.4 to 1.

- 48 states included technology standards for students in 2004–2005.

- In 2003, 8 percent of public schools lent laptop computers to students. . . .

- Schools in rural areas (12 percent) were more likely than city schools (5 percent) and urban fringe schools (7 percent) to lend laptops.

- In 2003, 10 percent of public schools provided a handheld computer to students or teachers.

- 16 states had at least one cyber-charter school operating in 2004–2005.

- 22 states had established virtual schools in 2004–2005.

- 56 percent of 2- and 4-year degree-granting institutions offer distance education courses, with 90 percent of public institutions offering distance education courses. . . .

Distance Learning

- 36% of school districts and 9% of all public schools have students enrolled in distance education courses.

- There were an estimated 328,000 enrollments in distance education courses by K–12 students during the 2001–2002 school year.

- 68% of the enrollments were in high school with an additional 29% in combined or ungraded schools.

- 45,300 enrollments in distance education were Advanced Placement or college-level courses.

- A greater proportion of rural area districts had students enrolled in distance education courses than did urban and suburban districts.

- 42% of districts that have students enrolled in distance-education courses are high poverty districts.

- When small districts offer distance learning, they are more likely to involve a greater proportion of schools.

- 80% of public school districts offering online courses said that offering courses not available at their schools is one of the most important reasons for having distance education.

- 50% of public school districts offering online courses cited distance learning as very important in making Advanced Placement or other college-level courses available to all students.

- 92% of districts enrolled in online distance education courses had students access online courses from school.

- 24% of districts with students accessing online courses from home provided or paid for a computer for all students, while an additional 8% did so for some students.

Friendship Through Education

- Using the Internet to connect students in the U.S. and Arab nations to develop mutual understandings of one another's cultures.

SOURCE C

Rosandich, Dan. "EDUCATION CARTOONS." *Danscartoons.com.* Web. 16
Oct. 2010. *(Reprinted with permission.)*

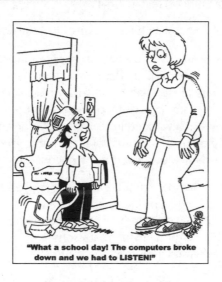

"What a school day! The computers broke
down and we had to LISTEN!"

SOURCE D

Johnson, Doug. "School Media Services for the "Net Generation" Part
One." *Doug Johnson Website.* 1 Jan. 2007. Web. 15 Oct. 2010.

---

*This passage is excerpted from an article by Doug Johnson, who has been
director of media and technology for the Mankato (Minnesota) Public Schools
since 1991.*

. . . kids expect fast communication responses, tune out when things
aren't interesting, and may be more visually than verbally literate. For
them, technology is a tool for learning on any topic they choose. (Are
you reading anything you don't already know from the media or from
personal observation?)

. . . Our current crop of students believes "teachers are vital," "computers can't replace humans," and motivation is critical in learning. They like group activities, believing building social skills is a part of schooling. They identify with their parents' values. And they are achievement oriented, feeling it is "cool to be smart." And although they are fascinated with new technologies, their knowledge of them is often "shallow."

(Who actually maintains the computers in your home or school?)

Finally, the studies point to how this generation learns—or likes to learn. Our current crop of students with their hypertext minds like inductive discovery rather than being told what they should know. In other words, they want to learn by doing rather than simply listening or reading. They enjoy working in teams, on "things that matter," often informally, and not just during school hours. And given their quick response requirements, they need to be encouraged to reflect.

It is my firm belief that schools will be more productive if educators acknowledge the unique attributes and preferences of the Net Generation and adapt educational environments to suit students instead of trying to change their basic natures. So what are some implications for NG (Net Generation) library media centers?

To a large degree, media centers may be the most NG-oriented places in schools. . . . Given their preference to work in groups, the NG media center should provide spaces for collaboration on school projects and socialization. It should contain the tools necessary for the production of information, not just its consumption—computers with the processing power and software to edit digital movies and photographs, scanners, and high-quality printers and projection devices—and, of course, assistance in the use of these tools.

. . . It should have comfy chairs, and be a friendly atmosphere, low-stress, safe, and forgiving—and yes, in high schools, an in-house coffee shop. Spaces for story times, puppetry, plays, and games along with computer stations with age-appropriate software and websites are just as important in elementary schools. If the "room" is not a wonderful place to be, students and teachers will stay on the Internet or in the classroom. Period. (And given the rise in online schools, is there a lesson here for classrooms as well?)

SOURCE E

Miller, Ed, and Joan Almon. "Child Advocates Challenge Current Ed Tech Standards" (press release). Alliance for Childhood. 30 Sept. 2004. Retrieved 21 Jan. 2011 at *http://drupal6.allianceforchildhood.org*. Reprinted by permission.

The following passage has been excerpted from a press release from the Alliance for Childhood, a non-profit organization concerned with healthy child development.

The high-tech, screen-centered life style of today's children—at home and at school—is a health hazard and the polar opposite of the education they need to take part in making ethical choices in a high-tech democracy, according to a new report released today by the Alliance for Childhood.

Tech Tonic: Towards a New Literacy of Technology challenges education standards and industry assertions that all teachers and children, from preschool up, should use computers in the classroom to develop technology literacy. That expensive agenda ignores evidence that high-tech classrooms have done little if anything to improve student achievement, the report says.

The report strongly criticizes the extensive financial and political connections between education officials and school technology vendors. It urges citizens to wake up to the increasing influence of corporations in policymaking for public education.

"The lack of evidence or an expert consensus that computers will improve student achievement—despite years of efforts by high-tech companies and government agencies to demonstrate otherwise—is itself compelling evidence of the need for change," *Tech Tonic* states. "It's time to scrap . . . national, state, and local policies that require all students and all teachers to use computers in every grade, and that eliminate even the possibility of alternatives."

At the same time, the Alliance suggests, high-tech childhood is making children sick—promoting a sedentary life at a time when childhood obesity is at epidemic levels

Today's children will inherit social and ecological crises that involve tough moral choices and awesome technological power, *Tech Tonic* warns. To confront problems like the proliferation of devastating weapons and global warming, children will need all the "wisdom, compassion, courage, and creative energy" they can muster, it adds. Blind faith in technology will not suffice.

"A new approach to technology literacy, calibrated for the 21st century, requires us to help children develop the habits of mind, heart, and action that can, over time, mature into the adult capacities for moral reflection, ethical restraint, and compassionate service," the report states.

The Alliance for Childhood is a nonprofit partnership of educators, researchers, health professionals, and other advocates for children, based in Maryland. *Tech Tonic* is a follow-up to the Alliance's widely noted 2000 report *Fool's Gold*. In *Tech Tonic* the Alliance proposes a new definition of technology literacy as "the mature capacity to participate creatively, critically, and responsibly in making technological choices that serve democracy, ecological sustainability, and a just society."

Tech Tonic proposes seven reforms in education and family life. These will free children from a passive attachment to screen-based entertainment and teach them about their "technological heritage" in a new way, rooted in the study and practice of technology "as social ethics in action" and in a renewed respect for nature.

The seven reforms:

- Make human relationships and a commitment to strong communities a top priority at home and school.
- Color childhood green to refocus education on children's relationships with the rest of the living world.
- Foster creativity every day, with time for the arts and play.

- Put community-based research and action at the heart of the science and technology curriculum.

- Declare one day a week an electronic entertainment-free zone.

- End marketing aimed at children.

- Shift spending from unproven high-tech products in the classroom to children's unmet basic needs.

"To expect our teachers, our schools, and our nation to strive to educate all of our children, leaving none behind, is a worthy goal," *Tech Tonic* says. "To insist that they must at the same time spend huge amounts of money and time trying to integrate unproven classroom technologies into their teaching, across the curriculum with preschoolers on up, is an unwise and costly diversion from that goal. It comes at the expense of our neediest children and schools, for whom the goal is most distant."

The report proposes 10 guiding principles for the new technology literacy and offers examples of each. It also includes suggestions for educators, parents, and other citizens to develop their own technology literacy, with a similar emphasis on social ethics in action.

"Today's children will face complex and daunting choices, in a future of biotechnology, robotics, and microchips, for which we are doing very little to prepare them," says Joan Almon, head of the Alliance. "We immerse them in a virtual, high-tech world and expect them to navigate the information superhighway with little guidance and few boundaries. It is time for a new definition of technology literacy that supports educational and family habits that are healthy both for children and for the survival of the Earth."

"It is within the context of relationships that children learn best," adds Dr. Marilyn Benoit, past president of the American Academy of Child and Adolescent Psychiatry and vice president of the Alliance Board of Trustees. "As we shift more towards the impersonal use of high technology as a major tool for teaching young children, we will lose that critical context of interactive relationship that so reinforces early learning."

SOURCE F

"NEA's policy recommendations" from "Technology in Schools: The
Ongoing Challenge of Access, Adequacy and Equity," An NEA policy brief,
2008, *http://www.nea.org.*

---

*The following information is excerpted from a policy brief released by the
National Education Association.*

1. Improve access to technology

Educators have been remarkably creative with limited computer
access, but if technology is to be integrated into instruction, more
computers must be made available for students' use, whether that is
through stand-alone computers or portable and wireless technologies.
States and school districts should pay more attention to building wireless
infrastructures that can support increased access to technology.

2. Increase Internet access, address software issues, and expand technical support

Programs designed to close the achievement gaps must begin
addressing equity issues related to Internet access, software, and technical
support. Educators across the board should have greater access to
computer software for planning and instruction. Educators in urban
schools, in particular, need better instructional software, and more
instructional staff should be involved in making decisions about software
purchases for their schools. Educators in elementary schools should have
more age-appropriate software for students, but, just as importantly, they
need more high-speed Internet services.

Maintenance support for computers must be adequate to ensure that
computers function properly and reliably. Quality technical support for
computers and other technologies should be available in every school.
Particular attention should be given to senior high schools, as well as to
schools located in urban areas, where maintenance and technical support
are less likely to be provided. One option is for districts or schools to make
use of their students' technical expertise by formally arranging for qualified

students to provide technical assistance where needed. Another important point is separating the instructional support role of paraprofessionals from that of providing maintenance and technical support.

3. Expand professional development in technology

Technology training, most commonly offered for administration, communications, and research, should focus more on applications for instruction. And those entering the profession, as well as experienced educators, should have access to high-quality professional development in technology. Particular attention should be paid to training opportunities provided for educators working in schools located in urban and rural areas, where educators believe the technology training in their schools has not been adequate.

4. Capitalize on teachers' and students' enthusiasm about technology

Schools should seek more ways to use technology for the greatest gain in student achievement, particularly in urban and rural/small-town schools. State and district leaders should encourage schools to use technology in more creative ways by permitting more flexibility in instruction and by providing incentives that support technology-enriched programs. More ways should be found to motivate the most experienced educators to use technology through better training and more curriculum-related opportunities.

5. Involve educators as advocates

Teacher organizations, such as NEA and its state affiliates, can be a valuable ally in the goal of fully integrating technology into education. State and local associations can also help educate parents and the business community about the benefits of better integrating technology into teaching and learning. They can actively support district and state efforts to secure more funding for school technology by lobbying state legislatures, establishing partnerships with commercial and private enterprises, and seeking federal and private grants.

SAMPLE ESSAY RESPONSE

Anyone who has ever been issued a dog-eared or graffiti-filled[1] ten-year-old textbook for a class would certainly agree that being provided with an iPad or a laptop would be a huge improvement in educational tools. Even if the textbook were brand new, it is still a finite resource, whereas an Internet-connected device is a potentially limitless resource that encompasses all subject areas. As more and more schools turn to technology and tools like iPads, opponents have expressed concern that plugged-in students are at a disadvantage compared with their pre-Internet peers. While a tech-driven curricula might carry some dangers, the educational benefits to students, rich and poor, far outweigh the risks.[2]

No student will learn anything if his or her attention is not focused on the lesson. A student must be engaged in the learning process to benefit.[3] According to Source A[4] "students in schools where laptops were being used were clearly more engaged." Part of that engagement comes from the way today's students consume information.[5] Johnson points out that the Net Generation (NG) expects information to be fast. What's more, he says students "tune out when things aren't interesting" (Source D). Because technology can entice and maintain student interest, it may, for the NG generation particularly, be an educational necessity.[6] In addition, since Internet[7]

---

[1] Writer uses imagery to engage readers as well as appeal to their common experience as students.

[2] The thesis shows that the writer understands that technology use is not perfect, but expresses a clear claim: benefits to all students outweigh risks. The writer also hints that some element of economic disparity will enter the argument later on.

[3] The first two sentences in this first body paragraph state a claim: students must be engaged to learn. Paraphrasing the first sentence doubles the effect of the claim.

[4] The writer makes an attribution statement (according to) to integrate evidence from a source.

[5] The writer uses a transition sentence to help explain the evidence and link the two pieces of evidence. Note that this writer has synthesized evidence from more than one source to defend an assertion.

[6] In this sentence, the writer is clarifying the argument by drawing a conclusion.

[7] Finally, the writer concludes this paragraph by using a partial quote that supports one last point.

connected devices provide students with "immediate access to the most recent information" (Source A), that information is potentially more relevant and more interesting to students.

Internet connected devices don't only provide access to information, such devices also provide something potentially more important, especially to schools in rural areas or to schools with a high percentage of students in poverty. Internet connected devices effectively break down the walls of a school and give students the ability to learn from home (distance learning), to take advanced classes, or even engage with students from other countries.[8] The US Department of Education reports that in 2004, 22 states had established virtual schools and that 36 percent of school districts have students enrolled in distance education programs (Source B). Online courses would allow students to learn from home, if necessary, but these programs are also a benefit to those going on to one of the many colleges that also provide similar online courses (Source B).

Distance education is beneficial in other ways as well. In such cases where a school cannot afford to offer higher-level courses, its students can join more than 45 thousand other students enrolled in online Advanced Placement courses (Source B).[9] Perhaps the greatest impact that technology can have in schools is to give all students equal learning opportunities. Source B points out that "42% of districts that have students enrolled in distance-education courses are high poverty districts," which implies[10] these schools have found a way to offer their students more despite limited resources. Just like their peers in wealthier schools, these students will leave high school or college and enter a workplace

---

[8] In the second body paragraph, the writer advances the argument by listing several advantages to giving students Internet-connected devices. The advantages listed were part of available information in the sources, but this writer focuses on the advantages of distance learning and defends assertions with evidence.

[9] While all of the evidence for claims in this paragraph comes from one source, there are multiple uses of the source, and the writer uses only what is necessary in support.

[10] In this paragraph, the writer is clearly drawing an inference about the data given in Source B. In a clear ethical appeal, the writer suggests that technology will provide equal education opportunities for all students. The final sentence in this paragraph reinforces the ethical appeal.

where computers have become commonplace (Source A).[11] To fail to integrate similar technologies into all schools seems to ignore a real world educational need.

Nevertheless,[12] there are those who argue that a strong, singular focus on technology could actually be harmful to children. Miller and Almon point out "a lack of evidence or an expert consensus that computers will improve student achievement" (Source E). They also say that since using computers is a sedentary activity, high technology use might be "making children sick" and be exacerbating the childhood obesity problem (Source E). However, it seems the technology trend is here to stay and once schools have fully embraced digital learning, no doubt convincing evidence for its effectiveness will emerge. As for the health claim, surely no school would chain its students to their computers all day. As always, striking a balance between bookwork and physical activity is important. The fact that the book is a computer makes no difference.

Today's world[13] is information driven, and business and commerce rely on computers or other devices to access this information. While there is still great value in traditional styles of learning, schools that do not allow students to learn using the tools of their future offer are doing them a great disservice.

---

[11] To explain why access to technology is important, the writer uses information from a second source in this paragraph.

[12] In the third body paragraph, the writer transitions to the counterargument, and acknowledges that some believe technology in schools is harmful. The writer presents two of the opponents' claims: 1) lack of evidence that technology is effective and 2) a sedentary learning style is harmful to children's health. Rather than offer solid evidence to refute these claims, the writer of this essay appeals to common-sense alternatives.

[13] The conclusion to this essay is short, but it furthers the writer's ethical appeal by suggesting that to deny students access to computers is a disservice.

ADDITIONAL COMMENTARY

Take note of how well organized this essay is. The writer's claim is clearly stated in the introduction. The argument progresses logically and evidence is used convincingly. This writer makes use of direct quotations, summaries, and paraphrases, but is careful to document the source of all evidence. It is easy to see how this writer has synthesized evidence to support the central argument. This writer has not strung together a summary of the sources, but has clearly shown independent thought throughout the essay. Ethical appeals enhance this writer's ethos. As for the writer's syntax, sentences are varied and effective. The writer's choice of words (*encompasses* and *exacerbates*, for example) shows an ability to use sophisticated language. As you read this essay, you may be thinking that the writer could have made other points or could have taken an entirely different approach. You're right. There is always more than one way to respond to the synthesis prompt, and your observation shows your engagement in these ideas.

Free-Response Question 2:
Rhetorical Analysis

Get the habit of analysis—analysis will in time enable synthesis to become your habit of mind.—Frank Lloyd Wright

OVERVIEW

The purpose of this chapter is to give you a closer look at the particulars of Free-Response Question 2: the Rhetorical Analysis. However, you will need to study more than just this chapter to be successful with this essay. While the entire book aims to help you be a stronger reader, writer, and thinker, please also review the following chapters in combination with this one:

- Chapter 5 on rhetorical strategies;

- Chapter 7 on logical fallacies;

- Chapter 11 on engaged and active reading;

- Chapter 15 on satire;

- Chapter 16 on prompts (focusing on those for Question 2).

REVIEWING QUESTION 2

Question 2 is nearly always an exercise in analysis. You will typically be asked to do one of three tasks:

1. After reading a short text, identify the writer's claim and defend, challenge (refute), or qualify it. (These terms are defined below.)

2. After reading a short text, analyze the rhetorical strategies the author employs to make his or her point. (It will be rare for you to be given a list of strategies.)

3. You will read two short texts that share elements such as topic, style, purpose, etc. You then will be asked to compare and contrast them, while also analyzing the writer's or speaker's purpose, attitude or point of view, and strategies.

DEFEND/CHALLENGE/QUALIFY

- Defend: To defend is to agree, to show that the claim is correct.

- Challenge (or sometimes refute): To challenge is to disagree or show that the claim is incorrect or unsound.

- Qualify: To qualify is to show how an argument is partially valid or right, but also partially invalid or wrong.

GUIDING YOUR ANALYSIS

To analyze is to examine the parts of something in order to understand how they function in the whole. So, to analyze an effective satirical essay, for example, you'll first need to recognize that it is satire. Next, you need to ask the right questions as you read, such as "Who or what is the satirical target?" and "Which techniques are employed and where?" Reading so you have an intelligent understanding of the text is necessary for your success with this essay.

No matter what text you're provided, you must isolate the author's thesis and the rhetorical strategies and stylistic techniques he or she uses to achieve the desired effect.

DETERMINE THE GENRE OR PATTERN OF EXPOSITION

As you read the passage for this question, identify the genre or expository pattern. While it won't be necessary to actually present this information in your essay, knowing what the genre is will help you know what to look for: what typical strategies might be found, etc. Making this determination should take you literally only seconds. Do not labor over this aspect of the text.

1. A persuasive **argument**?
   - Look for appeals.

- Watch for logical fallacies.
- What is it the writer wants you to believe or do?

2. An **expository** essay (one that explains or explores a topic using a variety of methods):

- Description
    - Used commonly by nature and environmental writers, description relies on imagery to get the reader to "see" the subject.
- Narrative
    - The writer will explore a topic using the framework of a story, perhaps a look at one person's life as a model or example of the main subject.
- Cause and Effect
    - Look for a problem or a current issue and the writer's theories about the underlying causes.
    - You will probably be asked to defend, challenge, or qualify.
- Problem/Solution
    - An obvious problem, in policy usually, will be presented along with one or more viable solutions.
    - You will probably be asked to defend, challenge, or qualify.
- Process analysis
    - The writer shows how something is done or how something works.
- Definition
    - This pattern is used when an idea is too abstract for people to grasp or when there are conflicting explanations for a term. For example, many people might benefit from having "supply-side economics" defined more fully. The writer is, of course, giving her point of view.

- Compare/Contrast

  — Quite commonly found on the exam, compare/
  contrast simply asks you to consider the obvious
  (and not so obvious) connections between two texts
  and to draw conclusions about what is revealed or
  communicated in the process. Look in Chapter 17 for
  a quick guide to writing compare/contrast essays.

3. **Satire?**

   - Who or what is the satirical target?
   - What aspect of the social contract is flawed or broken?
   - What specific method does the writer use to criticize the target?
   - What does the satirist want the reader to understand, know, or do?

SOAPSTONE: A METHOD OF ANALYSIS

Memorize the acronym SOAPSTONE to remind you to look for and identify key components of any nonfiction text. As you read, annotate the text using these main points.

S = Speaker

O = Occasion

A = Audience

P = Purpose

S = Subject

T(ONE) = Tone

Chapter 4 has a chart you can use for studying major texts.

RHETORIC

Review Chapter 6 for a detailed explanation of rhetoric and rhetorical strategies. Briefly, Aristotle defined three components of rhetoric:

- Logos (appeal to reason, using facts, verifiable evidence, expert opinion, etc.)
- Ethos (the credibility of the writer, the tone or spirit in which the writer presents the argument)
- Pathos (appeals to emotion)

Take caution: Do not simply say "the writer uses pathos in line three" or the like. Logos, Ethos, and Pathos are broad concepts encompassing particular aspects of effective argument. Be sure you understand Aristotle's framework in a holistic way.

ORGANIZING THE ESSAY

You will need to present a defensible claim as in any other essay for this exam. **DO NOT simply proceed to answer a question.** You will earn few, if any, points if you do. Your essay must be well organized, with an introduction, body paragraphs in support, and a conclusion. (See Chapter 17 for general essay writing tips.)

I strongly suggest you create a mini-outline or concept map to guide your general explanation or argument. Such an outline will help you stay focused. If you follow it, you should be less likely to repeat yourself or leave out cogent points.

Your introduction must acknowledge your specific task. If you are asked to defend, challenge or qualify, it should be clear in your introduction which of the three you have chosen to do.

You need not use the words "defend," "challenge," or "qualify," as doing so might be clunky. For example, you would not write, "Author argues for a ban on soda for children, and I plan to challenge that assertion." A better option would be to write something such as: "Author argues that a ban on soda for children under the age of 18 necessary to protect their health. Such a ban is not only unwarranted, it interferes with parents' ability to determine what is right for their children."

Notice how the second example does not use the word "challenge," even though it is clear that is what the writer intends to do.

The evidence for your rhetorical analysis essay will come from the text itself. If you state, for example, that the author makes an ethical appeal, you will need to show exactly where that is as well as explain how that appeal serves the overall purpose.

MORE TIPS FOR QUESTION 2

The following tips come from AP readers' commentaries on Question 2.

DO:

- Read the text carefully, first (if you fail to do this, you run a high risk of misunderstanding not only the text, but also the prompt).
- Provide specific examples, rather than general.
- Offer cogent insights.
- Provide convincing analysis.

DO NOT:

- Drop in quotations from the passage without providing any meaningful commentary or explanation.
- Write personal comments (asides) about the content of the passage. Note: You may feel compelled to do this if the subject of the text conflicts with your views or values. Please remember that your job is to analyze, not necessarily agree. Control biases that prevent you from objectively managing your task.
- Paraphrase or summarize instead of analyze.
- Identify features of the text without explanation.

SAMPLE RHETORICAL ANALYSIS PROMPT

QUESTION 2

(Suggested time: 40 minutes.)

The essay below, written in 2011 by Peter Singer, bioethics professor at Princeton University, examines the ethical nature of legal access to cigarettes. Read the essay carefully and write an essay in which you analyze how Singer crafts the text to express his view that cigarettes should be banned.

PRINCETON—US President Barack Obama's doctor confirmed last month that the president no longer smokes. At the urging of his wife, Michelle Obama, the president first resolved to stop smoking in 2006, and has used nicotine replacement therapy to help him. If it took Obama,
5   a man strong-willed enough to aspire to and achieve the US presidency, five years to kick the habit, it is not surprising that hundreds of millions of smokers find themselves unable to quit.

Although smoking has fallen sharply in the US, from about 40% of the population in 1970 to only 20% today, the proportion of smokers stopped
10 dropping around 2004. There are still 46 million American adult smokers, and smoking kills about 443,000 Americans each year. Worldwide, the number of cigarettes sold—six trillion a year, enough to reach the sun and back—is at an all-time high. Six million people die each year from smoking—more than from AIDS, malaria, and traffic accidents combined.
15 Of the 1.3 billion Chinese, more than one in ten will die from smoking.

Earlier this month, the US Food and Drug Administration announced that it would spend $600 million over five years to educate the public about the dangers of tobacco use. But Robert Proctor, a historian of science at Stanford University and the author of a forthcoming
20 blockbuster entitled *Golden Holocaust: Origins of the Cigarette Catastrophe and the Case for Abolition,* argues that to use education as one's only weapon against a highly addictive and often lethal drug is unpardonably insufficient.

"Tobacco control policy," Proctor says, "too often centers on
25 educating the public, when it should be focused on fixing or eliminating the product." He points out that we don't just educate parents to keep toys painted with lead-based paints away from their children's mouths; we ban the use of lead-based paint. Similarly, when thalidomide was found to cause major birth defects, we did not just educate women to avoid using
30 the drug when pregnant.

Proctor calls on the FDA to use its new powers to regulate the contents of cigarette smoke to do two things. First, because cigarettes are designed to create and maintain addiction, the FDA should limit the amount of nicotine that they contain to a level at which they would cease to be
35 addictive. Smokers who want to quit would then find it easier to do so.

Second, the FDA should bear history in mind. The first smokers did not inhale tobacco smoke; that became possible only in the nineteenth century, when a new way of curing tobacco made the smoke less alkaline. That tragic discovery is already responsible for about 150 million deaths,
40 with many times that toll still to come, unless something drastic is done. The FDA should therefore require that cigarette smoke be more alkaline, which would make it less easily inhaled, and so make it harder for cigarette smoke to reach the lungs.

Much of Proctor's book, which will be published in January, is based on
45 a vast archive of tobacco-industry documents, released during litigation. More than 70 million pages of industry documents are now available online.

The documents show that, as early as the 1940s, the industry had evidence suggesting that smoking causes cancer. In 1953, however, a
50 meeting of the chief executives of major American tobacco companies took a joint decision to deny that cigarettes are harmful. Moreover, once the scientific evidence that smoking causes cancer became public, the industry tried to create the impression that the science was inconclusive, in much the same way that those who deny that human activities are
55 causing climate change deliberately distort the science today.

As Proctor says, cigarettes, not guns or bombs, are the deadliest artifacts in the history of civilization. If we want to save lives and improve health, nothing else that is readily achievable would be as effective as an international ban on the sale of cigarettes. (Eliminating extreme poverty
60 worldwide is about the only strategy that might save more lives, but it would be far more difficult to accomplish.)

For those who recognize the state's right to ban recreational drugs like marijuana and ecstasy, a ban on cigarettes should be easy to accept. Tobacco kills far more people than these drugs.

65 Some argue that as long as a drug harms only those who choose to use it, the state should let individuals make their own decisions, limiting its role to ensuring that users are informed of the risks that they are running. But tobacco is not such a drug, given the dangers posed by secondhand smoke, especially when adults smoke in a home with young children.

70 Even setting aside the harm that smokers inflict on nonsmokers, the free-to-choose argument is unconvincing with a drug as highly addictive as tobacco, and it becomes even more dubious when we consider that

most smokers take up the habit as teenagers and later want to quit. Reducing the amount of nicotine in cigarette smoke to a level that was
75 not addictive might meet this objection.

The other argument for the *status quo* is that a ban on tobacco might result in the same kind of fiasco as occurred during Prohibition in the US. That is, like the effort to ban alcohol, prohibiting the sale of tobacco would funnel billions of dollars into organized crime and fuel corruption in
80 law-enforcement agencies, while doing little to reduce smoking.

But that may well be a false comparison. After all, many smokers would actually like to see cigarettes banned because, like Obama, they want to quit.

Peter Singer is a professor of bioethics at Princeton University and Laureate Professor at the University of Melbourne. His books include Animal Liberation, Practical Ethics, *and* The Life You Can Save.

Copyright: Project Syndicate, 2011. *www.project-syndicate.org.* For a podcast of this commentary in English, please use this link: *http://traffic.libsyn.com/ projectsyndicate/singer80.mp3.*

SAMPLE ESSAY RESPONSE

In "Should We Ban Cigarettes?," Peter Singer's[1] main claim is that since smoking kills nearly a half million citizens each year, the United States government should prohibit the sale of cigarettes as the only way to solve the problem.[2] However, until that time, he argues specifically that the US Food and Drug Administration (FDA) should use its powers to make cigarettes less powerful and addictive. Singer targets his message[3] to all citizens, as everyone is affected in one way or another by the problem, but perhaps most particularly to smokers, since without their willingness to accept a ban, it would not likely come to pass.

---

[1] The introduction includes the title of the article and the author's full name. All subsequent mentions of the author use only his last name.

[2] In this thesis statement, the writer summarizes Singer's main claim. Since this essay is an analysis, you are required to state the author's thesis, which becomes, in a way, your thesis.

[3] The writer acknowledges Singer's potential audience.

In order to point out the magnitude of the problem, Singer provides a sharp visual representation of a fact by describing how the six trillion cigarettes sold each year would be enough "to reach to the sun and back" (Lines 12–13).[4] However, Singer somewhat inflates the danger to US citizens since the six trillion represents the number of cigarettes sold worldwide, not just in the US.[5]

In support of his claim, Singer gives evidence of the extensive problem. He says that smoking kills more people each year than "AIDS, malaria, and traffic accidents combined" (14). He does not, however, cite the source for this statistic. In addition to pointing out that smoking is a killer, Singer says the fight against smoking is expensive. He cites an announcement by the FDA (from November 2011) that the agency "would spend $600 million over five years to educate the public about the dangers of tobacco use." And yet, as Singer explains, education doesn't work, despite the money spent on it.[6]

Singer provides expert testimony[7] for his argument that education is ineffective by citing Stanford University's Robert Proctor, whose book *Golden Holocaust: Origins of the Cigarette Catastrophe and the Case for Abolition* details the failure of previous attempts to educate the public about the dangers of smoking and the need for a federal ban. Singer uses Proctor's analogy[8] to suggest it is ridiculous to try to save people from the dangers of smoking through education, just as we would not "educate parents to keep toys painted with lead-based paints away from their children's mouths" (25–26). Instead, we banned the dangerous element and saved countless children from devastating effects. In an ethical appeal, Singer implies through this comparison

---

[4] In the first line citation in the essay, the writer uses the word "Lines," but in all further line citations, the numbers only are used.

[5] Here the writer is seen to be a critical reader and thinker by pointing out a discrepancy in Singer's illustration.

[6] This sentence serves as a transition to the next paragraph, which will further analyze the education aspect of Singer's argument.

[7] The writer clarifies the type of evidence Singer uses.

[8] The writer of this essay clearly understands the source of the analogy, but acknowledges its effectiveness in Singer's argument.

that it is immoral to simply let people become ill or die from smoking cigarettes, which the tobacco industry has known since the 1940s "causes cancer" (49).

While Singer[9] would like an overall ban on cigarettes, he realizes an all-out ban might be too difficult to achieve. Therefore, he argues that the FDA must take two important policy changes to make cigarettes less harmful: make them more alkaline so that people are less likely to inhale (to replicate pre-19th century tobacco before technology existed to reduce harsh alkalinity) and limit nicotine to make cigarettes less addictive (33–34). Singer does not provide proof of the addictive nature of cigarettes, but references Proctor, whose book includes documentation that proves the tobacco industry knew "as early as the 1940s . . . that smoking causes cancer," underscoring the fact that smoking is a deadly habit (48–49).

Singer concedes[10] that these days fewer people smoke, about 20% of the population versus 40% in 1970, but in his view, there are still far too many deaths to discount the importance of the issue. In a clear emotional appeal, Singer refers to the "tragic" fact that historically, 150 million people have died from cigarettes (39).

Singer acknowledges the opposition's argument.[11] He realizes that some believe that "as long as a drug harms only those who use it, the state should let individuals make their own decisions" regarding its use (65–66). This logic is flawed, says Singer, who points out that most smokers begin their habit as teenagers "and later want to quit" (73). His implication is that people begin smoking when they're least likely to be able to make reasonable judgments regarding their health, and before they realize it, teens

---

[9] This paragraph analyzes complex aspects of Singer's argument and synthesizes a couple of key points. Singer wants the FDA to make cigarettes less harmful and addictive, which is important because cigarettes cause cancer.

[10] The writer recognizes that Singer makes a concession to the fact that the issue is not as dire as it once was, but shows that Singer refutes that stance through emotional appeal by saying that too many still die needlessly.

[11] In this paragraph, the writer shows how Singer acknowledges another opposing view and refutes it.

are addicted. The smoking habit, as Singer points out in a logical appeal in paragraph one,[12] is even difficult for an adult like President Obama, "a man strong-willed enough to aspire to and achieve the US presidency" (5), so then how much harder for ordinary people, particularly teens.

To support his notion that a ban would be acceptable to US citizens, Singer says in his conclusion, many smokers "want to quit." However, he fails to say that there are also many smokers who enjoy smoking and do not want the government to control their access to cigarettes.[13]

To conclude,[14] the author could have made an appeal to ethics by pointing out the known fact that second-hand smoke inflicts damage on nonsmokers or how unfair it is for healthy nonsmokers to have to share in the growing health care costs that result from the unwillingness (or inability) of smokers to quit a habit they know is harmful to themselves and others. Nevertheless, Singer effectively adds to an important discussion about what can be done to reduce smoking deaths, since education is not an effective option in combatting a known health hazard to US citizens.

---

[12] The writer cites the source of the information from the paragraph, not the specific line. This is also an acceptable method if the paragraph is easily located, such as the first, second, or last. Never make someone count to find the seventh paragraph, for example. Take note also that reference is made to the kind of appeal Singer uses.

[13] The writer points out that Singer makes a generalization.

[14] While not required, this writer signals the conclusion. In this conclusion, the student points out other arguments Singer could have made, which shows critical thinking. Finally, the essay wraps up by tying back to the essence of Singer's thesis.

Free-Response Question 3:
The Persuasive Essay

*Writing, to me, is simply thinking through
my fingers.*—Isaac Asimov

OVERVIEW

Question 3 is where you show off your own rhetorical skills by creating an argument of your own. This is not to say that your other essays lack an argument. That's not what I mean. For each essay you write on the exam, you will establish a claim to defend. But this essay is different. There is no safety net—all your evidence must come from your head.

This chapter focuses on the key elements of Question 3. You will still need to study other chapters in this book to be more fully prepared to write this essay.

REVIEWING QUESTION 3

For Question 3, you will be presented with a question or an idea and asked to develop your own argument or explanation. Sometimes the question or idea is paired with a brief quotation or passage from a text.

Evidence for your claims for this essay come from your reading, your general knowledge, and your experience. See Chapter 16 for a summary of specific prompts over the past ten years.

PROVIDE APPROPRIATE EVIDENCE

What is evidence? It is the data, examples, and other information that you use to prove your claim. You will be given no resources for this essay. All you may have as a reference will be a short excerpt or one (or two) quotations. You may cite the provided passage as evidence. The rest of your evidence will come from your reading, your general knowledge, and your life experiences. In other words, your proof will come from everything you know. All evidence that you use must be relevant, current, credible, and reliable.

EXAMPLES:

1. Real life: these examples come from what you've experienced or observed.

2. Hypothetical (what if?): a hypothetical example needs to be logical, realistic, and based upon patterns of cause and effect, not fantasy or random anecdotes.

3. Specific: referring to particular people or events.

4. General: referring to types of people or events.

ABOUT PERSONAL EXAMPLES

A personal example differs from a real-life example in that it is from your own, personal experience. Be cautious when using personal examples, and avoid using private examples. Any information that should not be publicly shared is inappropriate in this context.

Personal examples are more limited in their universal value. Your experience, in other words, might just be your experience and may not be overly persuasive in your argument for that reason. On the other hand, an example from real life that involves significant events or large numbers of people is going to carry more weight.

If your personal example is compelling and unique, it might be excellent evidence.

STATISTICS

You will not have access to any resources, so you won't be able to look up any information. But that doesn't mean that you can't cite some facts if you know them. A good strategy for citing facts, especially if you're not 100 percent sure of the numbers, is to qualify your statements with terms such as "approximately," "about," "in general," etc. For example, you might remember that you heard on a news broadcast that one in three middle- and high-school students reported being bullied. If you're not sure, you can say "approximately one in three." Don't forget to mention the source. If you can't remember which network broadcast the story, refer in general, by saying, "In a recent television news broadcast, it was reported that . . . "

OTHER RHETORICAL STRATEGIES

- Appeals to values, needs, emotions: review Chapter 6.

- Effective syntax: review Chapter 9.

- Effective diction and language: review Chapter 17.

Test Tip

Prepare for Question 3 by being well read. Read not only nonfiction works from your English course, but also from your other courses. For example, maybe you will read A Sand County Almanac *in your environmental studies class. Don't think of that as just a science-oriented text. Everything you read is potentially valuable to you on this exam. See Chapter 4 for a list of authors and texts. In addition to reading books, articles, editorials, etc., as you read, contemplate the various ways the ideas in these works connect with your life. Try to engage personally with everything you read. What do YOU THINK?*

MAKE YOUR THINKING TRANSPARENT

One weakness of immature, nervous, or hurried writers is that they sometimes assume that their ideas, arguments, and connections are self-evident. They may think that if they get it, everyone will get it. Confusion occurs if your understanding of an idea lies in unstated connections, or in conclusions that you have only thought about but not shown in writing. DO NOT forget to explain. If you have not explicitly stated your interpretations and conclusions, you are hiding your thinking, not showing it. Again, if you haven't put your thinking on paper, you haven't made it transparent.

TRANSITIONAL WORDS AND PHRASES

By using transitional words and phrases in your writing, you will be less likely to write confusing or woolly prose. Chapter 17 gives you a list of common transitional words and phrases. Do not disregard their importance. Transitions not only lead your reader through your thinking, they also help you organize your argument.

TRANSITIONS IN ACTION

1. They bridge paragraph changes.

2. Transitions signal new ideas.

3. They establish logical relationships.

4. They make it easy for you to reiterate a previous idea.

POINT OF VIEW

BLENDING FIRST AND THIRD PERSON

You know that writing in the third person gives you an authoritative voice, but there are times when you need to use the first person. It would be impossible to relate a personal example without it. Think about your essay as a blending of the two, relying mostly upon using third person.

UNIVERSAL FIRST PERSON

When you include yourself in the community of human beings, whether a small society such as your high school student population or the entire population of the globe, you will use the pronouns "we," "us," and "our." This is appropriate and necessary if you desire to take a stance from such a point of view. But, as with any deviation from authoritative third person, do not go overboard.

AUTHORITATIVE VOICE

Do not express opinions with qualifiers. If you do, you lessen the strength of your statement. An opinion, expressed in your essay, unless attributed to someone else, is obviously your opinion. It's your essay. Notice in the examples below how the statements on the right sound more authoritative.

No	Yes
I think the general population is experiencing ennui when it comes to the Green Movement.	The general population is experiencing ennui when it comes to the Green Movement.
It is my opinion that students should be allowed to use computers to write all exams, even AP exams.	Students should be allowed to use computers to write all exams, even AP exams.

If you are an avid gamer, maybe it's time to leave the dusky shadows of your virtual environment for awhile and play the game of life by talking with your parents, grandparents, neighbors, teachers, coaches, and friends about the issues of the day. Does your family "get into it" at dinner about politics or religion? Instead of shirking away in avoidance, use those heated moments as opportunities for analysis and reflection. If your family tends toward the left in their views, read what those on the right are thinking. In other words, add to your perspective by actively thinking about and studying those opinions right under your nose.

ABOUT YOUR AUDIENCE

Your audience is a well-read, experienced adult who is accustomed to engaging with intelligent and sophisticated texts. Therefore, your ethos as a writer is very important. You must believe in the ideas you present in this essay. If you don't, everything about your essay will ring false or seem insincere. This exam is not a place for you to charm your reader with platitudes and flowery phrases. AP readers will see this tactic immediately for what it is, which is an evasion of your task. Instead, wow them with your honest exploration of ideas.

Your ethos is evident in the following ways:

- Level of knowledge (your credibility);
- Truthfulness (honesty);
- Sincere intentions.

GENERAL QUALITIES OF GOOD WRITING

Some items below come from commentaries on sample essays for Question 3 by AP readers.

STRIVE FOR:

- Varied and effective sentence structure.
- Rich, but standard vocabulary.
  - — Avoid specialized terms or jargon, unless their use is warranted and you clarify their meanings.
- More than a few examples or other details in support.
- Explain evidence.
- Present a coherent, compelling argument.

AVOID:

- Unnecessary repetition or redundancy. This is generally a result of getting your thinking tires stuck in the mud. Avoid this situation by referring often to your mini outline or concept map.
- Overly short paragraphs (one or two sentences). If a claim is worth stating, it is worth exploring and supporting fully.
- Stating generalizations as claims. Claims must be specific and supported.
- Discursive and overly general introductions that "talk" around the subject.

- Repeating the prompt, either directly or in paraphrase.

- Summary conclusions—Instead, strive to present an insightful idea in your conclusion that originates logically from your argument.

SAMPLE PERSUASIVE PROMPT

QUESTION 3

(Suggested time: 40 minutes.)

Consider the distinct perspectives expressed in the following statements.

Advice is seldom welcome; and those who want it the most always like it the least.

Philip Dormer Stanhope, Earl of Chesterfield (1694–1773)

I have lived some thirty years on this planet, and I have yet to hear the first syllable of valuable or even earnest advice from my seniors.

Henry David Thoreau (1817–1862)

In a well-organized essay, take a position on the importance of advice, using the above quotes as a starting point. Support your argument with appropriate examples.

SAMPLE ESSAY RESPONSE

"Take my advice." You hear it from your elders from childhood on. The idea that you are in dire need of their wisdom and experience can be irritating, particularly if you are an independent, headstrong person. However, it is best to listen closely to the advice you are given. If experience is the best teacher, certainly you can learn from someone else's experience and the advice that comes out of it.

Most people like to think for themselves, make their own decisions, learn from their own mistakes. As Chesterfield asserts, "advice is seldom welcome." Young people in particular tend to believe that they know what is best for themselves, and they chafe at following the advice of some busybody or know-it-all. Yet as Chesterfield also observes, the people who need advice the most like it the least. It is precisely the headstrong, overconfident person who could use a bit of wise counsel, who blunders ahead despite what anyone advises. A moment's reflection on some helpful advice might lead that person to make a life-improving decision. In junior high, I had my heart set on making the basketball team, but my uncle suggested that my small size and agility were better suited to soccer. After some long nights of thinking (and some choice words for my uncle's unwanted advice), I finally decided to give soccer a try. The result was a fun career in a sport I still enjoy.

Thoreau's quote is the perfect encapsulation of the headstrong attitude many young people have. Thoreau claims to have never heard "the first syllable of valuable or earnest advice" from his elders. In this way, he seems to be one of the very people that Chesterfield is describing in his quote. And apparently Thoreau still held his view about advice at the relatively advanced age of thirty. Nevertheless, most young people, lacking the genius of Thoreau, could surely benefit from the advice of older, wiser people. Even Thoreau must have learned something from reading older writers or following the example of some admired person. You could say that much classical literature is a form of advice from the past, from our "seniors."

Human nature being what it is, young people will doubtless go on ignoring or despising advice from their elders. But that doesn't mean that advice isn't necessary. Like a dose of bitter medicine, a piece of helpful advice can prevent much worse consequences in the future.

ADDITIONAL COMMENTARY

The student's response to the prompt makes good use of the opposed quotes on advice from Chesterfield and Thoreau. First, the student sets out a viewpoint on the importance of advice in the first paragraph: "However, it is best to listen closely to the advice you are given." Next, the student organizes the second paragraph around the two parts of Chesterfield's quote — that "advice is seldom welcome" and that the people who need it the most like it the least. The student points out that helpful advice can lead to a life-changing decision for the better, and then the student offers an example from his own experience that reinforces the point. In the third paragraph, the student examines the Thoreau quote and criticizes the idea that advice from elders is not valuable. The student makes the canny point that "much classical literature is a form of advice from the past, from our 'seniors.'" In the final paragraph, the student briefly summarizes the main idea that advice can be helpful. Overall the essay is forcefully argued and well organized.

Six Tips for Better Essays

Excellence is the gradual result of always striving
to do better.—Pat Riley

OVERVIEW

The purpose of this short chapter is to review some basic concepts that, if followed, should help you earn higher scores on your essays. This advice comes from various AP readers whose experience can be helpful to you. The main point of these tips is that you can't skip steps or take short cuts. You need to be committed to a standard of excellence that a typical high school course may not set for you.

SIX TIPS FOR BETTER ESSAYS

TIP 1

Master the prompt by underlining key verbs and words and paraphrasing your task. If you do not understand the prompt, your essay will most likely be off task and could score as low as a 1 or 2.

TIP 2

Create a mini-outline, semantic web, or other graphic organizer to guide your writing. There will be space in your green booklet (what you are given for Part Two of the exam) to do this step. One quality of essays that get high scores is that they are clear and concise. They aren't full of repetition or digression. They are focused on the main claim and support. The brief time you spend planning your main points will pay off in the end and will probably save you time in the long run, since you will not be searching for what to say next.

TIP 3

Once you've made a plan, **check back often**. Instead of relying on your memory, which is only your fleeting short-term memory, you need to actually look at what you planned. Your memory may fail, but your plan is still there. This step of checking back keeps you from repeating and digressing. However, as you write, you may discover a new, even better point you want to make. Do not let your initial plan hinder you from the new course. Fix your outline to reflect the new idea and continue writing.

TIP 4

Feel free to **revise or rewrite**. If you have misstated something or used the wrong word, ~~cross out the word or line~~ and rewrite. AP readers know that your essay is a draft and they expect to see some evidence of ongoing revision, which shows you are thinking as you write. It also shows your commitment to excellence and scholarship. On the other hand, if your essay is a tangled mass of scribbles and cross-outs, that sends another message: you did not know what to say or how to say it. (Don't forget tip No. 2: Make a plan.) When you need to revise, make your cross-outs neat. Draw a single line; don't scribble.

Remember, revision is an ongoing mental process in which good writers naturally engage. While you don't want to second guess every little word choice, you **do** want to have a critical eye on your own writing as you compose.

TIP 5

Introductions are important, so be sure you are not using vague, empty language that says nothing. Don't say, for example, "Throughout history people have striven for peace and freedom." That may be true, but so what? Every sentence you write in your short 40 minutes needs to have a purpose. When AP readers assess your writing, they are less concerned about length than they are about a solid argument that is well-supported and well-phrased.

We can write a lot of words and still say nothing.

It is an excellent strategy to write your introduction last. To be good at this strategy, practice it before exam day. Be sure to give yourself enough room on your paper to insert it later. You will want it to come first. Don't just draw a star and tell your reader to look at the end for the introduction. The reason for writing your introduction last is that as you compose, you will discover more clearly what you want to say in your essay. By saving the introduction until last, you will write one that more effectively fits your essay. However, this strategy should not be used for the first time on the exam. If you like the idea, try it out several times first with your in-class practice essays.

TIP 6

This exam is the place for you to **show off your composition skills**. AP readers expect to be reading college-level essays. This is what they want to see:

- **Mastery of Conventions:** You must know how to use punctuation properly, how to write complete sentences, how to write in active voice, how to weave in textual evidence, and more. See Chapters 9, 10, and 17.

- **Advanced Vocabulary:** One primary attribute of essays that score in the 8 and 9 range is the sophistication of the writer's **word choice**. You not only need to be able to understand big words, but you need to be able to use them effectively. See Chapter 12.

- **Sentence Variety:** You are expected to be able to vary your sentence structure to match your purpose. One of the key elements of **syntax** is emphasis. Learn how writers use devices like repetition, parallel structure, and other patterns for effect. Learning sentence fluency and variety takes time. This is something you can study and practice, however, and it will be worth your time. See Chapters 9 and 10.

- **Control of Tone and Diction:** Chapter 6 explains that **ethos** is the character of the writer that convinces the reader to believe him or her. One way to control your tone is to actually believe in what you are writing. If you are just "answering a question" on a test instead of writing an essay, your lack of commitment will be revealed in your word choice. Much like your true feelings are readily apparent to others through your facial expressions and body language, your attitude about the topic, the task, even the exam itself, will be laid bare one way or another. To state it bluntly, if AP readers perceive that you don't care about what you're writing, they probably won't care about it either. That logically leads to a lower score, doesn't it?

PART V:

MASTERING THE MULTIPLE-CHOICE SECTION

General Test-Taking Strategies

The beginning of knowledge is the discovery of something we do not understand.—Frank Herbert

OVERVIEW

You've been taking standardized tests since you were in elementary school. No one knows more about test taking than a high school student. However, the stakes for this exam are higher than others you've taken, so it seems appropriate to review the skills and strategies needed to answer multiple-choice questions. Some of what you find in this chapter will seem familiar, as if you've read it in other chapters. But these tips bear repeating.

You will want to have these strategies ingrained in your brain. Test day presents its own stresses. You should not have to worry, for example, about a guessing strategy. Use this chapter in combination with Chapter 24 to ensure your best possible score for Part One of the exam.

STRATEGIC READING

Before you answer the first question, you will carefully read excerpts from a variety of nonfiction texts. The smart way to read is to read actively. If you do, you should only need to read an entire prose text once. Active and strategic reading means you are reading with a pen in hand. Use whatever annotation techniques with which you are comfortable, but **do** mark the text as you read. This process of close and active reading will help you remember what you've read and also help you identify key aspects of a particular text. Chapter 11 gives you a more detailed explanation of active reading.

WHAT TO NOTE/MARK:

- Circle and link related words. Five words or phrases with a sarcastic tone in a passage are worth noting, for example.

- Underline key statements (anything that seems to be significant).

- Any shift in speaker, point of view, tone, or purpose is important to note in the margin. Also comment on what you think is happening because of this shift.

- Don't forget **SOAPST**ONE: Even if you don't write each thing down as you read, in your head you should know the speaker, the occasion, the audience, the purpose, the subject, and the tone.

- Write your own questions in the margin, even questions as simple as "Why?" or "What does this mean?" Your questions show you are thinking and may be answered as you read further, which will provide a logical link for you.

USE THE QUESTIONS TO SHARPEN YOUR FOCUS

- Regard the questions as sources of information. They may provide insight into the passage and improve your reading comprehension. In other words, the questions themselves could provide hints as to the author's purpose, the speaker's point of view, etc.

- Skimming the questions before you read each text can give you a stronger purpose for reading and will help you know how to annotate as you read.

TIPS ON ANSWERING QUESTIONS

- While it sounds like common sense, be sure to read the questions carefully. Ascertain what a question is asking for. Cursory reading creates careless errors. See Chapter 24 for an analysis of question types.

- As a matter of procedure, cross out answers that you know right away are wrong. If you automatically do this, you are not adding extra work, and you are likely to achieve a higher level of accuracy.

- If you really don't know the answer but can eliminate two or more answers, taking a 50–50 guess might be better than skipping the question. Points are not deducted for wrong answers. Your score for Part One is based only on what you answer correctly. Making an educated guess is still a good strategy.

- Many of the really tough questions provide two similar answers that you think are correct. In this case, you must choose *the most correct* answer. "Most correct" means the answer is more precise or more detailed. If another answer is only "sort of" right, then that is most likely not the one to choose.

- Don't over-think a question. Some questions are really, really easy. Most students think they couldn't possibly put such an easy question on the exam, so they overthink it and get it wrong.

- If the question asks you to identify ironic elements, the statement in the answer will reveal the irony. In other words, the answer itself will sound ironic.

- Many questions are going to require a *rereading* of lines or paragraphs from the text. Do not skip this step. Your notes and markings of the text should help you navigate quickly as you reread.

PRACTICE FOR REAL

In the AP English Language and Composition Course Description (*apcentral.collegeboard.org*), you'll find 50 multiple-choice practice questions. Take the time to answer these questions. Allow yourself 50 minutes to replicate true test conditions.

When finished, analyze your results. When you look back at your answers, ask yourself two questions:

1. Why did I get it wrong?

2. Why did I get it right?

It is important to understand what you understood as much as what you did not understand. Your careful analysis of your results is as important to your learning as actually taking the practice test.

Look through the practice exam for literary terms you are not familiar with or words you do not understand. Add them to your "to do" list and learn them.

Types of Questions
in the Multiple-Choice Section

*You must train your intuition—you must trust the small
voice inside you which tells you exactly what to say,
what to decide.*—Ingrid Bergman

OVERVIEW

The following information comes from an analysis of five released
AP English Language and Composition exams. Questions are organized
according to purpose. Below, you'll find a prevalence rating scale which
should help you focus your study. The number of stars relates to the number
of times a question type was found in released exams. The more stars a
question type has, the more likely it is to appear on future tests.

While I have organized this chapter according to types of questions,
most of the questions you'll encounter on the exam have one main goal
in mind—they want to know if you understand why and how the passage
means what it means. In other words, the multiple-choice section is a
reading comprehension test. However, you must also know details, such
as rhetorical strategies and literary devices. It all goes hand in hand.

PREVALENCE RATING SCALE

★ = 1–5 instances

★★ = 6–10 instances

★★★ = 11–15 instances

★★★★ = 16+ instances

BASIC QUESTION TYPES

1. **Double Answers** (★★★) Answer choices are given in pairs, such as "civil but angry" or "genial yet self-interested." Often the pairs contain one element that cannot be correct. Tip: If one part of a double answer is wrong, the entire thing is wrong.

2. **All of the following EXCEPT. . .** (★★★) Be sure to recognize this type of question and carefully consider which answer is *not* like the others.

3. **Of the following, which is LEAST. . .** (★)

4. **I only; I and II; I, II, and III, etc.** (★) These can be tricky and time-consuming. They used to be more prevalent on older tests. You are expected to reread to make an informed decision. It is my understanding that the College Board has eliminated this type of question, but it's good to be aware nevertheless.

DEFINING TERMS

ANALYZE, IDENTIFY, AND DETERMINE

1. When you *analyze,* you look at component parts of a whole to see how one part works to achieve an effect or purpose.

2. When you *identify,* you are recognizing, selecting, or pointing out what exists.

3. When you are asked to *determine,* you will most likely have to infer or interpret to get the answer.

TYPES OF QUESTIONS BY PURPOSE

Notes: Each of the following items begins with the phrase, **"The question asks you to. . ."**, but I've left it off the descriptions to make them simpler and easier to understand.

LITERARY ELEMENTS:

1. Identify a rhetorical strategy/device. (★★★)

2. Determine the characterization of a speaker. (★)

3. Determine function/effect of diction. (★)

4. Identify a symbol. (★)

5. Identify tone/atmosphere.(★)

6. Identify a shift in tone. (★)

7. Determine ironic effect. (★)

8. Identify antithesis. (★)

9. Identify elements of extended metaphor. (★)

10. Determine the effect of an analogy. (★)

11. Identify style or elements of style. (★)

12. Identify imagery. (★)

RHETORICAL/GENERAL ANALYSIS:

1. Interpret or infer meaning. (★★★★)

2. Determine the effect/function of a passage, paragraph, sentence or phrase. (★★★★)

3. Analyze the author's argument or process. (★★★)

4. Determine the author's/speaker's purpose in a passage or statement. (★★★)

5. Determine the rhetorical function/purpose of a word/phrase in a passage. (★)

6. Determine the author's/speaker's rhetorical strategy. (★)

7. Determine the effect of a word or phrase in the meaning of a passage. (★)

8. Determine the effect of a specific detail. (★)

9. Identify a shift in rhetorical purpose. (★)

ORGANIZATION/STRUCTURE:

1. Identify a word/phrase reference. The question is often worded "the word '----' refers to . . ." (★★)

2. In context of the passage as a whole, determine meaning of a sentence or phrase. (★★)

3. Identify unifying elements. (★)

4. In context of a passage as a whole, determine the function of a sentence or phrase. (★)

5. Identify the relationship of one element of the passage to another. (★)

6. Identify a logical order or sequence (such as a list from large to small, grand to ordinary). (★)

7. Identify similar elements. (★)

8. Identify contrasting elements. (★)

9. Determine the effect/purpose of typography (italics, bold type, etc.) in a passage. (★)

POINT OF VIEW/PERSPECTIVE:

1. Identify the speaker or author's attitude, belief or point of view. (★★★)

2. Identify the author's/speaker's voice or tone. (★★)

3. Identify a shift in point of view. (★)

4. Determine the intended audience. (★)

GRAMMATICAL CONSTRUCTION:

1. Identify the subject of a sentence. (★)

2. Identify the antecedent of a pronoun. (★)

3. Determine the grammatical function of a word or phrase. (★)

RESEARCH AND CITATIONS:

1. Determine the purpose of a footnote. (★)

2. Identify the elements of a footnote. (★)

3. Determine the accuracy of a source citation. (★)

4. Determine the effect of a citation. (★)

SENTENCE AND SYNTAX:

1. Identify parallel structure/elements. (★★)

2. Identify syntactical elements (types of sentences, syntax patterns). (★)

3. Identify sentence construction. (★)

4. Determine the function/effect of syntax. (★)

DENOTATION AND CONNOTATION:

1. Determine the meaning or purpose of a word/phrase in context. (★★★)

2. Identify the connotation of a word/phrase. (★)

3. Determine the value/purpose of a word/phrase throughout the passage. (★)

GENRE/PATTERN/MODE:

1. Identify the genre/rhetorical mode. (★)

2. Identify the pattern of exposition. (★)

3. Determine the genre from which the passage is likely excerpted. (★)

Chapter 5

Practice Multiple-Choice Questions

In May, when you take your actual exam, you will have approximately five to six passages to read and 52–55 questions to answer. This chapter gives you a shorter experience, but familiarizing yourself with multiple-choice questions will help you succeed on the actual exam. These questions also reinforce many of the key concepts in this book.

Questions: 25
Time: 35 minutes

Questions 1–5: Read the following excerpt from "Night and Moonlight" by Henry David Thoreau. Then use it to answer questions 1–5.

I complain of Arctic voyagers that they do not enough remind us of the constant peculiar dreariness of the scenery, and the perpetual twilight of the Arctic night. So he whose theme is moonlight, though he may find it difficult, must, as it were, illustrate it with the light of the moon alone.

5   Many men walk by day; few walk by night. It is a very different season. Take a July night, for instance. About ten o'clock—when man is asleep, and day fairly forgotten—the beauty of moonlight is seen over lonely pastures where cattle are silently feeding. On all sides novelties present themselves. Instead of the sun there are the moon and stars, instead of the wood-thrush there is the whip-poor-will—instead of butterflies in the meadows, fire-flies, winged sparks of fire! Who would have believed it? What kind of cool deliberate life dwells in those dewy abodes associated with a spark of fire? So man has fire in his eyes, or blood, or brain. Instead of singing birds, the half-throttled note of a cuckoo flying over, the croaking of frogs, and the intenser dream of crickets. But above all, the wonderful trump of the bullfrog, ringing from Maine to Georgia. The potato-vines stand upright, the corn grows apace, the bushes loom, the grain-fields are boundless. On our open river terraces once cultivated by the Indian, they appear to occupy the ground like an army—their heads nodding in the breeze. Small

20 trees and shrubs are seen in the midst overwhelmed as by an inundation.
The shadows of rocks and trees, and shrubs and hills, are more conspicuous
than the objects themselves. The slightest irregularities in the ground are
revealed by the shadows, and what the feet find comparatively smooth
appears rough and diversified in consequence. For the same reason the
25 whole landscape is more variegated and picturesque than by day. The
smallest recesses in the rocks are dim and cavernous; the ferns in the wood
appear of tropical size. The sweet fern and indigo in overgrown wood-
paths wet you with dew up to your middle. The leaves of the shrub-oak
are shining as if a liquid were flowing over them. The pools seen through
30 the trees are as full of light as the sky. "The light of the day takes refuge in
their bosoms," as the Purana says of the ocean. All white objects are more
remarkable than by day. A distant cliff looks like a phosphorescent space
on a hillside. The woods are heavy and dark. Nature slumbers. You see the
moonlight reflected from particular stumps in the recesses of the forest, as
35 if she selected what to shine on. These small fractions of her light remind
one of the plant called moon-seed—as if the moon were sowing it in such
places. . . .

It does not concern men who are asleep in their beds, but it is
very important to the traveler, whether the moon shines brightly or is
40 obscured. It is not easy to realize the serene joy of all the earth, when she
commences to shine unobstructedly, unless you have often been abroad
alone in moonlight nights. She seems to be waging continual war with
the clouds in your behalf. Yet we fancy the clouds to be her foes also. She
comes on magnifying her dangers by her light, revealing, displaying them
45 in all their hugeness and blackness, then suddenly casts them behind into
the light concealed, and goes her way triumphant through a small space
of clear sky.

1. What task does the author set himself in the first paragraph?

(A) to list and analyze all the facts he knows about the moon

(B) to present the theme of moonlight by describing effects of
moonlight at night

(C) to compare the dreariness of an Arctic night to a moonlit night in
a forest

(D) to describe themes of moonlight in poetry and romantic fiction

(E) to walk through an unfamiliar landscape at night guided only by
the moonlight

2. In line 8, the word "novelties" refers to

   (A) the moon and stars

   (B) tricks of the light

   (C) birds and animals that look like toys

   (D) wonders rarely seen

   (E) new ideas for describing the moonlight

3. Which of the following best conveys the main idea in lines 21–28?

   (A) The moonlight reduces every feature of the landscape to a rough and shadowy sameness.

   (B) The landscape is easier to negotiate in the moonlight than by day.

   (C) Shadows take on frightening shapes in the moonlight.

   (D) The moonlight makes everything appear smooth and silvery.

   (E) The moonlight serves to exaggerate the features of the landscape.

4. In the last paragraph, the author personifies the moon as

   (A) a traveler

   (B) a fighter

   (C) a servant with a lantern

   (D) a heartless conqueror

   (E) a peaceful mistress

5. The style of the passage as a whole is most accurately characterized as

   (A) clever and satirical

   (B) disjointed and querulous

   (C) lyrical and descriptive

   (D) terse and transparent

   (E) complex and scholarly

Questions 6–10: Read the following excerpt from *In Search of Schrödinger's Cat: Quantum Physics and Reality* by John Gribbin. Then use it to answer questions 6–10.

Although it all sounds reasonably neat and tidy from the perspective of the 1980s, by 1925 quantum theory was in a mess. There was no great highway of progress, but rather many individuals each hacking a separate path through the jungle. The top researchers knew this only too well, and
5   expressed their concern publicly; but the great leap forward was to come, with one exception, from the new generation who entered research after the First World War and were, perhaps as a result, open to new ideas. In 1924, Max Born commented that "at the moment one possesses only a few unclear hints" about the way classical laws need to be modified to
10   explain atomic properties, and in his textbook on atomic theory published in 1925 he promised a second volume to complete the job, one that he thought would "remain unwritten for several years yet."[1]

. . . The two great authorities were Einstein and [Niels] Bohr, but by 1925 they had begun to differ markedly in their scientific views.
15   First, Bohr was one of the strongest opponents of the light quantum; then, as Einstein began to be concerned about the role of probability in quantum theory Bohr became its great champion. The statistical methods (ironically, introduced by Einstein) became the cornerstone of quantum theory, but as early as 1920 Einstein wrote to Born, "That business about
20   causality causes me a lot of trouble, too . . . I must admit that . . . I lack the courage of my convictions," and the dialogue between Einstein and Bohr on this theme continued for thirty-five years, until Einstein's death.[2]

Max Jammer describes the situation at the beginning of 1925 as "a lamentable hodgepodge of hypotheses, principles, theorems and
25   computational recipes."[3] Every problem in quantum physics had to be first "solved" using classical physics, and then be reworked by the judicious insertion of quantum numbers more by inspired guesswork than cool reasoning. The quantum theory was neither autonomous nor logically consistent, but existed as a parasite on classical physics, an exotic bloom
30   without roots. No wonder Born thought that it would be years before he could write his second, definitive volume on atomic physics. . . .

---

[1] Quotes in this section taken from the epilogue to volume 1 of Mehra and Rechenberg.

[2] Einstein expressed these doubts also in his correspondence with Born, published as *The Born-Einstein Letters*. The quote here is from page 23 of the Macmillan edition.

[3] *The Conceptual Development of Quantum Mechanics,* page 196.

6. Read the following sentence from lines 2–4 of the passage.

   > There was no great highway of progress, but rather many individuals each hacking a separate path through the jungle.

   Which of the following best represents the author's meaning in this sentence?

   (A) Had researchers worked together from the beginning, quantum theory could have been developed much more quickly.

   (B) Scientific research on quantum theory was like blindly trying to cut a path through a jungle to a highway.

   (C) The road to progress on quantum theory developed only after many researchers reached dead ends in their work.

   (D) Progress on quantum theory didn't result from a single focused effort, but instead required hard work by many different researchers.

   (E) Developing the quantum theory was like building a superhighway through a jungle.

7. The interpretation of footnote 1 that is most likely correct is

   (A) the quotes in this section are from two scientists named Mehra and Rechenberg.

   (B) the quotes in this section are discussed more fully in the epilogue to this book, which includes material by writers named Mehra and Rechenberg.

   (C) the quotes in this section are taken from the epilogue of a biography about two scientists named Mehra and Rechenberg.

   (D) the quotes in this section are from volume 1 of a work published by a company named Mehra and Rechenberg.

   (E) the quotes in this section come from volume 1 of a work that is by two authors named Mehra and Rechenberg and is listed in the bibliography.

8. Why does the author place the word "solved" (line 26) in quotation marks?

   (A) The word is Einstein's, not the author's.

   (B) The author is signaling to the reader that the problems had already been solved by classical physics.

   (C) The problems were solved only provisionally; there was more work to be done on each.

   (D) None of the problems could ever be solved satisfactorily.

   (E) The author does not believe that quantum theory can solve any problem in physics.

9. In lines 29–30, the phrase "an exotic bloom without roots" refers to

   (A) classical physics

   (B) quantum theory

   (C) a hodgepodge of hypotheses and principles

   (D) Born's projected second volume

   (E) inspired guesswork

10. The author's overall tone in this passage is primarily one of

   (A) fluent authority

   (B) mocking skepticism

   (C) turgid pretension

   (D) admiring puffery

   (E) judicious criticism

Questions 11–18: Read the following excerpt from a female essayist of the early twentieth century. Then use it to answer questions 11–18.

That woman, then, who was born with a gift of poetry in the sixteenth century, was an unhappy woman, a woman at strife against herself. All the conditions of her life, all her own instincts, were hostile to the state of mind which is needed to set free whatever is in the brain. But
5   what is the state of mind that is most propitious to the act of creation? I asked. Can one come by any notion of the state that furthers and makes possible that strange activity? Here I opened the volume containing the Tragedies of Shakespeare. What was Shakespeare's state of mind, for instance, when he wrote LEAR and ANTONY AND CLEOPATRA? It
10   was certainly the state of mind most favourable to poetry that there has ever existed. But Shakespeare himself said nothing about it. We only know casually and by chance that he "never blotted a line." Nothing indeed was ever said by the artist himself about his state of mind until the eighteenth century perhaps. Rousseau perhaps began it. At any
15   rate, by the nineteenth century self-consciousness had developed so far that it was the habit for men of letters to describe their minds in confessions and autobiographies. Their lives also were written, and their letters were printed after their deaths. Thus, though we do not know what Shakespeare went through when he wrote LEAR, we do know what
20   Carlyle went through when he wrote the FRENCH REVOLUTION; what Flaubert went through when he wrote MADAME BOVARY; what Keats was going through when he tried to write poetry against the coming death and the indifference of the world. . . .

And one gathers from this enormous modern literature of confession
25   and self-analysis that to write a work of genius is almost always a feat of prodigious difficulty. Everything is against the likelihood that it will come from the writer's mind whole and entire. Generally material circumstances are against it. Dogs will bark; people will interrupt; money must be made; health will break down. Further, accentuating all these difficulties and
30   making them harder to bear is the world's notorious indifference. It does not ask people to write poems and novels and histories; it does not need them. It does not care whether Flaubert finds the right word or whether Carlyle scrupulously verifies this or that fact. Naturally, it will not pay for what it does not want. And so the writer, Keats, Flaubert, Carlyle, suffers,
35   especially in the creative years of youth, every form of distraction and discouragement. A curse, a cry of agony, rises from those books of analysis and confession. "Mighty poets in their misery dead"—that is the burden

of their song. If anything comes through in spite of all this, it is a miracle, and probably no book is born entire and uncrippled as it was conceived.

40   But for women, I thought, looking at the empty shelves, these difficulties were infinitely more formidable. In the first place, to have a room of her own, let alone a quiet room or a sound-proof room, was out of the question, unless her parents were exceptionally rich or very noble, even up to the beginning of the nineteenth century. Since her pin
45   money, which depended on the goodwill of her father, was only enough to keep her clothed, she was debarred from such alleviations as came even to Keats or Tennyson or Carlyle, all poor men, from a walking tour, a little journey to France, from the separate lodging which, even if it were miserable enough, sheltered them from the claims and tyrannies of their
50   families. Such material difficulties were formidable; but much worse were the immaterial. The indifference of the world which Keats and Flaubert and other men of genius have found so hard to bear was in her case not indifference but hostility. The world did not say to her as it said to them, Write if you choose; it makes no difference to me. The world said with a
55   guffaw, Write? What's the good of your writing? . . .

        Thus, I concluded . . . it is fairly evident that even in the nineteenth century a woman was not encouraged to be an artist. On the contrary, she was snubbed, slapped, lectured and exhorted. Her mind must have been strained and her vitality lowered by the need of opposing this,
60   of disproving that. For here again we come within range of that very interesting and obscure masculine complex which has had so much influence upon the woman's movement; that deep-seated desire, not so much that SHE shall be inferior as that HE shall be superior, which plants him wherever one looks, not only in front of the arts, but barring the way
65   to politics too, even when the risk to himself seems infinitesimal and the suppliant humble and devoted. . . . The spectacle is certainly a strange one, I thought. The history of men's opposition to women's emancipation is more interesting perhaps than the story of that emancipation itself.

[from "A Room of One's Own" by Virginia Woolf]

11. Which of the following sentences is the clearest statement of the author's theme in this passage?

    (A) What was Shakespeare's state of mind, for instance, when he wrote LEAR and ANTONY AND CLEOPATRA?

    (B) And one gathers from this enormous modern literature of confession and self-analysis that to write a work of genius is almost always a feat of prodigious difficulty.

    (C) Further, accentuating all these difficulties and making them harder to bear is the world's notorious indifference.

    (D) But for women, I thought, looking at the empty shelves, these difficulties were infinitely more formidable.

    (E) The history of men's opposition to women's emancipation is more interesting perhaps than the story of that emancipation itself.

12. In line 7, the author refers to the act of creation as "that strange activity" in order to

    (A) emphasize that it is not a casual or ordinary pursuit for the true artist

    (B) suggest that all artists are perverse in some way

    (C) affirm that society views all artists as outcasts and vagabonds

    (D) introduce the idea that Shakespeare's art is like magic to the ordinary reader

    (E) describe the heightened sensitivity of the artist's mind to outside sensations

13. In line 13, "the artist" is a reference to

    (A) Jean-Jacques Rousseau

    (B) William Shakespeare

    (C) a generic writer

    (D) the author

    (E) nature

14. Which of the following characteristics associated with a writer's work is most emphasized in paragraph 3?

   (A) the satisfactions of reaching a large audience despite its initial indifference

   (B) the importance of self-analysis and self-consciousness to a writer

   (C) the difficulty of writing successfully in an indifferent world

   (D) the agony of working toward an artistic goal that keeps changing

   (E) the irritations of finding precisely the right words and checking every fact

15. In line 40, the phrase "looking at the empty shelves" serves to reinforce what important point that the author seeks to make?

   (A) There are not enough readers in the world to make a writer's vocation worthwhile.

   (B) It is foolish to go through all the difficulties of writing when most bookshelves will be filled with inferior books.

   (C) The hostile world will not allow books by women to take up space on bookshelves.

   (D) Most books, both good and bad, will eventually be tossed out and forgotten.

   (E) Many potential works by women writers remain unwritten because of external circumstances.

16. In lines 44–45, the colloquial term "pin money" essentially means

   (A) savings

   (B) an allowance

   (C) a salary

   (D) winnings from gambling

   (E) an inheritance

17. What is the best interpretation of the phrase "state of mind" in the context of the passage as a whole?

    (A) inborn talent

    (B) ability to create, despite external forces

    (C) stable mental health

    (D) mindful attention to detail

    (E) intelligence

18. In lines 60–68, the author resorts to which logical fallacy to make a point?

    (A) overgeneralization

    (B) begging the question

    (C) ad hominem attack

    (D) slippery slope argument

    (E) bandwagon appeal

Refer to the following footnote to answer questions 19–20.

[1] Garry Wills, "Rome's Gossip Columnist," *The American Scholar* (Spring 2008): 68–76.

19. What kind of source is referenced in this footnote?

    (A) book

    (B) newspaper

    (C) journal

    (D) film

    (E) encyclopedia

20. From reading this footnote, you can ascertain all of the following EXCEPT

    (A) the subject of the article

    (B) the title of the publication

    (C) the author's name

    (D) the title of the article

    (E) the pages on which the article appears

21. Which of the following sentences has correct parallel structure?

    (A) The team discovered a problem, its causes were then researched, and a solution was found.

    (B) A problem was discovered, its causes were researched, and the team found a solution.

    (C) The team discovered a problem, researched its causes, and a solution was found.

    (D) The team discovered a problem, researched its causes, and found a solution.

    (E) A problem was discovered by the team, the team researched its causes, and a solution was found.

Read the following sentence and use it to answer questions 22 and 23.

Great fanfare surrounded the law that Congress passed, the law actually accomplished very little.

22. What is the problem with this sentence?

    (A) not parallel in construction

    (B) comma splice

    (C) run-on sentence

    (D) passive voice

    (E) unclear pronoun reference

23. Which of the following is the best correction for the sentence on the previous page?

    (A) Great fanfare surrounded the law that Congress passed the law actually accomplished very little.

    (B) Due to the great fanfare that surrounded the law that Congress passed, the law actually accomplished very little.

    (C) Great fanfare surrounded the law that Congress passed. It actually accomplished very little.

    (D) The great fanfare that surrounded the law that Congress passed actually accomplished very little.

    (E) Although great fanfare surrounded the law that Congress passed, the law actually accomplished very little.

24. The best way to approach counterarguments in a persuasive essay is to

    (A) restate them in your own words

    (B) ignore them entirely

    (C) anticipate them and answer them early in the essay

    (D) anticipate them and rebut them toward the end of the essay

    (E) discredit the source of the counterarguments

25. Often a prompt requires the writer to "defend, refute, or qualify" the position an author takes in a passage. If the writer chooses to "qualify" the argument in the passage, he or she will

    (A) rewrite the argument in more transparent language

    (B) invert the argument to make the opposite point

    (C) partially agree and partially disagree with the argument

    (D) use inductive reasoning to make a counterargument

    (E) criticize the author's reasoning on every point

ANSWERS TO PRACTICE QUESTIONS

1. (B)

The author "complains" at the beginning of the passage about arctic voyagers who do not focus enough on the "peculiar dreariness" of the arctic landscape. He then declares that "he whose theme is moonlight"—i.e., himself—must illustrate that theme "with the light of the moon alone." The author then proceeds to "present the theme of moonlight" by describing in great detail a moonlit July night. Answer choice (B) is correct. The author doesn't list all the facts he knows about the moon (A), and he is not comparing an arctic night to a moonlit night in a forest (C). Poetry and romantic fiction are not referenced (D). He does seem to be walking through a strange landscape at night guided only by moonlight, but this is not the task that is related to the ideas in the first paragraph (E).

2. (D)

The author says, "On all sides novelties present themselves," referring to the very different sights that a person walking on a moonlit night might see. He then goes on to describe some of the unusual things—in other words, "wonders rarely seen" (D). These wonders include, but are not limited to, the moon and the stars (A) and various tricks of the moonlight (B). He does not compare birds and animals to toys (C), and the "novelties" are not new ideas for describing the moonlight (E).

3. (E)

The author points out that the shadows of things in the moonlight "are more conspicuous than the objects themselves," and that the smooth ground "appears rough and diversified." The whole landscape looks different, and the "smallest recesses in rocks are dim and cavernous," and thus exaggerated in size and effect. Answer choice (E) is correct. The moonlight does the opposite of reducing features to a sameness (A). With the exaggerated shadows, the landscape is probably *harder*, not easier, to negotiate at night (B). The idea is not that the shadowy shapes are frightening (C), and things do not all appear smooth and silvery (D).

4. (B)

To personify is to give human qualities to animals, objects, or ideas. The author personifies the moon as a fighter when he writes, "She seems to be waging continual war with the clouds in your behalf." Answer choice (B) is correct. The moon is waging war but is not described as a heartless conqueror (D). The other answers do not describe the personification correctly.

5. (C)

The author employs many lyrical, or poetic, images and comparisons in his portrayal of a moonlit night: "You see the moonlight reflected from particular stumps in the recesses of the forest, as if she selected what to shine on. These small fractions of her light remind one of the plant called moon-seed—as if the moon were sowing it in such places." He also provides lots of descriptive details, such as, "The potato-vines stand upright, the corn grows apace, the bushes loom, the grain-fields are boundless." Answer choice (C) is correct.

6. (D)

The author uses a metaphor to indicate that the work on quantum theory was not brisk and focused, like a stream of cars driving along a single highway, but rather difficult and separate, like individual paths being hacked through a jungle. Answer choice (D) restates this idea best. The sentence does not suggest that it was possible for all the researchers to work together, so (A) is incorrect. The metaphor also does not suggest that a path was being cut from the "jungle" to the "highway," so (B) is incorrect. No indication of dead ends is mentioned, as in (C). The highway is contrasted with the jungle in the metaphor; the highway is not being built "through a jungle," so (E) is not correct.

7. (E)

Since the names Mehra and Rechenberg are not italicized, as for a book title, and no book title is given, they doubtless refer to the authors of a multi-volume work that has a complete listing in the bibliography (and that probably has already been mentioned in the text, hence the simple reference to the authors). Answer choice (E) is correct.

8. (C)

The author points out that every problem in quantum physics had to be solved at first by using the principles of classical physics and then translated and reworked using quantum numbers. This indicates that the original "solutions" were not final but provisional. To show this, the author puts quotes around "solved," which usually means arriving at a final answer but here means something else. Answer choice (C) is correct.

The word is not quoted from Einstein (A). The author says that quantum problems had to be solved first according to classical physics principles, not that they had already been solved (B). The author doesn't suggest that the problems could never be solved (D), nor does he seem skeptical that quantum theory can solve problems in physics (E).

9. (B)

The question can be answered by reading the entire sentence where the phrase appears. It is the quantum theory that "existed as a parasite on classical physics, an exotic bloom without roots." Answer choice (B) is correct.

10. (A)

To be "fluent" is to handle language and source material easily and accurately, which the author does; his metaphors are particularly helpful to a reader unfamiliar with quantum theory. The range of his knowledge also gives his writing an authoritative tone. Answer choice (A) is correct. The author does not shy away from the messier aspects of quantum physics, but he does not sound skeptical of the theory—rather the contrary (B). His tone throughout is generally elevated, but phrases like "neat and tidy" and "was in a mess" save the passage from sounding pretentious (C). While he apparently has a healthy respect for the scientists who made the major discoveries in quantum theory, he does not seem guilty of "puffery," or building them up with nothing but praise (D). "Judicious criticism" (E) comes close to the tone of the passage in parts—such as the clear-eyed description of the disagreements between Einstein and Bohr, "the two great authorities" on quantum theory—but is not the major quality throughout.

11. (D)

The author's main theme in the passage overall is the particular difficulty faced by women who want to write. She goes on to discuss the social conditions ("In the first place, to have a room of her own, let alone a quiet room or a sound-proof room, was out of the question, unless her parents were exceptionally rich or very noble") and societal attitudes ("The world said with a guffaw, Write? What's the good of your writing?") that made the vocation of writing so hard for women to pursue. Answer choice (D) is correct. The theme is not about Shakespeare in particular (A), nor is it focused on the difficulty in general of writing "a work of genius" (B) or the world's indifference to an artist's travails (C). The history of men's opposition to women's rights is tangential to the main theme (E).

12. (A)

The author, obviously a creative writer herself, is emphasizing the "strangeness" of an activity that requires tremendous dedication and a certain state of mind that enables the imagination to function at its best. She wants to underline the difficulties inherent in the creative act for any writer in order to affirm the special problems faced by women who want to write. Answer choice (A) is correct. While the author does question the state of mind necessary for creation, she doesn't seem to view it as perverse in some way (B). The phrase does not point to society's view of artists (C). The sentence in which the phrase appears does introduce a section on Shakespeare's art, but the phrase does not refer specifically to Shakespeare (D). Answer choice (E) is close to the author's intention, but the phrase suggests the overall activity of writing and creation, not just sensitivity to outside sensations.

13. (C)

The author is referring to a generic writer, making the point that no writer (or "artist") had described the creative "state of mind" in detail until the eighteenth century, when Rousseau perhaps became the first to do so. Even though at first it seems as if "the artist" refers to Shakespeare (A), who has just been discussed, it actually means any artist. Answer choice (C) is correct. Of course, the introduction points out that the author is a woman, so "the artist himself" could not be the author (D).

14. (C)

The author begins paragraph 3 by describing the difficulties of writing when material circumstances are against it. Then she focuses on "the world's notorious indifference," which is the main emphasis of this paragraph. The author points out that the world "does not ask people to write" works and "does not need them." It does not care how hard a writer must work to create a finished book. Answer choice (C) is correct. There is no mention of the satisfactions of reaching a large audience (A). The importance of self-analysis is mentioned only to emphasize a writer's difficulties (B). The agony referenced here is in regard to outside circumstances, not inner artistic goals (D). Finding the right words and checking facts—the obsessions of writers such as Flaubert and Carlyle—

are mentioned but are not the part of a writer's work that is most emphasized (E).

15. (E)

When the author pointedly glances at "the empty shelves" in the course of discussing difficulties that are "infinitely more formidable" than those male writers face, she is planting the idea that many potentially great books by women never got written at all. This accords with her overall theme. Answer choice (E) is correct. Choice (C) is close to this idea, but it suggests that the world rejects books by women rather than preventing them from being written in the first place.

16. (B)

The term here means a modest allowance, which for a typical young woman "depended on the goodwill of her father," who paid it. The term dates back to the age of Henry VIII when wives were given money to buy pins, which were expensive for the time. The author employs the term to show how women were dependent on their families.

17. (B)

Some evidence exists for the need to mindfully concentrate (D) in a quiet space, but the author suggests a positive state of mind can flourish even without a "room of her own." The author does not directly discuss intelligence (E) or mental health (C) in the passage. While the author praises Shakespeare, the implication in the passage is that all writers possess talent (A). The best interpretation is (B) because the majority of the passage exposes how external forces work more powerfully against women than men, making it harder for women to maintain the mental focus necessary to create.

18. (A)

Overgeneralization is the logical fallacy in which it is assumed that all individuals are alike or react in the same way. The author here generalizes about an "obscure masculine complex" and "that deep-seated desire" of all men to feel, and in fact be, superior to women. She uses this technique as a shortcut to express her dismay at males who are opposed to "women's emancipation." The correct answer is (A).

19. (C)

The source is not a book (A), film (D), or encyclopedia (E) because the date—(Spring 2008)—is in the style of a periodical. The two possibilities for the type of periodical are newspaper (B) and journal (C), which is often a magazine. The number of pages listed for the article indicates the source is a journal, so (C) is the correct answer. In fact, *The American Scholar* is a journal published by Phi Beta Kappa.

20. (A)

From the information provided in the footnote, it is impossible to tell exactly what the subject of the article is. (The subject is actually the first-century Roman poet Martial, whose topical epigrams Garry Wills likens to a modern gossip column.) All the other types of information can be gleaned from the footnote.

21. (D)

Parallel structure means that sentence elements that are alike in function are also alike in construction. This adds to the clarity, economy, and force of a piece of writing. Answer choice (D) has correct parallel structure: The team *discovered* a problem, *researched* its causes, and *found* a solution. All three verbs are in active voice, performing the action of the sentence.

22. (B)

The sentence is a comma splice, in which two independent clauses are joined with only a comma. The correct answer is (B).

23. (E)

Choice (E) is the simplest and best correction for the sentence, adding the word *Although* to form a complex sentence that retains the correct sense. Answer choice (E) is correct. Choice (A) is still a run-on sentence. Choice (B) indicates that the fanfare caused the law to accomplish very little. Choice (C) creates ambiguity about whether the law or the fanfare accomplished very little. Choice (D) incorrectly says that the fanfare, not the law, accomplished very little.

24. (D)

It is a good idea to anticipate objections or counterarguments to your viewpoint in an essay and then rebut these arguments toward the end after you have presented your own case. Including possible counterarguments can actually strengthen your argument by demonstrating that you have thought of all sides of the question. The correct answer is (D). It is not important how the counterarguments are stated (A) as long as they are included. They should not be ignored completely (B). Answering them early in the essay before you have presented your own argument completely is not a good idea (C). Discrediting the source of counterarguments (E) is a logical fallacy that does not bolster your argument.

25. (C)

To "qualify" an argument in an essay means to modify it in some way, or to support part of it and oppose part of it. Usually a qualified argument falls somewhere in between the two extremes, pointing out the merits and problems with both sides and offering a compromise position. Answer choice (C) is correct. Qualifying an argument is not merely rewriting or restating it in other words (A). To invert the argument to make the opposite point (B) or criticize every point of it (E) is to refute the argument. Using inductive reasoning (D) is not necessarily a part of qualifying the argument.

Reiteration: Advice Worth Restating

The purpose of this section is to summarize some of the best advice I can leave with you. Most of these points you have already read in this book, but sometimes what we read last we remember best. The starred items (★) refer to reminders for the exam itself.

RHETORICAL READING

Prepare for your exam by reading complex texts from various writers and perspectives. Challenge yourself with pre-20th century texts. There will always be several such texts on the exam. These older texts typically feature more difficult syntax and vocabulary. If you are jumping into this challenge at the last minute, find the Essential Reading list in Chapter 4. While it is best to read more than what is on that list, if you literally do not have time for more, those texts are excellent "last minute" choices.

★ Do not skip over introductions to any selection given in the exam. Introductory material, as well as footnotes, are added purposefully and often provide important comprehension clues.

★ Do not forget to annotate. By making even just a few quick notes to underscore key points and the author's strategies, you'll make your analysis task easier.

Consider that everything you read is an argument in one way or another. As you "read" your world, consider the following for each genre you encounter: audience, author's purpose (main point), and the rhetorical tools/strategies he or she uses to create the effect.

RHETORICAL ANALYSIS

★ An analysis is not a listing of rhetorical elements or strategies, but requires students to describe how the writer's rhetorical tools accomplish his or her overall purpose.

Bolster your ability to develop your analysis by improving your vocabulary—and not just general vocabulary. For this exam it is crucial that you have a working knowledge of terms one uses to write about effective rhetoric. Review Chapters 5 and 6, as well as all key terms throughout this book.

★ All the texts you encounter were created within a context: historical as well as cultural. Do not make the mistake of layering your own culture and history over the text and expect it to conform. The more you read, the more you will improve your ability to comprehend diverse perspectives.

WRITING PERSUASIVELY

★ AP readers are looking for students to construct clear, rhetorically valid arguments that support an assertion. Evidence in support should be convincing, and essays should explain the argument logically and persuasively.

★ When providing illustrative examples for question #3 (the persuasive essay), choose texts that are relevant in subject and weight. For example, a reference to *The Hunger Games* could be construed in context as insignificant. In other words, take care to use evidence from AP level texts that effectively complement your argument. All the texts in Chapter 4's Essential Reading list are AP level texts.

★ Avoid broad generalized conclusions. Words like *all, none, always, never,* or other absolute terms are typically not effective.

★ Any example (or citation of evidence) in your argument is not automatically self-evident. You must always provide an explanation that shows "why" or "how."

★ Don't forget to synthesize evidence for the synthesis essay. In the simplest terms, this means to blend evidence from more than one source as you argue an assertion/claim.

GENERAL REMINDERS

★ Take enough time to read and understand the expectations of a prompt. You will always be given explicit or implicit guidance in the prompt. If you veer from the expectations set forth in the prompt, you risk writing an essay considered "off topic," which would rarely score higher than a 1.

In many ways, since the AP English Language and Composition exam is a test of one's ability to think, it is by default a test of your ability to use (or at least regard as value) everything you learn in every class in school. In math, you learn to read and infer the consequence of data presented in graphs. That's a perfect skill necessary in the synthesis prompt. In your civics or social studies classes, you learn about world events and leaders of consequence. Often, such people will be featured in passages on the AP English Language exam.

Your ability to draw on all your school and other learning experiences and to see your education as one integrated experience is at the heart of your ability to do well on this exam. This exam does not test something separate and discrete from your full experience, which makes it a challenge, but also a wonderful opportunity for you to show what you know and what you can do.

Finally, the AP English Language and Composition exam is only one test of what you know and can do at this particular point in your life. It does not define you or what you will be capable of in the future. Relax and bring your best to the experience.

Best of luck to you!

References

Chrisomalis, Stephen. "Philosophical Isms" *The Phrontistery.* 2007, accessed August 5, 2010, *http://phrontistery.info/isms.html.*

Decker, Randall E. *Patterns of Exposition 10.* Boston: Little, Brown and Company, 1986.

Donovan, M. *A Philosophical Timeline of Lives and Texts,* accessed July 24, 2010, *http://www.santarosa.edu/~mdonovan/whatis/line.htm.*

Fieser, James, ed., *Internet Encyclopedia of Philosophy,* accessed July 19, 2010, *http://www.iep.utm.edu/.*

Fowler, H. Ramsey, ed., *The Little Brown Handbook.* Boston: Little, Brown and Company, 1980.

Gaarder, Jostein. *Sophie's World: A Novel About the History of Philosophy.* New York: Berkley, 1994.

Harris, Robert. "The Purpose and Method of Satire" *VirtualSalt,* 2004, accessed August 14, 2010, *http://www.virtualsalt.com/satire.htm.*

Marvin, Christopher. "The Window: Philosophy on the Internet" *Timeline,* 2000, accessed July 24, 2010, *http://www.trincoll.edu/depts/phil/philo/timeline.html.*

Miller, Robert K. *The Informed Argument.* San Diego: Harcourt Brace Jovanovich, Publishers, 1986.

Rottenberg, Annette T. *Elements of Argument.* Boston: Bedford/St. Martin's, 2000.

Purdue OWL: Verb Tenses. Purdue University, 2018. Web. 18 Apr. 2018. *https://owl.english.purdue.edu/owl/resource/601/04/*

Shertzer, M., ed. *The Elements of Grammar.* New York: Macmillan Publishing Company, 1986.

Notes

Notes

Notes

Notes

Notes

Notes

Notes

Notes

Notes

Notes

Notes